C-1782 CAREER EXAMINATION SERIES

*This is your*
***PASSBOOK for...***

# Senior Management Analyst

***Test Preparation Study Guide***
***Questions & Answers***

NATIONAL LEARNING CORPORATION®

**National Learning Corporation**

212 Michael Drive, Syosset, NY 11791
(516) 921-8888 • www.passbooks.com
E-mail: info@passbooks.com

# PASSBOOK® SERIES

THE *PASSBOOK® SERIES* has been created to prepare applicants and candidates for the ultimate academic battlefield – the examination room.

At some time in our lives, each and every one of us may be required to take an examination – for validation, matriculation, admission, qualification, registration, certification, or licensure.

Based on the assumption that every applicant or candidate has met the basic formal educational standards, has taken the required number of courses, and read the necessary texts, the *PASSBOOK® SERIES* furnishes the one special preparation which may assure passing with confidence, instead of failing with insecurity. Examination questions – together with answers – are furnished as the basic vehicle for study so that the mysteries of the examination and its compounding difficulties may be eliminated or diminished by a sure method.

This book is meant to help you pass your examination provided that you qualify and are serious in your objective.

The entire field is reviewed through the huge store of content information which is succinctly presented through a provocative and challenging approach – the question-and-answer method.

A climate of success is established by furnishing the correct answers at the end of each test.

You soon learn to recognize types of questions, forms of questions, and patterns of questioning. You may even begin to anticipate expected outcomes.

You perceive that many questions are repeated or adapted so that you can gain acute insights, which may enable you to score many sure points.

You learn how to confront new questions, or types of questions, and to attack them confidently and work out the correct answers.

You note objectives and emphases, and recognize pitfalls and dangers, so that you may make positive educational adjustments.

Moreover, you are kept fully informed in relation to new concepts, methods, practices, and directions in the field.

You discover that you are actually taking the examination all the time: you are preparing for the examination by "taking" an examination, not by reading extraneous and/or supererogatory textbooks.

In short, this PASSBOOK®, used directedly, should be an important factor in helping you to pass your test.

# SENIOR MANAGEMENT ANALYST

DUTIES:

Under general supervision, an incumbent of this class is responsible for analyzing and evaluating the policies and procedures of a County department by performing complex organizational studies to provide management with recommendations regarding departmental protocols, compliance issues, automated systems requirements and needs; facility management, staffing resources and training, and other issues impacting overall departmental operations. In addition, this position is responsible for fiscal and budgetary analyses as it relates to overall operations and developing procedures to ensure effective processes and cost controls are in place to facilitate operations, and to ensure mandated reporting requirements are met. Incumbents are also responsible for applying and ensuring relevant federal, state and local laws, rules and regulations are considered in providing recommendations. This position differs from Management Analyst by the scope and complexity of assignment as well as the overall level of participation in departmental operations. Supervision may be exercised over subordinate staff.

An employee in this class supervises and participates in surveys and analyses of methods and procedures involving departmental operations. The employee is responsible for the development, coordination and implementation of intra-County and inter-departmental administrative systems and procedures. The incumbent exercises independent initiative and judgment in evaluating existing and new systems and recommending changes in methods and policies. Supervision is exercised over several Management Analysts in the performance of concurrent projects. Work is reviewed by superiors through consultations and periodic reports. Does related work as required.

SUBJECT OF EXAMINATION:

The written test will be designed to test for knowledge, skills and/or abilities in such areas as:

1. **Evaluating conclusions in light of known facts** - These questions will consist of a set of facts and a conclusion. You must decide if the conclusion is proved by the facts, disproved by the facts or if the facts are not sufficient to prove or disprove the conclusion. The questions will not be specific to a particular field.
2. **Preparing written material** - These questions test for the ability to present information clearly and accurately, and to organize paragraphs logically and comprehensibly. For some questions, you will be given information in two or three sentences followed by four restatements of the information. You must then choose the best version. For other questions, you will be given paragraphs with their sentences out of order. You must then choose, from four suggestions, the best order for the sentences.
3. **Supervision** - These questions test for knowledge of the principles and practices employed in planning, organizing, and controlling the activities of a work unit toward predetermined objectives. The concepts covered, usually in a situational question format, include such topics as assigning and reviewing work; evaluating performance; maintaining work standards; motivating and developing subordinates; implementing procedural change; increasing efficiency; and dealing with problems of absenteeism, morale, and discipline.

4. **Understanding and interpreting tabular material** - These questions test your ability to understand, analyze, and use the internal logic of data presented in tabular form. You may be asked to perform tasks such as completing tables, drawing conclusions from them, analyzing data trends or interrelationships, and revising or combining data sets. The concepts of rate, ratio, and proportion are tested. Mathematical operations are simple, and computational speed is not a major factor in the test.
5. **Understanding and interpreting written material** - These questions test for the ability to understand and interpret written material. You will be presented with brief reading passages and will be asked questions about the passages. You should base your answers to the questions only on what is presented in the passages and not on what you may happen to know about the topic.

# HOW TO TAKE A TEST

## I. YOU MUST PASS AN EXAMINATION

### *A. WHAT EVERY CANDIDATE SHOULD KNOW*

Examination applicants often ask us for help in preparing for the written test. What can I study in advance? What kinds of questions will be asked? How will the test be given? How will the papers be graded?

As an applicant for a civil service examination, you may be wondering about some of these things. Our purpose here is to suggest effective methods of advance study and to describe civil service examinations.

Your chances for success on this examination can be increased if you know how to prepare. Those "pre-examination jitters" can be reduced if you know what to expect. You can even experience an adventure in good citizenship if you know why civil service exams are given.

### *B. WHY ARE CIVIL SERVICE EXAMINATIONS GIVEN?*

Civil service examinations are important to you in two ways. As a citizen, you want public jobs filled by employees who know how to do their work. As a job seeker, you want a fair chance to compete for that job on an equal footing with other candidates. The best-known means of accomplishing this two-fold goal is the competitive examination.

Exams are widely publicized throughout the nation. They may be administered for jobs in federal, state, city, municipal, town or village governments or agencies.

Any citizen may apply, with some limitations, such as the age or residence of applicants. Your experience and education may be reviewed to see whether you meet the requirements for the particular examination. When these requirements exist, they are reasonable and applied consistently to all applicants. Thus, a competitive examination may cause you some uneasiness now, but it is your privilege and safeguard.

### *C. HOW ARE CIVIL SERVICE EXAMS DEVELOPED?*

Examinations are carefully written by trained technicians who are specialists in the field known as "psychological measurement," in consultation with recognized authorities in the field of work that the test will cover. These experts recommend the subject matter areas or skills to be tested; only those knowledges or skills important to your success on the job are included. The most reliable books and source materials available are used as references. Together, the experts and technicians judge the difficulty level of the questions.

Test technicians know how to phrase questions so that the problem is clearly stated. Their ethics do not permit "trick" or "catch" questions. Questions may have been tried out on sample groups, or subjected to statistical analysis, to determine their usefulness.

Written tests are often used in combination with performance tests, ratings of training and experience, and oral interviews. All of these measures combine to form the best-known means of finding the right person for the right job.

## II. HOW TO PASS THE WRITTEN TEST

### *A. NATURE OF THE EXAMINATION*

To prepare intelligently for civil service examinations, you should know how they differ from school examinations you have taken. In school you were assigned certain definite pages to read or subjects to cover. The examination questions were quite detailed and usually emphasized memory. Civil service exams, on the other hand, try to discover your present ability to perform the duties of a position, plus your potentiality to learn these duties. In other words, a civil service exam attempts to predict how successful you will be. Questions cover such a broad area that they cannot be as minute and detailed as school exam questions.

In the public service similar kinds of work, or positions, are grouped together in one "class." This process is known as *position-classification*. All the positions in a class are paid according to the salary range for that class. One class title covers all of these positions, and they are all tested by the same examination.

### *B. FOUR BASIC STEPS*

**1) Study the announcement**

How, then, can you know what subjects to study? Our best answer is: "Learn as much as possible about the class of positions for which you've applied." The exam will test the knowledge, skills and abilities needed to do the work.

Your most valuable source of information about the position you want is the official exam announcement. This announcement lists the training and experience qualifications. Check these standards and apply only if you come reasonably close to meeting them.

The brief description of the position in the examination announcement offers some clues to the subjects which will be tested. Think about the job itself. Review the duties in your mind. Can you perform them, or are there some in which you are rusty? Fill in the blank spots in your preparation.

Many jurisdictions preview the written test in the exam announcement by including a section called "Knowledge and Abilities Required," "Scope of the Examination," or some similar heading. Here you will find out specifically what fields will be tested.

**2) Review your own background**

Once you learn in general what the position is all about, and what you need to know to do the work, ask yourself which subjects you already know fairly well and which need improvement. You may wonder whether to concentrate on improving your strong areas or on building some background in your fields of weakness. When the announcement has specified "some knowledge" or "considerable knowledge," or has used adjectives like "beginning principles of..." or "advanced ... methods," you can get a clue as to the number and difficulty of questions to be asked in any given field. More questions, and hence broader coverage, would be included for those subjects which are more important in the work. Now weigh your strengths and weaknesses against the job requirements and prepare accordingly.

**3) Determine the level of the position**

Another way to tell how intensively you should prepare is to understand the level of the job for which you are applying. Is it the entering level? In other words, is this the position in which beginners in a field of work are hired? Or is it an intermediate or advanced level? Sometimes this is indicated by such words as "Junior" or "Senior" in the class title. Other jurisdictions use Roman numerals to designate the level – Clerk I, Clerk II, for example. The word "Supervisor" sometimes appears in the title. If the level is not indicated by the title, check the description of duties. Will you be working under very close supervision, or will you have responsibility for independent decisions in this work?

**4) Choose appropriate study materials**

Now that you know the subjects to be examined and the relative amount of each subject to be covered, you can choose suitable study materials. For beginning level jobs, or even advanced ones, if you have a pronounced weakness in some aspect of your training, read a modern, standard textbook in that field. Be sure it is up to date and has general coverage. Such books are normally available at your library, and the librarian will be glad to help you locate one. For entry-level positions, questions of appropriate difficulty are chosen – neither highly advanced questions, nor those too simple. Such questions require careful thought but not advanced training.

If the position for which you are applying is technical or advanced, you will read more advanced, specialized material. If you are already familiar with the basic principles of your field, elementary textbooks would waste your time. Concentrate on advanced textbooks and technical periodicals. Think through the concepts and review difficult problems in your field.

These are all general sources. You can get more ideas on your own initiative, following these leads. For example, training manuals and publications of the government agency which employs workers in your field can be useful, particularly for technical and professional positions. A letter or visit to the government department involved may result in more specific study suggestions, and certainly will provide you with a more definite idea of the exact nature of the position you are seeking.

## III. KINDS OF TESTS

Tests are used for purposes other than measuring knowledge and ability to perform specified duties. For some positions, it is equally important to test ability to make adjustments to new situations or to profit from training. In others, basic mental abilities not dependent on information are essential. Questions which test these things may not appear as pertinent to the duties of the position as those which test for knowledge and information. Yet they are often highly important parts of a fair examination. For very general questions, it is almost impossible to help you direct your study efforts. What we can do is to point out some of the more common of these general abilities needed in public service positions and describe some typical questions.

1) General information

Broad, general information has been found useful for predicting job success in some kinds of work. This is tested in a variety of ways, from vocabulary lists to questions about current events. Basic background in some field of work, such as sociology or economics, may be sampled in a group of questions. Often these are principles which have become familiar to most persons through exposure rather than through formal training. It is difficult to advise you how to study for these questions; being alert to the world around you is our best suggestion.

2) Verbal ability

An example of an ability needed in many positions is verbal or language ability. Verbal ability is, in brief, the ability to use and understand words. Vocabulary and grammar tests are typical measures of this ability. Reading comprehension or paragraph interpretation questions are common in many kinds of civil service tests. You are given a paragraph of written material and asked to find its central meaning.

3) Numerical ability

Number skills can be tested by the familiar arithmetic problem, by checking paired lists of numbers to see which are alike and which are different, or by interpreting charts and graphs. In the latter test, a graph may be printed in the test booklet which you are asked to use as the basis for answering questions.

4) Observation

A popular test for law-enforcement positions is the observation test. A picture is shown to you for several minutes, then taken away. Questions about the picture test your ability to observe both details and larger elements.

5) Following directions

In many positions in the public service, the employee must be able to carry out written instructions dependably and accurately. You may be given a chart with several columns, each column listing a variety of information. The questions require you to carry out directions involving the information given in the chart.

6) Skills and aptitudes

Performance tests effectively measure some manual skills and aptitudes. When the skill is one in which you are trained, such as typing or shorthand, you can practice. These tests are often very much like those given in business school or high school courses. For many of the other skills and aptitudes, however, no short-time preparation can be made. Skills and abilities natural to you or that you have developed throughout your lifetime are being tested.

Many of the general questions just described provide all the data needed to answer the questions and ask you to use your reasoning ability to find the answers. Your best preparation for these tests, as well as for tests of facts and ideas, is to be at your physical and mental best. You, no doubt, have your own methods of getting into an exam-taking mood and keeping "in shape." The next section lists some ideas on this subject.

## IV. KINDS OF QUESTIONS

Only rarely is the "essay" question, which you answer in narrative form, used in civil service tests. Civil service tests are usually of the short-answer type. Full instructions for answering these questions will be given to you at the examination. But in case this is your first experience with short-answer questions and separate answer sheets, here is what you need to know:

**1) Multiple-choice Questions**

Most popular of the short-answer questions is the "multiple choice" or "best answer" question. It can be used, for example, to test for factual knowledge, ability to solve problems or judgment in meeting situations found at work.

A multiple-choice question is normally one of three types—

- It can begin with an incomplete statement followed by several possible endings. You are to find the one ending which *best* completes the statement, although some of the others may not be entirely wrong.
- It can also be a complete statement in the form of a question which is answered by choosing one of the statements listed.

- It can be in the form of a problem – again you select the best answer.

Here is an example of a multiple-choice question with a discussion which should give you some clues as to the method for choosing the right answer:

> When an employee has a complaint about his assignment, the action which will *best* help him overcome his difficulty is to
> A. discuss his difficulty with his coworkers
> B. take the problem to the head of the organization
> C. take the problem to the person who gave him the assignment
> D. say nothing to anyone about his complaint

In answering this question, you should study each of the choices to find which is best. Consider choice "A" – Certainly an employee may discuss his complaint with fellow employees, but no change or improvement can result, and the complaint remains unresolved. Choice "B" is a poor choice since the head of the organization probably does not know what assignment you have been given, and taking your problem to him is known as "going over the head" of the supervisor. The supervisor, or person who made the assignment, is the person who can clarify it or correct any injustice. Choice "C" is, therefore, correct. To say nothing, as in choice "D," is unwise. Supervisors have and interest in knowing the problems employees are facing, and the employee is seeking a solution to his problem.

**2) True/False Questions**

The "true/false" or "right/wrong" form of question is sometimes used. Here a complete statement is given. Your job is to decide whether the statement is right or wrong.

SAMPLE: A roaming cell-phone call to a nearby city costs less than a non-roaming call to a distant city.

This statement is wrong, or false, since roaming calls are more expensive.

This is not a complete list of all possible question forms, although most of the others are variations of these common types. You will always get complete directions for answering questions. Be sure you understand *how* to mark your answers – ask questions until you do.

## V. RECORDING YOUR ANSWERS

Computer terminals are used more and more today for many different kinds of exams.

For an examination with very few applicants, you may be told to record your answers in the test booklet itself. Separate answer sheets are much more common. If this separate answer sheet is to be scored by machine – and this is often the case – it is highly important that you mark your answers correctly in order to get credit.

An electronic scoring machine is often used in civil service offices because of the speed with which papers can be scored. Machine-scored answer sheets must be marked with a pencil, which will be given to you. This pencil has a high graphite content which responds to the electronic scoring machine. As a matter of fact, stray dots may register as answers, so do not let your pencil rest on the answer sheet while you are pondering the correct answer. Also, if your pencil lead breaks or is otherwise defective, ask for another.

Since the answer sheet will be dropped in a slot in the scoring machine, be careful not to bend the corners or get the paper crumpled.

The answer sheet normally has five vertical columns of numbers, with 30 numbers to a column. These numbers correspond to the question numbers in your test booklet. After each number, going across the page are four or five pairs of dotted lines. These short dotted lines have small letters or numbers above them. The first two pairs may also have a "T" or "F" above the letters. This indicates that the first two pairs only are to be used if the questions are of the true-false type. If the questions are multiple choice, disregard the "T" and "F" and pay attention only to the small letters or numbers.

Answer your questions in the manner of the sample that follows:

32. The largest city in the United States is
    A. Washington, D.C.
    B. New York City
    C. Chicago
    D. Detroit
    E. San Francisco

1) Choose the answer you think is best. (New York City is the largest, so "B" is correct.)
2) Find the row of dotted lines numbered the same as the question you are answering. (Find row number 32)
3) Find the pair of dotted lines corresponding to the answer. (Find the pair of lines under the mark "B.")
4) Make a solid black mark between the dotted lines.

## VI. BEFORE THE TEST

Common sense will help you find procedures to follow to get ready for an examination. Too many of us, however, overlook these sensible measures. Indeed, nervousness and fatigue have been found to be the most serious reasons why applicants fail to do their best on civil service tests. Here is a list of reminders:

- Begin your preparation early – Don't wait until the last minute to go scurrying around for books and materials or to find out what the position is all about.
- Prepare continuously – An hour a night for a week is better than an all-night cram session. This has been definitely established. What is more, a night a week for a month will return better dividends than crowding your study into a shorter period of time.
- Locate the place of the exam – You have been sent a notice telling you when and where to report for the examination. If the location is in a different town or otherwise unfamiliar to you, it would be well to inquire the best route and learn something about the building.
- Relax the night before the test – Allow your mind to rest. Do not study at all that night. Plan some mild recreation or diversion; then go to bed early and get a good night's sleep.
- Get up early enough to make a leisurely trip to the place for the test – This way unforeseen events, traffic snarls, unfamiliar buildings, etc. will not upset you.
- Dress comfortably – A written test is not a fashion show. You will be known by number and not by name, so wear something comfortable.

- Leave excess paraphernalia at home – Shopping bags and odd bundles will get in your way. You need bring only the items mentioned in the official notice you received; usually everything you need is provided. Do not bring reference books to the exam. They will only confuse those last minutes and be taken away from you when in the test room.
- Arrive somewhat ahead of time – If because of transportation schedules you must get there very early, bring a newspaper or magazine to take your mind off yourself while waiting.
- Locate the examination room – When you have found the proper room, you will be directed to the seat or part of the room where you will sit. Sometimes you are given a sheet of instructions to read while you are waiting. Do not fill out any forms until you are told to do so; just read them and be prepared.
- Relax and prepare to listen to the instructions
- If you have any physical problem that may keep you from doing your best, be sure to tell the test administrator. If you are sick or in poor health, you really cannot do your best on the exam. You can come back and take the test some other time.

## VII. AT THE TEST

The day of the test is here and you have the test booklet in your hand. The temptation to get going is very strong. Caution! There is more to success than knowing the right answers. You must know how to identify your papers and understand variations in the type of short-answer question used in this particular examination. Follow these suggestions for maximum results from your efforts:

**1) Cooperate with the monitor**

The test administrator has a duty to create a situation in which you can be as much at ease as possible. He will give instructions, tell you when to begin, check to see that you are marking your answer sheet correctly, and so on. He is not there to guard you, although he will see that your competitors do not take unfair advantage. He wants to help you do your best.

**2) Listen to all instructions**

Don't jump the gun! Wait until you understand all directions. In most civil service tests you get more time than you need to answer the questions. So don't be in a hurry. Read each word of instructions until you clearly understand the meaning. Study the examples, listen to all announcements and follow directions. Ask questions if you do not understand what to do.

**3) Identify your papers**

Civil service exams are usually identified by number only. You will be assigned a number; you must not put your name on your test papers. Be sure to copy your number correctly. Since more than one exam may be given, copy your exact examination title.

**4) Plan your time**

Unless you are told that a test is a "speed" or "rate of work" test, speed itself is usually not important. Time enough to answer all the questions will be provided, but this does not mean that you have all day. An overall time limit has been set. Divide the total time (in minutes) by the number of questions to determine the approximate time you have for each question.

**5) Do not linger over difficult questions**

If you come across a difficult question, mark it with a paper clip (useful to have along) and come back to it when you have been through the booklet. One caution if you do this – be sure to skip a number on your answer sheet as well. Check often to be sure that you have not lost your place and that you are marking in the row numbered the same as the question you are answering.

**6) Read the questions**

Be sure you know what the question asks! Many capable people are unsuccessful because they failed to *read* the questions correctly.

**7) Answer all questions**

Unless you have been instructed that a penalty will be deducted for incorrect answers, it is better to guess than to omit a question.

**8) Speed tests**

It is often better NOT to guess on speed tests. It has been found that on timed tests people are tempted to spend the last few seconds before time is called in marking answers at random – without even reading them – in the hope of picking up a few extra points. To discourage this practice, the instructions may warn you that your score will be "corrected" for guessing. That is, a penalty will be applied. The incorrect answers will be deducted from the correct ones, or some other penalty formula will be used.

**9) Review your answers**

If you finish before time is called, go back to the questions you guessed or omitted to give them further thought. Review other answers if you have time.

**10) Return your test materials**

If you are ready to leave before others have finished or time is called, take ALL your materials to the monitor and leave quietly. Never take any test material with you. The monitor can discover whose papers are not complete, and taking a test booklet may be grounds for disqualification.

## VIII. EXAMINATION TECHNIQUES

1) Read the general instructions carefully. These are usually printed on the first page of the exam booklet. As a rule, these instructions refer to the timing of the examination; the fact that you should not start work until the signal and must stop work at a signal, etc. If there are any *special* instructions, such as a choice of questions to be answered, make sure that you note this instruction carefully.

2) When you are ready to start work on the examination, that is as soon as the signal has been given, read the instructions to each question booklet, underline any key words or phrases, such as *least, best, outline, describe* and the like. In this way you will tend to answer as requested rather than discover on reviewing your paper that you *listed without describing*, that you selected the *worst* choice rather than the *best* choice, etc.

3) If the examination is of the objective or multiple-choice type – that is, each question will also give a series of possible answers: A, B, C or D, and you are called upon to select the best answer and write the letter next to that answer on your answer paper – it is advisable to start answering each question in turn. There may be anywhere from 50 to 100 such questions in the three or four hours allotted and you can see how much time would be taken if you read through all the questions before beginning to answer any. Furthermore, if you come across a question or group of questions which you know would be difficult to answer, it would undoubtedly affect your handling of all the other questions.

4) If the examination is of the essay type and contains but a few questions, it is a moot point as to whether you should read all the questions before starting to answer any one. Of course, if you are given a choice – say five out of seven and the like – then it is essential to read all the questions so you can eliminate the two that are most difficult. If, however, you are asked to answer all the questions, there may be danger in trying to answer the easiest one first because you may find that you will spend too much time on it. The best technique is to answer the first question, then proceed to the second, etc.

5) Time your answers. Before the exam begins, write down the time it started, then add the time allowed for the examination and write down the time it must be completed, then divide the time available somewhat as follows:
   - If 3-1/2 hours are allowed, that would be 210 minutes. If you have 80 objective-type questions, that would be an average of 2-1/2 minutes per question. Allow yourself no more than 2 minutes per question, or a total of 160 minutes, which will permit about 50 minutes to review.
   - If for the time allotment of 210 minutes there are 7 essay questions to answer, that would average about 30 minutes a question. Give yourself only 25 minutes per question so that you have about 35 minutes to review.

6) The most important instruction is to *read each question* and make sure you know what is wanted. The second most important instruction is to *time yourself properly* so that you answer every question. The third most important instruction is to *answer every question.* Guess if you have to but include something for each question. Remember that you will receive no credit for a blank and will probably receive some credit if you write something in answer to an essay question. If you guess a letter – say "B" for a multiple-choice question – you may have guessed right. If you leave a blank as an answer to a multiple-choice question, the examiners may respect your feelings but it will not add a point to your score. Some exams may penalize you for wrong answers, so in such cases *only,* you may not want to guess unless you have some basis for your answer.

7) Suggestions
   a. Objective-type questions
      1. Examine the question booklet for proper sequence of pages and questions
      2. Read all instructions carefully
      3. Skip any question which seems too difficult; return to it after all other questions have been answered
      4. Apportion your time properly; do not spend too much time on any single question or group of questions

5. Note and underline key words – *all, most, fewest, least, best, worst, same, opposite,* etc.
6. Pay particular attention to negatives
7. Note unusual option, e.g., unduly long, short, complex, different or similar in content to the body of the question
8. Observe the use of "hedging" words – *probably, may, most likely,* etc.
9. Make sure that your answer is put next to the same number as the question
10. Do not second-guess unless you have good reason to believe the second answer is definitely more correct
11. Cross out original answer if you decide another answer is more accurate; do not erase until you are ready to hand your paper in
12. Answer all questions; guess unless instructed otherwise
13. Leave time for review

b. Essay questions
1. Read each question carefully
2. Determine exactly what is wanted. Underline key words or phrases.
3. Decide on outline or paragraph answer
4. Include many different points and elements unless asked to develop any one or two points or elements
5. Show impartiality by giving pros and cons unless directed to select one side only
6. Make and write down any assumptions you find necessary to answer the questions
7. Watch your English, grammar, punctuation and choice of words
8. Time your answers; don't crowd material

8) Answering the essay question

Most essay questions can be answered by framing the specific response around several key words or ideas. Here are a few such key words or ideas:

M's: manpower, materials, methods, money, management
P's: purpose, program, policy, plan, procedure, practice, problems, pitfalls, personnel, public relations

a. Six basic steps in handling problems:
1. Preliminary plan and background development
2. Collect information, data and facts
3. Analyze and interpret information, data and facts
4. Analyze and develop solutions as well as make recommendations
5. Prepare report and sell recommendations
6. Install recommendations and follow up effectiveness

b. Pitfalls to avoid
1. *Taking things for granted* – A statement of the situation does not necessarily imply that each of the elements is necessarily true; for example, a complaint may be invalid and biased so that all that can be taken for granted is that a complaint has been registered

2. *Considering only one side of a situation* – Wherever possible, indicate several alternatives and then point out the reasons you selected the best one
3. *Failing to indicate follow up* – Whenever your answer indicates action on your part, make certain that you will take proper follow-up action to see how successful your recommendations, procedures or actions turn out to be
4. *Taking too long in answering any single question* – Remember to time your answers properly

## IX. AFTER THE TEST

Scoring procedures differ in detail among civil service jurisdictions although the general principles are the same. Whether the papers are hand-scored or graded by machine we have described, they are nearly always graded by number. That is, the person who marks the paper knows only the number – never the name – of the applicant. Not until all the papers have been graded will they be matched with names. If other tests, such as training and experience or oral interview ratings have been given, scores will be combined. Different parts of the examination usually have different weights. For example, the written test might count 60 percent of the final grade, and a rating of training and experience 40 percent. In many jurisdictions, veterans will have a certain number of points added to their grades.

After the final grade has been determined, the names are placed in grade order and an eligible list is established. There are various methods for resolving ties between those who get the same final grade – probably the most common is to place first the name of the person whose application was received first. Job offers are made from the eligible list in the order the names appear on it. You will be notified of your grade and your rank as soon as all these computations have been made. This will be done as rapidly as possible.

People who are found to meet the requirements in the announcement are called "eligibles." Their names are put on a list of eligible candidates. An eligible's chances of getting a job depend on how high he stands on this list and how fast agencies are filling jobs from the list.

When a job is to be filled from a list of eligibles, the agency asks for the names of people on the list of eligibles for that job. When the civil service commission receives this request, it sends to the agency the names of the three people highest on this list. Or, if the job to be filled has specialized requirements, the office sends the agency the names of the top three persons who meet these requirements from the general list.

The appointing officer makes a choice from among the three people whose names were sent to him. If the selected person accepts the appointment, the names of the others are put back on the list to be considered for future openings.

That is the rule in hiring from all kinds of eligible lists, whether they are for typist, carpenter, chemist, or something else. For every vacancy, the appointing officer has his choice of any one of the top three eligibles on the list. This explains why the person whose name is on top of the list sometimes does not get an appointment when some of the persons lower on the list do. If the appointing officer chooses the second or third eligible, the No. 1 eligible does not get a job at once, but stays on the list until he is appointed or the list is terminated.

## X. HOW TO PASS THE INTERVIEW TEST

The examination for which you applied requires an oral interview test. You have already taken the written test and you are now being called for the interview test – the final part of the formal examination.

You may think that it is not possible to prepare for an interview test and that there are no procedures to follow during an interview. Our purpose is to point out some things you can do in advance that will help you and some good rules to follow and pitfalls to avoid while you are being interviewed.

*What is an interview supposed to test?*

The written examination is designed to test the technical knowledge and competence of the candidate; the oral is designed to evaluate intangible qualities, not readily measured otherwise, and to establish a list showing the relative fitness of each candidate – as measured against his competitors – for the position sought. Scoring is not on the basis of "right" and "wrong," but on a sliding scale of values ranging from "not passable" to "outstanding." As a matter of fact, it is possible to achieve a relatively low score without a single "incorrect" answer because of evident weakness in the qualities being measured.

Occasionally, an examination may consist entirely of an oral test – either an individual or a group oral. In such cases, information is sought concerning the technical knowledges and abilities of the candidate, since there has been no written examination for this purpose. More commonly, however, an oral test is used to supplement a written examination.

*Who conducts interviews?*

The composition of oral boards varies among different jurisdictions. In nearly all, a representative of the personnel department serves as chairman. One of the members of the board may be a representative of the department in which the candidate would work. In some cases, "outside experts" are used, and, frequently, a businessman or some other representative of the general public is asked to serve. Labor and management or other special groups may be represented. The aim is to secure the services of experts in the appropriate field.

However the board is composed, it is a good idea (and not at all improper or unethical) to ascertain in advance of the interview who the members are and what groups they represent. When you are introduced to them, you will have some idea of their backgrounds and interests, and at least you will not stutter and stammer over their names.

*What should be done before the interview?*

While knowledge about the board members is useful and takes some of the surprise element out of the interview, there is other preparation which is more substantive. It *is* possible to prepare for an oral interview – in several ways:

**1) Keep a copy of your application and review it carefully before the interview**

This may be the only document before the oral board, and the starting point of the interview. Know what education and experience you have listed there, and the sequence and dates of all of it. Sometimes the board will ask you to review the highlights of your experience for them; you should not have to hem and haw doing it.

**2) Study the class specification and the examination announcement**

Usually, the oral board has one or both of these to guide them. The qualities, characteristics or knowledges required by the position sought are stated in these documents. They offer valuable clues as to the nature of the oral interview. For example, if the job involves supervisory responsibilities, the announcement will usually indicate that knowledge of modern supervisory methods and the qualifications of the candidate as a supervisor will be tested. If so, you can expect such questions, frequently in the form of a hypothetical situation which you are expected to solve. NEVER go into an oral without knowledge of the duties and responsibilities of the job you seek.

**3) Think through each qualification required**

Try to visualize the kind of questions you would ask if you were a board member. How well could you answer them? Try especially to appraise your own knowledge and background in each area, *measured against the job sought*, and identify any areas in which you are weak. Be critical and realistic – do not flatter yourself.

**4) Do some general reading in areas in which you feel you may be weak**

For example, if the job involves supervision and your past experience has NOT, some general reading in supervisory methods and practices, particularly in the field of human relations, might be useful. Do NOT study agency procedures or detailed manuals. The oral board will be testing your understanding and capacity, not your memory.

**5) Get a good night's sleep and watch your general health and mental attitude**

You will want a clear head at the interview. Take care of a cold or any other minor ailment, and of course, no hangovers.

*What should be done on the day of the interview?*

Now comes the day of the interview itself. Give yourself plenty of time to get there. Plan to arrive somewhat ahead of the scheduled time, particularly if your appointment is in the fore part of the day. If a previous candidate fails to appear, the board might be ready for you a bit early. By early afternoon an oral board is almost invariably behind schedule if there are many candidates, and you may have to wait. Take along a book or magazine to read, or your application to review, but leave any extraneous material in the waiting room when you go in for your interview. In any event, relax and compose yourself.

The matter of dress is important. The board is forming impressions about you – from your experience, your manners, your attitude, and your appearance. Give your personal appearance careful attention. Dress your best, but not your flashiest. Choose conservative, appropriate clothing, and be sure it is immaculate. This is a business interview, and your appearance should indicate that you regard it as such. Besides, being well groomed and properly dressed will help boost your confidence.

Sooner or later, someone will call your name and escort you into the interview room. *This is it.* From here on you are on your own. It is too late for any more preparation. But remember, you asked for this opportunity to prove your fitness, and you are here because your request was granted.

*What happens when you go in?*

The usual sequence of events will be as follows: The clerk (who is often the board stenographer) will introduce you to the chairman of the oral board, who will introduce you to the other members of the board. Acknowledge the introductions before you sit down. Do not be surprised if you find a microphone facing you or a stenotypist sitting by. Oral interviews are usually recorded in the event of an appeal or other review.

Usually the chairman of the board will open the interview by reviewing the highlights of your education and work experience from your application – primarily for the benefit of the other members of the board, as well as to get the material into the record. Do not interrupt or comment unless there is an error or significant misinterpretation; if that is the case, do not hesitate. But do not quibble about insignificant matters. Also, he will usually ask you some question about your education, experience or your present job – partly to get you to start talking and to establish the interviewing "rapport." He may start the actual questioning, or turn it over to one of the other members. Frequently, each member undertakes the questioning on a particular area, one in which he is perhaps most competent, so you can expect each member to participate in the examination. Because time is limited, you may also expect some rather abrupt switches in the direction the questioning takes, so do not be upset by it. Normally, a board member will not pursue a single line of questioning unless he discovers a particular strength or weakness.

After each member has participated, the chairman will usually ask whether any member has any further questions, then will ask you if you have anything you wish to add. Unless you are expecting this question, it may floor you. Worse, it may start you off on an extended, extemporaneous speech. The board is not usually seeking more information. The question is principally to offer you a last opportunity to present further qualifications or to indicate that you have nothing to add. So, if you feel that a significant qualification or characteristic has been overlooked, it is proper to point it out in a sentence or so. Do not compliment the board on the thoroughness of their examination – they have been sketchy, and you know it. If you wish, merely say, "No thank you, I have nothing further to add." This is a point where you can "talk yourself out" of a good impression or fail to present an important bit of information. Remember, *you close the interview yourself.*

The chairman will then say, "That is all, Mr. ______, thank you." Do not be startled; the interview is over, and quicker than you think. Thank him, gather your belongings and take your leave. Save your sigh of relief for the other side of the door.

*How to put your best foot forward*

Throughout this entire process, you may feel that the board individually and collectively is trying to pierce your defenses, seek out your hidden weaknesses and embarrass and confuse you. Actually, this is not true. They are obliged to make an appraisal of your qualifications for the job you are seeking, and they want to see you in your best light. Remember, they must interview all candidates and a non-cooperative candidate may become a failure in spite of their best efforts to bring out his qualifications. Here are 15 suggestions that will help you:

**1) Be natural – Keep your attitude confident, not cocky**

If you are not confident that you can do the job, do not expect the board to be. Do not apologize for your weaknesses, try to bring out your strong points. The board is interested in a positive, not negative, presentation. Cockiness will antagonize any board member and make him wonder if you are covering up a weakness by a false show of strength.

**2) Get comfortable, but don't lounge or sprawl**

Sit erectly but not stiffly. A careless posture may lead the board to conclude that you are careless in other things, or at least that you are not impressed by the importance of the occasion. Either conclusion is natural, even if incorrect. Do not fuss with your clothing, a pencil or an ashtray. Your hands may occasionally be useful to emphasize a point; do not let them become a point of distraction.

**3) Do not wisecrack or make small talk**

This is a serious situation, and your attitude should show that you consider it as such. Further, the time of the board is limited – they do not want to waste it, and neither should you.

**4) Do not exaggerate your experience or abilities**

In the first place, from information in the application or other interviews and sources, the board may know more about you than you think. Secondly, you probably will not get away with it. An experienced board is rather adept at spotting such a situation, so do not take the chance.

**5) If you know a board member, do not make a point of it, yet do not hide it**

Certainly you are not fooling him, and probably not the other members of the board. Do not try to take advantage of your acquaintanceship – it will probably do you little good.

**6) Do not dominate the interview**

Let the board do that. They will give you the clues – do not assume that you have to do all the talking. Realize that the board has a number of questions to ask you, and do not try to take up all the interview time by showing off your extensive knowledge of the answer to the first one.

**7) Be attentive**

You only have 20 minutes or so, and you should keep your attention at its sharpest throughout. When a member is addressing a problem or question to you, give him your undivided attention. Address your reply principally to him, but do not exclude the other board members.

**8) Do not interrupt**

A board member may be stating a problem for you to analyze. He will ask you a question when the time comes. Let him state the problem, and wait for the question.

**9) Make sure you understand the question**

Do not try to answer until you are sure what the question is. If it is not clear, restate it in your own words or ask the board member to clarify it for you. However, do not haggle about minor elements.

**10) Reply promptly but not hastily**

A common entry on oral board rating sheets is "candidate responded readily," or "candidate hesitated in replies." Respond as promptly and quickly as you can, but do not jump to a hasty, ill-considered answer.

**11) Do not be peremptory in your answers**

A brief answer is proper – but do not fire your answer back. That is a losing game from your point of view. The board member can probably ask questions much faster than you can answer them.

**12) Do not try to create the answer you think the board member wants**

He is interested in what kind of mind you have and how it works – not in playing games. Furthermore, he can usually spot this practice and will actually grade you down on it.

**13) Do not switch sides in your reply merely to agree with a board member**

Frequently, a member will take a contrary position merely to draw you out and to see if you are willing and able to defend your point of view. Do not start a debate, yet do not surrender a good position. If a position is worth taking, it is worth defending.

**14) Do not be afraid to admit an error in judgment if you are shown to be wrong**

The board knows that you are forced to reply without any opportunity for careful consideration. Your answer may be demonstrably wrong. If so, admit it and get on with the interview.

**15) Do not dwell at length on your present job**

The opening question may relate to your present assignment. Answer the question but do not go into an extended discussion. You are being examined for a *new* job, not your present one. As a matter of fact, try to phrase ALL your answers in terms of the job for which you are being examined.

*Basis of Rating*

Probably you will forget most of these "do's" and "don'ts" when you walk into the oral interview room. Even remembering them all will not ensure you a passing grade. Perhaps you did not have the qualifications in the first place. But remembering them will help you to put your best foot forward, without treading on the toes of the board members.

Rumor and popular opinion to the contrary notwithstanding, an oral board wants you to make the best appearance possible. They know you are under pressure – but they also want to see how you respond to it as a guide to what your reaction would be under the pressures of the job you seek. They will be influenced by the degree of poise you display, the personal traits you show and the manner in which you respond.

## ABOUT THIS BOOK

This book contains tests divided into Examination Sections. Go through each test, answering every question in the margin. We have also attached a sample answer sheet at the back of the book that can be removed and used. At the end of each test look at the answer key and check your answers. On the ones you got wrong, look at the right answer choice and learn. Do not fill in the answers first. Do not memorize the questions and answers, but understand the answer and principles involved. On your test, the questions will likely be different from the samples. Questions are changed and new ones added. If you understand these past questions you should have success with any changes that arise. Tests may consist of several types of questions. We have additional books on each subject should more study be advisable or necessary for you. Finally, the more you study, the better prepared you will be. This book is intended to be the last thing you study before you walk into the examination room. Prior study of relevant texts is also recommended. NLC publishes some of these in our Fundamental Series. Knowledge and good sense are important factors in passing your exam. Good luck also helps. So now study this Passbook, absorb the material contained within and take that knowledge into the examination. Then do your best to pass that exam.

# EXAMINATION SECTION

# EXAMINATION SECTION

## TEST 1

DIRECTIONS: Each question or incomplete statement is followed by several suggested answers or completions. Select the one that BEST answers the question or completes the statement. *PRINT THE LETTER OF THE CORRECT ANSWER IN THE SPACE AT THE RIGHT.*

1. If an analyst recommends to the head of a newly established agency that the latter institute a line type of organization, he should also point out that this structure has the following MAJOR disadvantage: 1.____
   A. Delay will be encountered in reaching decisions.
   B. Coordination will be difficult to secure.
   C. Authority and responsibility will be diffused.
   D. Discipline will be hard to maintain.

2. Of the following statements which relate to the use of office space, the one that is LEAST valid is: 2.____
   A. A request for a conference room on the basis of privacy for meetings usually cannot be justified, for most private offices are suitable for meetings.
   B. Private offices are objectionable because they tend to slow up the work by interfering with supervisory effectiveness.
   C. The reception room should not handle ordinary and necessary traffic between different areas in the office.
   D. The space utilization of private offices is about 35 to 50 percent of that of the open area arrangement.

3. In preparing the layout for a small office, PARAMOUNT consideration should be given to a design that will 3.____
   A. accommodate the flows representing the largest volumes of work
   B. cause work to progress through its production cycle regardless of backtracking in a straight line or U
   C. increase the speed and movement of papers involved in the flow of work to the shortest compass feasible
   D. take into account vertical relationships of floor locations in the work flow

4. When centralization of office activities is instituted, which one of the following conditions will MOST likely occur? 4.____
   A. Confidentiality of office work will decrease.
   B. Equitable wage schedules will be undermined.
   C. Office machine maintenance costs will increase.
   D. Training of office employees will be delayed.

5. Descriptor is a term COMMONLY used in 5.____
   A. information retrieval
   B. network analysis
   C. planning and forecasting
   D. systems analysis

6. Of the following, the BEST way to secure effective management is USUALLY to 6.____
   A. allow staff agencies to help solve the administrative problems of line management
   B. provide a good organization structure
   C. select capable managers and administrators
   D. set up conservative spans of control

7. The MOST effective way of graphically representing the division of total costs into component costs as they vary over a period of time is by means of a 7.____
   A. band chart
   B. pictograph
   C. pie diagram
   D. histogram

8. During the past 50 years, the rate of increase in the number of office workers has been much greater than that of our total working force. 8.____
   The LEAST likely reason to cause this increase is the
   A. dispersal of clerical operations which accompanied the growth in manufacturing
   B. development of "service industries"
   C. use of more factual information by managers
   D. expansion in business legislation and governmental regulatory agencies

9. In attempting to discover flaws in an organization, an organization chart has been prepared. 9.____
   The condition that will be LEAST likely to be disclosed through use of the organization chart will be
   A. executives who are burdened with details
   B. work schedules that are unmet
   C. promotional possibilities that are not being provided
   D. functions which are becoming secondary due to splitting among departmental units

10. The PRIMARY function of systems analysis in the Planning Programming Budgetary System is to 10.____
   A. cost out various alternatives
   B. develop a PERT chart for evaluating program content
   C. develop better alternatives than those which are in the currently approved program
   D. provide perspective in judging the validity of an expenditure

11. Systems analysis would be LEAST effective in solving which of these problems? The 11.____
   A. determination of need for a new pier
   B. problem of air pollution
   C. selection of a site for a police station
   D. selection of engineering personnel

12. In procedural analysis, when the purpose of a particular step has been shown to be justifiable to the end purpose of the procedure, the NEXT necessary step is usually to 12.____
   A. determine the time limits for the step
   B. weigh the value of the step against the expense involved
   C. sell the idea to the supervisory staff
   D. make it a part of the procedure

13. ▽ is a symbol used in records management flow diagrams to indicate 13.____
   A. destruction of paper
   B. filing and/or permanent storage
   C. inspection
   D. microfilming is necessary

14. The concept that decisions should be made at the lowest level in an organization where all the (required) information and competence are available is MOST particularly a general rule in 14.____
   A. communications theory
   B. decentralization of authority
   C. incremental decision-making
   D. span of control

15. An office quality control program may comprise several approaches. The one LEAST desirable of the following normally is to 15.____
   A. follow a policy of spot or sample checking
   B. follow a practice of 100% checking of all work to verify its correctness
   C. inspect the work by means of a statistical quality control program
   D. review and tally errors being detected from present checking operations to determine the amount of checking presently being followed and the results being obtained

16. When a form is to be completed by an electronic data processing machine, which of the following is LEAST necessary? 16.____
   A. Form number B. Form title C. Lines D. Margins

17. Under a PPBS system, the selection of the proper alternative program should be made by the 17.____
   A. administrator responsible for the program, with the approval of the mayor and city legislative body
   B. budget director, basing his decision according to the optimum alternative
   C. budget examiner who reviews the administration budget
   D. chief systems analyst who programmed the alternatives

18. Which of the following is LEAST applicable in describing PPBS as a general concept? A 18.____
   A. quantitative method of budgeting for the coming year
   B. system of defining long-range alternative programs and planning the allocation of resources on the basis of the cost of the long-range program versus the benefit derived over the planning period
   C. system of measuring budgeted performance against pre-established goals
   D. system that establishes the importance of a program in terms of the expected cost of executing

19. Under a PPBS system, substantive planning is NORMALLY defined as 19.____
    A. fiscal planning
    B. planning of future budgets
    C. planning of objectives—ultimate and intermediate
    D. planning of programs—ultimate and intermediate

20. The method of selection which would provide the TIGHTEST standard under the logging method of work measurement would be 20.____
    A. one-third array
    B. modal average
    C. selected arithmetic average
    D. upper quartile

21. A concept for the evaluation of managers whereby goals are set and agreed upon for each manager, and then his attainment of those goals is evaluated at a particular prearranged target date, is BEST termed 21.____
    A. management by objectives
    B. management evaluation planning
    C. managerial performance appraisal
    D. program evaluation

22. When work is organized so that the work is broken into a series of jobs, and each unit of work (a customer order, invoice, etc.) moves progressively to position until completion, we would NORMALLY refer to this as the 22.____
    A. parallel plan of work subdivision
    B. serial plan
    C. unit assembly plan
    D. unit process plan

23. The type of organization in which employees report to a nominal manager for administrative purposes but are assigned to *ad hoc* supervisors as various assignments arise is BEST termed the _____ type of organization. 23.____
    A. functional
    B. process
    C. project or task force
    D. unit assembly

24. The expression which BEST defines a generalized situation in which several programs may be executed simultaneously or concurrently is 24.____
    A. multiprocessing
    B. multiprogramming
    C. on-line, real time programming
    D. process overlap

25. The sampling technique which consists of taking selections at constant intervals (every nth unit) from a list of the universe is called _____ sampling. 25.____
    A. area
    B. quota
    C. stratified random
    D. systematic

26. A method of project scheduling and control which shows the MOST optimistic, MOST pessimistic, and MOST probable estimate of time for how long each task in a project will take is called 26.____
    A. CPM (Critical Path Method)
    B. Gantt charting
    C. Linear Responsibility Charting
    D. PERT

27. The idea that classic organizational structure tends to create work situations having requirements counter to those for psychological success and self-esteem, sometimes called the "organizational dilemma," is MOST closely associated with which one of the following persons? 27.____
A. Chris Argyris
B. Frederick Taylor
C. Luther Gulick
D. Max Weber

28. Charles J. Hitch is known PRIMARILY for his work in the area of 28.____
A. administrative behavior
B. behavioral sciences
C. organizational analysis
D. PPBS

Questions 29-30.

DIRECTIONS: Questions 29 and 30 are to be answered on the basis of the following paragraph.

If one were to observe the information, in all its variant forms, that flows to a manager in the typical American enterprise, he would have a word for it: chaos. Subordinates want to be helpful, or to promote themselves, or to reflect discredit somewhere, and they originate or serve as a transmission belt for information they think the manager should have. Furthermore, it is the nature of the business process that information is generated where it is most easily reflected and is very scarce in areas or phases where data are not readily available. If one could project a tape which showed information density through time, he would find areas of heavy concentration and areas of little or no cloudiness. This means two things: First, people seem to have an inner drive to report available information in many ways, many forms, and for many users. Note what an accountant or statistician can do with two figures—or a mathematician without any figures at all! Second, the lack of information in specific areas means only that it is not available; it does not mean that it is unnecessary. Indeed, the blind areas may be of the greatest importance for decision-making purposes.

29. The result of the state of affairs described in the above paragraph would MOST likely be 29.____
A. inconsequential
B. an impetus to proper decision-making
C. high costs and poor decisions
D. a successful uniform information system

30. The author in this paragraph is PRIMARILY concerned with 30.____
A. decision-making theory
B. communications
C. tape information systems
D. information gathering by accountants and statisticians

# KEY (CORRECT ANSWERS)

| | | | | | |
|---|---|---|---|---|---|
| 1. | B | 11. | D | 21. | A |
| 2. | A | 12. | B | 22. | B |
| 3. | A | 13. | B | 23. | C |
| 4. | A | 14. | B | 24. | B |
| 5. | A | 15. | B | 25. | D |
| 6. | C | 16. | C | 26. | D |
| 7. | A | 17. | A | 27. | A |
| 8. | A | 18. | A | 28. | D |
| 9. | B | 19. | C | 29. | C |
| 10. | C | 20. | D | 30. | B |

# TEST 2

DIRECTIONS: Each question or incomplete statement is followed by several suggested answers or completions. Select the one that BEST answers the question or completes the statement. *PRINT THE LETTER OF THE CORRECT ANSWER IN THE SPACE AT THE RIGHT.*

1. It has been decided to make a few important revisions in the methods and procedures of a particular work unit. 1.____
Of the following, the method of implementing these revisions which would probably be MOST desirable in terms of morale as well as efficiency is to
   A. give all the employees in the work unit individual instructions in the revised procedures, making sure that each employee fully understands the changes before instructing the next employee
   B. institute all the revisions at once, followed by on-the-job training for all the employees in the work unit
   C. introduce the revisions one at a time, accompanying each revision with an orientation for the employees
   D. set up a training course for the employees, instructing them in all aspects of the revised procedures prior to their implementation

2. In an administrative survey of a multiple-unit organization, which of the following is it usually MOST important to identify? The 2.____
   A. data and information used commonly by units, how used and by whom
   B. flow of data and information within a single organization unit
   C. type and volume of data used within individual units and transmitted between units
   D. way data and information are transmitted between units, how used and by whom

3. A noted authority has described a common method of making organizational policy in which the decision-maker tries to find some acceptable level of goal accomplishment short of ultimate fulfillment of all objectives and to frame policies toward such fulfillment. 3.____
Of the following, this method is BEST termed
   A. feedback
   B. incrementalism
   C. satisfying
   D. seriality

4. The managerial grid, as defined by Blake and Mouton, shows two concerns and a range of interaction between them as follows: The horizontal axis indicates a concern for _____, while the vertical axis indicates a concern for _____. 4.____
   A. hierarchy; people
   B. production; people
   C. organization; people
   D. people; P/L (profit or loss)

5. In the managerial grid, which managerial style is dominant for any given person in any particular situation can be determined by any one or several sets of conditions in combination. 5.____
The five conditions in CORRECT order are:
   A. Organization, management, values, chance, production
   B. Organization, situation, values, personality, chance
   C. Production, situation, personality, chance, individually
   D. Values, personality, variety, organization, chance

6. The analyst may be faced with a choice of either recommending service contracts or recommending on-call service for maintenance of equipment. 6.____
In making a decision, the one of the following factors which would mitigate MOST against the use of on-call service would be that
   A. equipment utilization is not heavy
   B. prompt service when breakdowns occur is seldom essential
   C. regular checkups and servicing are considered desirable based on past equipment history
   D. trade-ins are made frequently

7. The type of paper stock MOST commonly used for office forms work is _____ bond. 7.____
   A. cotton content
   B. duplicating or mimeo
   C. rag
   C. sulphite

8. In laying out an office, according to most authorities, the amount of space which NORMALLY should be allowed for a clerk would in the range of _____ square feet. 8.____
   A. 10 to15
   B. 25 to 100
   C. 110 to 125
   D. 130 to 150

9. A noted behavioral scientist believes that the MOST important element in job satisfaction, of those listed below, s 9.____
   A. job security
   B. responsibility or recognition
   C. salary
   D. type of supervision

10. The point of view that the average human being prefers to be directed, wishes to avoid responsibility, has relatively little ambition, and wants security above all has been described in Douglas MacGregor's classic book on human motivation in business. 10.____
He includes this point of view in what he calls
   A. Theory X
   B. Theory Y
   C. Theory Z
   D. Theory X and Y combined

11. New desk top electronic machines are of two main types—printing or display. Display type machines show the results by any of the following methods EXCEPT for 11.____
   A. cathode ray tube
   B. electro-mechanical
   C. mosaic or liquid crystal
   D. nixie

12. The type of chart that is normally MOST useful for studying the work assignments and job content of individual positions in a particular organizational unit when making a procedure analysis is the _____ chart. 12._____
    A. columnar flow
    B. procedure flow
    C. work distribution
    D. work process

13. To prepare a work distribution chart, two other types of lists generally must be prepared. 13._____
    In the usual order of preparation, they are FIRST a(n)
    A. flow diagram, then an activity list
    B. skills list, then a task list
    C. task list, then an activity list
    D. activity list, then a task list

14. The critical path is defined as that path (or those paths) through a network 14,_____
    A. showing the least number of time units
    B. showing the greatest number of time units
    C. which consists (or consist) entirely of sequential activities
    D. which links (or link) together activities in concurrent relationship to each other

15. A statistical quality control program in the office is valuable in alerting management that the level of quality for particular transactions has deteriorated. 15._____
    It is, however, LEAST likely to reveal
    A. when preventive action is necessary
    B. when a variation is due to other than chance
    C. when an assignable cause is present
    D. what the cause of the error is

16. In work measurement, the value of a TMU is _____ min. 16._____
    A. .0001
    B. .0006
    C. .0036
    D. .0100

17. The sheet version of microfilm is NORMALLY referred to as 17._____
    A. microfiche
    B. micro-sheet
    C. microdupe
    D. microspec

18. While a line and staff organization is generally considered to have the advantages of both a line organization and a functional organization, with the disadvantages of each eliminated, disadvantages, nevertheless, do exist. 18._____
    Of the following, the one that describes the MOST significant disadvantage of a line and staff type of organization is that
    A. fewer opportunities are afforded to match the capacities of personnel with the job, since a smaller number of jobs is required
    B. line orders and staff advice, although clearly known to managers, tend to be confused by non-management members
    C. staff officers may attempt to take over line authority
    D. staff officers may tend to follow the ideas of the line officers and not generate their own ideas

19. Which activities take the most time? Are skills being utilized properly? Are employees doing too many unrelated tasks? 19.____
Of the following, the BEST technique to find answers to all of these questions is the
    A. flow diagram
    B. skills chart
    C. work count
    D. work distribution chart

20. Operator participation in management improvement work is LEAST likely to do which one of the following? 20.____
    A. Assure the use of the best available management techniques
    B. Make installation of new procedures quicker and easier
    C. Overcome the stigma of the outside expert
    D. Take advantage of the desire of most operators to seek self-improvement

21. Which of the following BEST defines an organization chart? A 21.____
    A. chart depicting the informal channels of communications within an organization
    B. chart depicting the major functions of an organization and the normal work flow between subdivisions of the organization
    C. graphic presentation of the arrangement and interrelationships of the subdivisions and functions of an organization as they exist
    D. graphic presentation of the arrangement and relationships of al positions authorized in an organization

22. Under a PPBS system, fiscal planning is NORMALLY considered to be planning 22.____
    A. for anticipated fixed costs only
    B. for present personnel requirements, procurement, and construction
    C. of current income and expenditures
    D. of future budgets

23. In the selection of space within an office building, LEAST consideration, generally, should be given to which of the following factors? 23.____
    A. Future expansion
    B. Proximity to elevators and restrooms
    C. Stability of other tenants on other floors
    D. Ventilation

24. In office layout, an office unit consisting of a combined desk and file cabinet and small movable partitions may BEST be described as _____ unit. 24.____
    A. conference
    B. landscaped office
    C. modular office
    D. semi-private office

25. Which of the following is it generally MOST important to consider when allocating office space? 25.____
    A. Actual organizational relationships
    B. Lighting requirements
    C. Noise levels
    D. Preferences of employees with over ten years of seniority

26. In preparing office layouts, the one of the following general factors within the affected unit which should generally receive the LEAST consideration is 26.____
    A. lighting levels in the existing area
    B. major work flow—the processing of paper
    C. present and projected growth rate of the unit
    D. traffic patterns of employees and visitors

27. In reviewing a new office layout, the one of the following questions that should normally receive LEAST consideration is: 27.____
    A. Have several alternate move day plans been prepared showing possible new locations of each piece of office equipment?
    B. Has expansion been provided for?
    C. Have alternate schemes been adequately explored to try to achieve the best possible layout?
    D. Is there adequate aisle space for ingress and egress?

28. Which of the following is the LEAST important reason for preparing a written study report? The 28.____
    A. report documents findings and recommendations so that the client can review and comment on them
    B. report is of interest as an historical document
    C. report serves as a document useful in implementing the recommendations
    D. writing process itself helps the analyst structure his thinking and conclusions

29. According to the classic studies by Rensis Likert at the University of Michigan, the GREATEST factor making for good morale and increased productivity was having a 29.____
    A. good program of employee benefits and wage scales
    B. supervisor who gave his employees free rein, after they were fully trained, and did not interfere with them
    C. supervisor who was interested primarily in production
    D. supervisor who, while also interested in production, was primarily "employee-centered"

30. Organization structure deals with the relationship of functions and the personnel performing these functions. It is usually advisable to think first of functions, then of the individuals performing these functions.
    MOST implicit in this approach is the recognition that 30.____
    A. conditions outside the organization may necessitate changes in the organization structure
    B. functions need not always be coordinated for an organization to effectively carry out its objectives
    C. functions tend to change with time while the interests and abilities of personnel are usually permanent
    D. personnel emphasis often results in unusual combinations of duties that are difficult to manage

# KEY (CORRECT ANSWERS)

| | | | | | |
|---|---|---|---|---|---|
| 1. | D | 11. | B | 21. | C |
| 2. | A | 12. | C | 22. | D |
| 3. | C | 13. | C | 23. | C |
| 4. | B | 14. | A | 24. | C |
| 5. | B | 15. | D | 25. | A |
| 6. | C | 16. | B | 26. | A |
| 7. | D | 17. | A | 27. | A |
| 8. | B | 18. | C | 28. | B |
| 9. | B | 19. | D | 29. | D |
| 10. | A | 20. | A | 30. | D |

# EXAMINATION SECTION

## TEST 1

DIRECTIONS: Each question or incomplete statement is followed by several suggested answers or completions. Select the one that BEST answers the question or completes the statement. *PRINT THE LETTER OF THE CORRECT ANSWER IN THE SPACE AT THE RIGHT.*

1. In organizational theory, the optimum span of control, that is, the number of subordinates who can be effectively supervised by one man above the level of the first line supervisor is GENERALLY set at between 1.____
   A. 3 and 6 B. 6 and 12 C. 12 and 18 D. 18 and 24

2. Which of the following is LEAST desirable as a basic guide to normal conventional office layout? 2.____
   A. Arrange desks so that work flows in a normal fashion
   B. Place files nearest to the persons who will use them
   C. Utilize a number of small areas to provide privacy
   D. Utilize one single large area

3. *A set of objects together with relationships between the objects and between their attributes* is the definition of 3.____
   A. a perceptual whole and its subcomponents
   B. a system in the terms of specific systems theory
   C. an organism
   D. forms control

4. A technique of time study in which each employee maintains a record of his own time is GENERALLY known as _____ study. 4.____
   A. estimated time B. observed time
   C. time log D. wristwatch

5. An employee has approached a supervisor with a request for a change involving his personal status or with a suggestion for making an improvement in the work The supervisor knows that the suggestion cannot be granted. 5.____
   Of the following, the BEST procedure would be for the supervisor to
   A. refer the matter to the personnel department
   B. refer the matter to his superior for action
   C. reject the proposal, explaining the defects or objections which cannot be overcome
   D. shelve the idea so that the employee will realize it cannot be acted upon

6. There are, in general, a number of common methods of drawing samples for statistical work. 6.____
   The method in which a regularly ordered interval is maintained between the items chosen is BEST termed _____ sampling.
   A. random B. stratified or selective
   C. systematic D. work

7. The multi-column process chart can be put to all of the following general uses EXCEPT to 7.____
   A. improve office layout
   B. improve procedures
   C. standardize procedures
   D. train personnel

8. If one wished to show the percentage of change over a period of time, the MOST appropriate type of graph or chart GENERALLY would be the _____ chart. 8.____
   A. bar
   B. line or curve
   C. logarithmic or semilogarithmic
   D. pie

9. A chart designed for the explicit purpose of portraying graphically information relating to the degree of responsibility of key individuals for the performance of various functions is BEST described as a(n) _____ chart. 9.____
   A. linear responsibility
   B. work distribution
   C. work process
   D. staff

10. The technique of work measurement LEAST useful for setting up a program of office incentive pay GENERALLY would be 10.____
   A. log sheets
   B. stopwatch time study
   C. wristwatch time study
   D. work sampling

11. There are a number of steps to be taken in making a work sampling study in order to set production standards. Three of the steps listed below are peculiar only to work sampling, in contrast with other work measurement techniques. 11.____
   The one EXCEPTION is:
   A. Define the breakdown of work into the proper elements of work and no-work or delay to be observed
   B. Determine the required number of observations needed for the specified degree of reliability
   C. Establish the observation intervals
   D. Make a preliminary estimate of work and no-work or delay element percentages for step A

12. A number of standardized flow process chart symbols have been generally accepted. 12.____
   The symbol ▽ GENERALLY indicates a(n)
   A. delay
   B. storage or file
   C. inspection
   D. operation

13. The number of standardized flow process chart symbols have been generally accepted. 13.____
   The symbol ▭ GENERALLY indicates a(n)
   A. delay
   B. storage or file
   C. inspection
   D. operation

14. The type of work for which short interval scheduling generally would be LEAST applicable would be the work of a group of 14.____
A. calculating clerks B. order clerks
C. technically-oriented clerks D. typists

15. In writing a business report, the BEST expression to use, in general, of those listed below would NORMALLY be: 15.____
A. Because B. Inasmuch as
C. In view of the fact that D. With reference to

16. Of the following, the MAJOR advantage of a random access data processing system, as compared with a sequential-type system, is its 16.____
A. ability to use more than one input system
B. demand for more sophisticated systems and programming
C. greater storage capacity and access speed
D. potential for processing data on a *first come, first-served* basis

17. A good rule to remember with regard to decision making is that decisions should be made 17.____
A. at the highest level competent to make such a decision
B. at the lowest level competent to make such a decision
C. by the person responsible for carrying out the decision
D. by the person responsible for the work of the unit

18. Which of the following potential systems would LEAST likely be improved by being online? A(n) _____ system. 18.____
A. budgeting control B. welfare eligibility
C. employee payroll D. inventory control

19. A management information and control system essentially should be designed to provide management personnel with up-to-date information which will enable them to improve control over their operations. 19.____
In designing such a system, the FIRST step to determine is:
A. What information is needed to effectively control operations?
B. What information is presently available?
C. What organization changes are necessary to implement the system?
D. Who is presently processing the information that might be used?

20. In designing control reports, which of the following guidelines is of MOST importance? 20.____
A. Financial information should always be carried to the nearest penny.
B. The report should be a simple and concise statement of only the pertinent facts.
C. The report should indicate the source of original data and how the computations were made.
D. The report should have the broadest possible distribution at all levels of management.

21. A situation which enables a number of users at offsite locations to have access to an office computer network is called 21.____
    A. multiprocessing B. multiprogramming
    C. cloud connectivity D. remote access

22. Computer software that would typically be used for widespread dissemination of a business report is 22.____
    A. Microsoft Word B. Microsoft PowerPoint
    C. Adobe Elements D. Google Sheets

23. Which of the following steps is LEAST desirable in designing an electronic data processing system? 23.____
    A. Design the EDP system first, then relate it to current operations
    B. Develop a corollary chart for the corresponding flow of information
    C. Develop a flow chart for the functions affected by the system
    D. Obtain from available EDP equipment that which best fits current operations

24. Electronic data processing equipment can produce more information faster than can be generated by any other means. Because this is true, one wonders whether our ability to generate information has not far outstripped our ability to assimilate it. 24.____
    In view of this, a PERSISTENT danger management faces is in
    A. determining the budget for management information systems
    B. determining what information is of real worth
    C. finding enough computer personnel
    D. keeping their computers fully occupied

25. The one of the following that is an ADVANTAGE of a hybrid local/remote network setup over fully local access is 25.____
    A. the ability to access a network outside normal circumstances
    B. closer oversight of personnel
    C. more efficient workflow
    D. reduced costs for software and production equipment

# KEY (CORRECT ANSWERS)

1. A
2. C
3. A
4. C
5. C

6. C
7. A
8. C
9. A
10. A

11. A
12. B
13. C
14. C
15. A

16. D
17. B
18. C
19. A
20. B

21. D
22. A
23. A
24. B
25. A

# TEST 2

DIRECTIONS: Each question or incomplete statement is followed by several suggested answers or completions. Select the one that BEST answers the question or completes the statement. *PRINT THE LETTER OF THE CORRECT ANSWER IN THE SPACE AT THE RIGHT.*

1. In analyzing data for the acquisition of new equipment, an analyst gathers the facts, analyzes them, and develops new procedures which will be required when the new equipment arrives. 1.____
Inn analyzing the factors involved, which one of the following is normally LEAST important in the evaluation of new equipment?
   A. Cost factors
   B. Layout and installation factors
   C. Production planning
   D. Operational experience of manufacturers of allied equipment

2. If an analyst is required to recommend the selection of a machine for an office operation, he can BEST judge the expected output of a particular machine by pursuing which of the following courses of action? 2.____
Obtain
   A. an actual test run of the machine in his office
   B. data from the manufacturer of the machine
   C. information on the percentage of working time the machine will be used
   D. the experience of actual users of similar machines elsewhere

3. Of the following, the BEST definition of records management is 3.____
   A. storage of all types of records at minimum expense
   B. planned control of all types of records
   C. storage of records for maximum accessibility
   D. systematic filing of all types of records

4. The one of the following which is NOT a primary objective of a records retention and disposal system is to 4.____
   A. assure appropriate preservation of records having permanent value
   B. dispose of records not warranting further preservation
   C. establish retention standards for archives
   D. provide an opportunity to use miniaturization

5. Of the following functions of management, the one which should NORMALLY precede the others is 5.____
   A. coordinating B. directing C. organizing D. planning

6. One of the more famous studies of organizations is called the Hawthorne study. 6.____
This work was one of the first to point out the importance of
   A. employee's benefit and retirement programs
   B. informal organization among employees
   C. job engineering
   D. styles of position classification

7. In organization theory, the type of position in which an individual is appointed to give technical aid to management on a particular problem area is generally BEST termed a(n) 7.____
   A. administrative assistant
   B. assistant to
   C. staff assistant
   D. staff specialist

8. In organizing, doing what works in the particular situation, with due regard to both short- and long-range objective, is BEST termed 8.____
   A. ambivalence
   B. authoritarianism
   C. decentralization
   D. pragmatism

9. If an effort were made to reduce the number of private offices in a new layout, the LEAST effective substitute in offering privacy would be the use of 9.____
   A. an open area with lower movable partitions or railings separating each individual
   B. conference rooms
   C. larger desks
   D. modular desk units

10. The term *administrative substation* NORMALLY refers to 10.____
   A. a work station handling a number of office services for an office organization
   B. a work station where middle level supervisors are located
   C. an office for handling management trainees
   D. the functions allocated to particular levels of administrative managers

11. An operations research technique which would be applied to determine the optimum number of window clerks or interviewers to have in an agency serving the public would MOST likely be the use of 11.____
   A. line of balance
   B. queuing theory
   C. simulation
   D. work sampling

12. A type of file which permits the operator to remain seated while the file can be moved backward and forward as required is BEST termed a _____ file. 12.____
   A. lateral
   B. movable
   C. reciprocating
   D. rotary

13. The technique of work measurement in which the analyst observes the work at random times of the day is BEST termed 13.____
   A. indirect observation
   B. logging
   C. ratio delay
   D. wristwatch

14. Examples of predetermined time systems generally should include all of the following EXCEPT 14.____
   A. Master Clerical Data
   B. Methods Time Measurement
   C. Short Interval Data
   D. Work Factor

15. A technique by which the supervisor or an assistant distributes a predetermined batch of work to the employee at periodic intervals of the day is generally BEST known as 15.____
A. backlog control scheduling
B. production control scheduling
C. short interval schedule
D. workload balancing

16. E. Wright Bakke defined his *fusion process* as: The 16.____
A. work environment to some degree remakes the organization and the organization to some degree remakes the work environment
B. fusing of the interests of both management and labor unions
C. community of interest between first line supervisors and top management
D. organization to some degree remakes the individual and the individual to some degree remakes the organization

17. A pamphlet on issues related to 2020s-era office setup would likely be titled 17.____
A. Close Encounters: How Proximity Elevates Production
B. How Connectivity Spurs Inspiration
C. See Your Employees in a New Light With Open Floor Plans
D. From A to Zoom: The Terminology of the Hybrid Workplace

18. In planning office space for a newly established bureau, it would usually be LEAST desirable to 18.____
A. concentrate, rather than disperse, the chief sources of office noises
B. design an office environment with the same brightness as the office desk
C. designate as reception rooms, washrooms, and other service areas those areas that will receive lesser amounts of illumination than those areas in which private office work will be performed
D. eliminate natural light in cases where it is not the major light source

19. A private office should be used when its use is dictated by facts and unbiased judgment. It should never be provided simply because requests and sometimes pressure have been brought to bear. 19.____
Of the following reasons used to justify use of a private office, the one that requires the MOST care in determining whether a private office is actually warranted is
A. an office has always been provided for a particular job
B. prestige considerations
C. the confidential nature of the work
D. the work involves high concentration

20. Theoretically, an ideal organization structure can be set up for each enterprise. In actual practice, the ideal organization structure is seldom, if ever, obtained. 20.____
Of the following, the one that normally is of LEAST influence in determining the organization structure is the
A. existence of agreements and favors among members of the organization
B. funds available
C. opinions and beliefs of top executives
D. tendency of management to discard established forms in favor of new forms

21. An IMPORTANT aspect to keep in mind during the decision-making process is that 21.____
    A. all possible alternatives for attaining goals should be sought out and considered
    B. considering various alternatives only leads to confusion
    C. once a decision has been made, it cannot be retracted
    D. there is only one correct method to reach any goal

22. Implementation of accountability requires 22.____
    A. a leader who will not hesitate to take punitive action
    B. an established system of communication from the bottom to the top
    C. explicit directives from leaders
    D. too much expense to justify it

23. Of the following, the MAJOR difference between systems and procedures analysis and work simplification is: 23.____
    A. The former complicates organizational routine and the latter simplifies it
    B. The former is objective and the latter is subjective
    C. The former generally utilizes expert advice and the latter is a *do-it-yourself* improvement by supervisors and workers
    D. There is no difference other than in name

24. Systems development is concerned with providing 24.____
    A. a specific set of work procedures
    B. an overall framework to describe general relationships
    C. definitions of particular organizational functions
    D. organizational symbolism

25. Organizational systems and procedures should be 25.____
    A. developed as problems arise as no design can anticipate adequately the requirements of an organization
    B. developed jointly by experts in systems and procedures and the people who are responsible for implementing them
    C. developed solely by experts in systems and procedures
    D. eliminated whenever possible to save unnecessary expense

# KEY (CORRECT ANSWERS)

1. D
2. A
3. B
4. D
5. D

6. B
7. D
8. D
9. C
10. A

11. B
12. C
13. C
14. C
15. C

16. D
17. D
18. D
19. A
20. D

21. A
22. B
23. C
24. B
25. B

# TEST 3

DIRECTIONS: Each question or incomplete statement is followed by several suggested answers or completions. Select the one that BEST answers the question or completes the statement. *PRINT THE LETTER OF THE CORRECT ANSWER IN THE SPACE AT THE RIGHT.*

1. The CHIEF danger of a decentralized control system is that 1.____
   A. excessive reports and communications will be generated
   B. problem areas may not be detected readily
   C. the expense will become routine
   D. this will result in too many *chiefs*

2. Of the following, management guides and controls clerical work PRINCIPALLY through 2.____
   A. close supervision and constant checking of personnel
   B. spot checking of clerical procedures
   C. strong sanctions for clerical supervisors
   D. the use of printed forms

3. Which of the following is MOST important before conducting fact-finding interviews? 3.____
   A. Becoming acquainted with all personnel to be interviewed
   B. Explaining the techniques you plan to use
   C. Explaining to the operating officials the purpose and scope of the study
   D. Orientation of the physical layout

4. Of the following, the one that is NOT essential in carrying out a comprehensive work improvement program is 4.____
   A. standards of performance
   B. supervisory training
   C. work count/task list
   D. work distribution chart

5. Which of the following control techniques is MOST useful on large complex systems projects? 5.____
   A. A general work plan
   B. Gantt chart
   C. Monthly progress report
   D. PERT chart

6. The action which is MOST effective in gaining acceptance of a study by the agency which is being studied is 6.____
   A. a directive from the agency head to install a study based on recommendations included in a report
   B. a lecture-type presentation following approval of the procedures
   C. a written procedure in narrative form covering the proposed system with visual presentations and discussions
   D. procedural charts showing the *before* situation, forms, steps, etc. to the employees affected

7. Which of the following is NOT an advantage in the use of oral instructions as compared with written instructions? Oral instruction(s) 7.____
   A. can easily be changed
   B. is superior in transmitting complex directives
   C. facilitate exchange of information between a superior and his subordinate
   D. with discussions make it easier to ascertain understanding

8. Which organization principle is MOST closely related to procedural analysis and improvement? 8.____
   A. Duplication, overlapping, and conflict should be eliminated.
   B. Managerial authority should be clearly defined.
   C. The objectives of the organization should be clearly defined.
   D. Top management should be freed of burdensome detail.

9. Which one of the following is the MAJOR objective of operational audits? 9.____
   A. Detecting fraud
   B. Determining organization problems
   C. Determining the number of personnel needed
   D. Recommending opportunities for improving operating and management practices

10. Of the following, the formalization of organization structure is BEST achieved by 10.____
    A. a narrative description of the plan of organization
    B. functional charts
    C. job descriptions together with organization charts
    D. multi-flow charts

11. Budget planning is MOST useful when it achieves 11.____
    A. cost control
    B. forecast of receipts
    C. performance review
    D. personnel reduction

12. The UNDERLYING principle of sound administration is to 12.____
    A. base administration on investigation facts
    B. have plenty of resources available
    C. hire a strong administrator
    D. establish a broad policy

13. Although questionnaires are not the best survey tool the management analyst has to use, there are times when a good questionnaire can expedite the *fact-finding* phase of a management survey. 13.____
    Which of the following should be AVOIDED in the design and distribution of the questionnaire?
    A. Questions should be framed so that answers can be classified and tabulated for analysis.
    B. Those receiving the questionnaire must be knowledgeable enough to accurately provide the information desired.

C. The questionnaire should enable the respondent to answer in a narrative manner.
D. The questionnaire should require a minimum amount of writing.

14. Of the following, the formula which is used to calculate the arithmetic mean from data grouped in a frequency distribution is M = 14.____

A. $\frac{N}{\Sigma fx}$ B. $N(\Sigma fx)$ C. $\frac{\Sigma fx}{N}$ D. $\frac{\Sigma x}{fN}$

15. Arranging large groups of numbers in frequency distributions 15.____
A. gives a more composite picture of the total group than a random listing
B. is misleading in most cases
C. is unnecessary in most instances
D. presents the data in a form whereby further manipulation of the group is eliminated

16. After a budget has been developed, it serves to 16.____
A. assist the accounting department in posting expenditures
B. measure the effectiveness of department managers
C. provide a yardstick against which actual costs are measured
D. provide the operating department with total expenditure to date

17. Of the following, which formula is used to determine staffing requirements? 17.____

A. $\frac{\text{Hours per man-day}}{\text{Volume x Standard}}$ = Employees Needed

B. $\frac{\text{Hours per man-day x Standard}}{\text{Volume}}$ = Employees Needed

C. $\frac{\text{Hours per man-day x Volume}}{\text{Standard}}$ = Employees Needed

D. $\frac{\text{Volume x Standard}}{\text{Hours per man-day}}$ = Employees Needed

18. Of the following, which formula is used to determine the number of days required to process work? 18.____

A. $\frac{\text{Employees x Daily Output}}{\text{Volume}}$ = Days to Process Work

B. $\frac{\text{Employees x Volume}}{\text{Daily Output}}$ = Days to Process Work

C. $\frac{\text{Volume}}{\text{Employees x Daily Output}}$ = Days to Process Work

D. $\frac{\text{Volume x Daily Output}}{\text{Employees}}$ = Days to Process Work

19. Identify this symbol, as used in a Systems Flow Chart.
    A. Document
    B. Decision
    C. Preparation
    D. Process

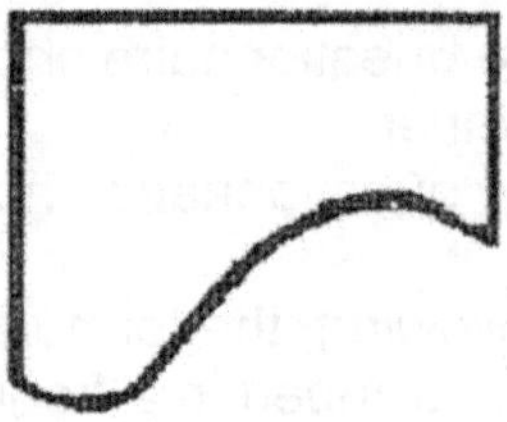

19.____

20. Of the following, the MAIN advantage of a form letter over a dictated letter is that a form letter
    A. is more expressive
    B. is neater
    C. may be mailed in a window envelope
    D. requires less secretarial time

20.____

21. The term that may be defined as a *systematic analysis of all factors affecting work being done or all factors that will affect work to be done, in order to save effort, time, or money* is
    A. flow process charting
    B. work flow analysis
    C. work measurement
    D. work simplification

21.____

22. Generally, the LEAST important basic factor to be considered in developing office layout improvements is to locate
    A. office equipment, reference facilities, and files as close as practicable to those using them
    B. persons as close as practicable to the persons from whom they receive their work
    C. persons as close as practicable to windows and/or adequate ventilation
    D. persons who are friendly with each other close together to improve morale

22.____

23. Of the following, the one which is LEAST effective in reducing administrative costs is
    A. applying objective measurement techniques to determine the time required to perform a given task
    B. establishing budgets on the basis of historical performance data
    C. motivating supervisors and managers in the importance of cost reduction
    D. selecting the best method—manual, mechanical, or electronic—to process the essential work

23.____

24. *Fire-fighting* is a common expression in management terminology. Of the following, which BEST describes *fire-fighting* as an analyst's approach to solving paperwork problems?
    A. A complete review of all phases of the department's processing functions
    B. A studied determination of the proper equipment to process the work
    C. An analysis of each form that is being processed and the logical reasons for its processing
    D. The solution of problems as they arise, usually at the request of operating personnel

24.____

25. Assume that an analyst with a proven record of accomplishment on many projects is having difficulties on his present assignment. 25.____
Of the following, the BEST course of action for his superior to take is to
   A. assume there is a personality conflict involved and transfer the analyst to another project
   B. give the analyst some time off
   C. review the nature of the project to determine whether or not the analyst is equipped to handle the assignment
   D. suggest that the analyst seek counseling

# KEY (CORRECT ANSWERS)

| | | | |
|---|---|---|---|
| 1. | B | 11. | A |
| 2. | D | 12. | A |
| 3. | C | 13. | C |
| 4. | B | 14. | C |
| 5. | D | 15. | A |
| 6. | C | 16. | C |
| 7. | B | 17. | D |
| 8. | A | 18. | C |
| 9. | D | 19. | A |
| 10. | C | 20. | D |
| 21. | D | | |
| 22. | D | | |
| 23. | B | | |
| 24. | D | | |
| 25. | C | | |

# EXAMINATION SECTION

## TEST 1

DIRECTIONS: Each question or incomplete statement is followed by several suggested answers or completions. Select the one that BEST answers the question or completes the statement. *PRINT THE LETTER OF THE CORRECT ANSWER IN THE SPACE AT THE RIGHT.*

1. Assume that a manager is preparing a list of reasons to justify making a major change in methods and procedures in his agency. 1.____
   Which of the following reasons would be LEAST appropriate on such a list?
   A. Improve the means for satisfying needs and wants of agency personnel
   B. Increase efficiency
   C. Intensify competition and stimulate loyalty to separate work groups
   D. Contribute to the individual and group satisfaction of agency personnel

2. Many managers recognize the benefits of decentralization but are concerned about the danger of over-relaxation of control as a result of increased delegation. 2.____
   Of the following, the MOST appropriate means of establishing proper control under decentralization is for the manager to
   A. establish detailed standards for all phases of operation
   B. shift his attention from operating details to appraisal of results
   C. keep himself informed by decreasing the time span covered by reports
   D. make unilateral decisions on difficult situations that arise in decentralized locations

3. In some agencies, the counsel to the agency head is given the right to bypass the chain of command and issue orders directly to the staff concerning matters that involve certain specific processes and practices. 3.____
   This situation MOST NEARLY illustrates the principle of _____ authority.
   A. the acceptance theory of
   B. multiple-linear
   C. splintered
   D. functional

4. Assume that a manager is writing a brief report to his superior outlining the advantages of matrix organization. 4.____
   Of the following, it would be INCORRECT to state that
   A. in matrix organization, a project is emphasized by designating one individual as the focal point for all matters pertaining to it
   B. utilization of manpower can be flexible in matrix organization because a reservoir of specialists is maintained in the line operations
   C. the usual line staff arrangement is generally reversed in matrix organization
   D. in matrix organization, responsiveness to project needs is generally faster due to establishing needed communication lines and decision points

5. It is commonly understood that communication is an important part of the administrative process. 5.____
Which of the following is NOT a valid principle of the communication process in administration?
   A. The channels of communication should be spontaneous.
   B. The lines of communication should be as direct and as short as possible.
   C. Communications should be authenticated.
   D. The persons serving in communications centers should be competent.

6. The PRIMARY purpose of the quantitative approach in management is to 6.____
   A. identify better alternatives for management decision-making
   B. substitute data for judgment
   C. match opinions to data
   D. match data to opinions

7. If an executive wants to make a strong case for running his agency as a flat type of structure, he should point out that the PRIMARY advantage of doing so is to 7.____
   A. provide less experience in decision-making for agency personnel
   B. facilitate frequent contact between each superior and his immediate subordinates
   C. improve communication and unify attitudes
   D. improve communication and diversify attitudes

8. In deciding how detailed his delegation of authority to a subordinate should be, a manager should follow the general principle that 8.____
   A. delegation of authority is more detailed at the top of the organizational structure
   B. detailed delegation of authority is associated with detailed work assignments
   C. delegation of authority should be in sufficient detail to prevent overlapping assignments
   D. detailed delegation of authority is associated with broad work assignments

9. In recent years, newer and more fluid types of organizational forms have been developed. One of these is a type of free-form organization. 9.____
Another name for this type of organization is the
   A. project organization
   B. semimix organization
   C. naturalistic structure
   D. semipermanent structure

10. Which of the following is the MAJOR objective of operational or management systems audits? 10.____
   A. Determining the number of personnel needed
   B. Recommending opportunities for improving operating and management practices
   C. Detecting fraud
   D. Determining organization problems

11. Assume that a manager observes that conflict exists between his agency and another operating agency of government. 11.____
Which of the following statements is the LEAST probable cause of this conflict?
    A. Incompatibility between the agencies' goals but similarity in their resource allocations
    B. Compatibility between agencies' goals and resources
    C. Status differences between agency personnel
    D. Differences in perceptions of each other's policies

12. Of the following, a MAJOR purpose of brainstorming as a problem-solving technique is to 12.____
    A. develop the ability to concentrate
    B. encourage creative thinking
    C. evaluate employees' ideas
    D. develop critical ability

13. The one of the following requirements which is LEAST likely to accompany regular delegation of work from a manager to a subordinate is a(n) 13.____
    A. need to review the organization's workload
    B. indication of what work the subordinate is to do
    C. need to grant authority to the subordinate
    D. obligation for the subordinate who accepts the work to try to complete it

14. Of the following, the one factor which is generally considered LEAST essential to successful committee operation is 14.____
    A. stating a clear definition of the authority and scope of the committee
    B. selecting the committee chairman carefully
    C. limiting the size of the committee to four persons
    D. limiting the subject matter to that which can be handled in group discussion

15. In using the program evaluation and review technique, the *critical path* is the path that 15.____
    A. requires the shortest time
    B. requires the longest time
    C. focuses most attention on social constraints
    D. focuses most attention to repetitious jobs

16. Which one of the following is LEAST characteristic of the management-by-objectives approach? 16.____
    A. The scope within which the employee may exercise decision-making is broadened.
    B. The employee starts with a self-appraisal of his performances, abilities, and potential.
    C. Emphasis is placed on activities performed; activities orientation is maximized.
    D. Each employee participates in determining his own objectives.

17. The function of management which puts into effect the decisions, plans, and programs that have previously been worked out for achieving the goals of the group is MOST appropriately called 17.____
    A. scheduling B. classifying C. budgeting D. directing

18. In the establishment of a plan to improve office productive efficiency, which of the following guidelines is LEAST helpful in setting sound work standards? 18.____
    A. Employees must accept the plan's objectives.
    B. Current production averages must be promulgated as work standards for a group.
    C. The work flow must generally be fairly constant.
    D. The operation of the plan must be expressed in terms understandable to the worker.

19. The one of the following activities which, generally speaking, is of *relatively* MAJOR importance at the lower-management level and of *somewhat* LESSER importance at higher-management levels is 19.____
    A. actuating B. forecasting C. organizing D. planning

20. Three styles of leadership exist: democratic, authoritarian, and laissez-faire. Of the following work situations, the one in which a democratic approach would normally be the MOST effective is when the work is 20.____
    A. routine and moderately complex B. repetitious and simple
    C. complex and not routine D. simple and not routine

21. Governmental and business organizations *generally* encounter the GREATEST difficulties in developing tangible measures of which one of the following? 21.____
    A. The level of expenditures B. Contributions to social welfare
    C. Retention rates D. Causes of labor unrest

22. Of the following, a *management-by-objectives* program is BEST described as 22.____
    A. a new comprehensive plan of organization
    B. introduction of budgets and financial controls
    C. introduction of long-range planning
    D. development of future goals with supporting and related progress reviews

23. Research and analysis is probably the most widely used technique for selecting alternatives when major planning decisions are involved. 23.____
    Of the following, a VALUABLE characteristic of research and analysis is that this technique
    A. places the problem in a meaningful conceptual framework
    B. involves practical application of the various alternatives
    C. accurately analyzes all important tangibles
    D. is much less expensive than other problem-solving methods

24. If a manager were assigned the task of using a systems approach to designing a new work unit, which of the following should he consider FIRST in carrying out his design? 24.____
   A. Networks
   B. Work flows and information processes
   C. Linkages and relationships
   D. Decision points and control loops

25. The MAIN distinction between Theory X and Theory Y approaches to organization, in accordance with Douglas McGregor's view, is that Theory Y 25.____
   A. considers that work is natural to people; Theory X assumes that people are lazy and avoid work
   B. leads to a tall, narrow organization structure, while Theory X leads to one that is flat
   C. organizations motivate people with money; Theory X organizations motivate people with good working conditions
   D. represents authoritarian management, while Theory X management is participative

---

## KEY (CORRECT ANSWERS)

| | | | |
|---|---|---|---|
| 1. | C | 11. | B |
| 2. | B | 12. | B |
| 3. | D | 13. | A |
| 4. | C | 14. | C |
| 5. | A | 15. | B |
| 6. | A | 16. | C |
| 7. | C | 17. | D |
| 8. | B | 18. | B |
| 9. | A | 19. | A |
| 10. | B | 20. | C |

| | |
|---|---|
| 21. | B |
| 22. | D |
| 23. | A |
| 24. | B |
| 25. | A |

# TEST 2

DIRECTIONS: Each question or incomplete statement is followed by several suggested answers or completions. Select the one that BEST answers the question or completes the statement. *PRINT THE LETTER OF THE CORRECT ANSWER IN THE SPACE AT THE RIGHT.*

1. Of the following, the stage in decision-making which is usually MOST difficult is 1.____
   A. stating the alternatives
   B. predicting the possible outcome of each alternative
   C. evaluating the relative merits of each alternative
   D. minimizing the undesirable aspects of the alternative selected

2. In a department where a clerk is reporting both to a senior clerk in charge of the mail room and also to a supervising clerk in charge of the duplicating section, there may be a breakdown of the management principle called 2.____
   A. horizontal specialization
   B. job enrichment
   C. unity of command
   D. Graicunas' Law

3. Of the following, the failure by line managers to accept and appreciate the benefits and limitations of a new program or system VERY frequently can be traced to the 3.____
   A. budgetary problems involved
   B. resultant need to reduce staff
   C. lack of controls it engenders
   D. failure of top management to support its implementation

4. Although there is general agreement that *management-by-objectives* has made a major contribution to modern management of large organizations, criticisms of the system during the past few years have resulted in 4.____
   A. mounting pressure for relaxation of management goals
   B. renewed concern with human values and the manager's personal needs
   C. over-mechanistic application of the perceptions of the behavioral scientists
   D. disillusionment with *management-by-objectives* on the part of a majority of managers

5. Of the following, which is usually considered to be a MAJOR obstacle to the systematic analysis of potential problems by managers? 5.____
   A. Managers have a tendency to think that all the implications of some proposed step cannot be fully understood.
   B. Rewards rarely go to those managers who are most successful at resolving current problems in management.
   C. There is a common conviction of manages that their goals are difficult to achieve.
   D. Managers are far more concerned about correcting today's problems than with preventing tomorrow's.

6. Which of the following should generally have the MOST influence on the selection of supervisors? 6.____
   A. Experience within the work unit where the vacancies exist
   B. Amount of money needed to effect the promotion
   C. Personal preferences of the administration
   D. Evaluation of capacity to exercise supervisory responsibilities

7. In questioning a potential administrator for selection purposes, the one of the following practices which is MOST desirable is to 7.____
   A. encourage the job applicant to give primarily *yes* or *no* replies
   B. get the applicant to talk freely and in detail about his background
   C. let the job applicant speak most of the time
   D. probe the applicant's attitudes, motivation, and willingness to accept responsibility

8. In implementing the managerial function of training subordinates, it is USEFUL to know that a widely agreed-upon definition of human learning is that learning 8.____
   A. is a relatively permanent change in behavior that results from reinforced practice or experience
   B. involves an improvement, but not necessarily a change in behavior
   C. involves a change in behavior, but not necessarily an improvement
   D. is a temporary change in behavior which must be subject to practice or experience

9. If a manager were thinking about using a committee of subordinates to solve an operating problem, which of the following would generally NOT be an advantage of such use of the committee approach? 9.____
   A. Improved coordination B. Low cost
   C. Increased motivation D. Integrated judgment

10. Which one of the following management approaches MOST often uses model-building techniques to solve management problems? 10.____
    _____ approach.
    A. Behavioral B. Fiscal C. Quantitative D. Process

11. Of the following, the MOST serious risk in using budgets as a tool for management control is the 11.____
    A. probable neglect of other good management practices
    B. likelihood of guesswork because of the need to plan far in advance
    C. possibility of undue emphasis on factors that are easiest to measure
    D. danger of making qualitative rather than quantitative assessments of performance

12. In government budgeting, the problem of relating financial transactions to the fiscal year in which they are budgeted is BEST met by 12.____
    A. determining the cash balance by comparing how much money has been received and how much has been paid out
    B. applying net revenue to the fiscal year in which they are collected as offset by relevant expenses

C. adopting a system whereby appropriations are entered when they are received and expenditures are entered when they are paid out
D. entering expenditures on the books when the obligation to make the expenditure is made

13. If the agency's bookkeeping system records income when it is received and expenditures when the money is paid out this system is USUALLY known as a _____ system. 13.____
A. cash
B. flow-payment
C. deferred
D. fiscal year income

14. An audit, as the term applies to budget execution, is MOST NEARLY a 14.____
A. procedure based on the budget estimates
B. control exercised by the executive on the legislature in the establishment of program priorities
C. check on the legality of expenditures and is based on the appropriations act
D. requirement which must be met before funds can be spent

15. In government budgeting, there is a procedure known as *allotment*. 15.____
Of the following statements which relate to allotment, select the one that is MOST generally considered to be correct.
Allotment
A. increases the practice of budget units coming back to the legislature branch for supplemental appropriations
B. is simply an example of red tape
C. eliminates the requirement of timing of expenditures
D. is designed to prevent waste

16. In government budgeting, the establishment of the schedules of allotments is MOST generally the responsibility of the 16.____
A. budget unit and the legislature
B. budget unit and the executive
C. budget unit only
D. executive and the legislature

17. Of the following statements relating to preparation of an organization's budget request, which is the MOST generally valid precaution? 17.____
A. Give specific instructions on the format or budget requests and required supporting data
B. Because of the complexity of preparing a budget request, avoid argumentation to support the requests
C. Put requests in whatever format is desirable
D. Consider that final approval will be given to initial estimates

18. Of the following statements which relate to the budget process in a well-organized government, select the one that is MOST NEARLY correct. 18.____
A. The budget cycle is the step-by-step process which is repeated each and every fiscal year.
B. Securing approval of the budget does not take place within the budget cycle.

C. The development of a new budget and putting it into effect is a two-step process known as the budget cycle.
D. The fiscal period, usually a fiscal year, has no relation to the budget cycle.

19. If a manager were asked what PPBS stands for, he would be RIGHT if he said _____ budgeting system. 19.____
A. public planning
B. planning programming
C. planning projections
D. programming procedures

Questions 20-21.

DIRECTIONS: Questions 20 and 21 are to be answered on the basis of the following information.

Sample Budget

| Refuse Collection | Amount |
|---|---|
| Personal Services | $30,000 |
| Contractual Services | 5,000 |
| Supplies and Materials | 5,000 |
| Capital Outlay | 10,000 |
| | $50,000 |

| Residential Collections | |
|---|---|
| Dwellings – 1 pickup per week | 1,000 |
| Tons of refuse collected per year | 375 |
| Cost of collections per ton | $ 8 |
| Cost per dwelling pickup per year | $ 3 |
| Total annual cost | $3,000 |

20. The sample budget shown is a simplified example of a _____ budget. 20.____
A. factorial B. performance C. qualitative D. rational

21. The budget shown in the sample differs CHIEFLY from line-item and program budgets in that it includes 21.____
A. objects of expenditure but not activities or functions
B. only activities, functions, and control
C. activities and functions but not objects of expenditures
D. levels of service

Question 22.

DIRECTIONS: Question 22 is to be answered on the basis of the following information.

Sample Budget

| | | |
|---|---|---|
| Environmental Safety | | |
| Air Pollution Protection | | |
| Personal Services | $20,000,000 | |
| Contractual Services | 4,000,000 | |
| Supplies and Materials | 4,000,000 | |
| Capital Outlay | 2,000,000 | |
| Total Air Pollution Protection | | $30,000,000 |
| Water Pollution Protection | | |
| Personal Services | $23,000,000 | |
| Supplies and Materials | 4,500,000 | |
| Capital Outlay | 20,500,000 | |
| Total Water Pollution Protection | | $48,000,000 |
| Total Environmental Safety | | $78,000,000 |

22. Based on the above budget, which is the MOST valid statement? 22.____
    A. Environmental Safety, Air Pollution Protection, and Water Pollution Protection could all be considered program elements.
    B. The object listings included water pollution protection and capital outlay.
    C. Examples of the program element listings in the above are personal services and supplies and materials
    D. Contractual Services and Environmental Safety were the program element listings.

23. Which of the following is NOT an advantage of a program budget over a line-item budget? 23.____
A program budget
    A. allows us to set up priority lists in deciding what activities we will spend our money on
    B. gives us more control over expenditures than a line-item budget
    C. is more informative in that we know the broad purposes of spending money
    D. enables us to see if one program is getting much less money than the others

24. If a manager were trying to explain the fundamental difference between traditional accounting theory and practice and the newer practice of managerial accounting, he would be MOST accurate if he said that 24.____
    A. traditional accounting practice focused on providing information for persons outside organizations, while managerial accounting focuses on providing information for people inside organizations
    B. traditional accounting practice focused on providing information for persons inside organizations while managerial accounting focuses on providing information for persons outside organizations

C. managerial accounting is exclusively concerned with historical facts while traditional accounting stresses future projections exclusively
D. traditional accounting practice is more budget-focused than managerial accounting

25. Which of the following formulas is used to determine the number of days required to process work? 25.____
_____ = Days to Process Work

A. $\frac{\text{Employees x Daily Output}}{\text{Volume}}$ B. $\frac{\text{Volume x Daily Output}}{\text{Volume}}$

C. $\frac{\text{Volume}}{\text{Employees x Daily Output}}$ D. $\frac{\text{Employees x Volume}}{\text{Daily Output}}$

# KEY (CORRECT ANSWERS)

1. C
2. C
3. D
4. B
5. D

6. D
7. D
8. A
9. B
10. C

11. C
12. D
13. A
14. C
15. D

16. C
17. A
18. A
19. B
20. B

21. D
22. A
23. B
24. A
25. C

# TEST 3

DIRECTIONS: Each question or incomplete statement is followed by several suggested answers or completions. Select the one that BEST answers the question or completes the statement. *PRINT THE LETTER OF THE CORRECT ANSWER IN THE SPACE AT THE RIGHT.*

1. Electronic data processing equipment can produce more information faster than can be generated by any other means. 1.____
In view of this, the MOST important problem faced by management at present is to
   A. keep computers fully occupied
   B. find enough computer personnel
   C. assimilate and properly evaluate the information
   D. obtain funds to establish appropriate information systems

2. A well-designed management information system ESSENTIALLY provides each executive and manager the information he needs for 2.____
   A. determining computer time requirements
   B. planning and measuring results
   C. drawing a new organization chart
   D. developing a new office layout

3. It is generally agreed that management policies should be periodically reappraised and restated in accordance with current conditions. 3.____
Of the following, the approach which would be MOST effective in determining whether a policy should be revised is to
   A. conduct interviews with staff members at all levels in order to ascertain the relationship between the policy and actual practice
   B. make proposed revisions in the policy and apply it to current problems
   C. make up hypothetical situations using both the old policy and a revised version in order to make comparisons
   D. call a meeting of top level staff in order to discuss ways of revising the policy

4. Every manager has many occasions to lead a conference or participate in a conference of some sort. 4.____
Of the following statements that pertain to conferences and conference leadership, which is generally considered to be MOST valid?
   A. Since World War II, the trend has been toward fewer shared decisions and more conferences.
   B. The most important part of a conference leader's job is to direct discussion.
   C. In providing opportunities for group interaction, management should avoid consideration of its past management philosophy.
   D. A good administrator cannot lead a good conference if he is a poor public speaker.

5. Of the following, it is usually LEAST desirable for a conference leader to 5.____
   A. turn the question to the person who asked it
   B. summarize proceedings periodically
   C. make a practice of not repeating questions
   D. ask a question without indicating who is to reply

6. The behavioral school of management thought bases its beliefs on certain assumptions. 6.____
   Which of the following is NOT a belief of this school of thought?
   A. People tend to seek and accept responsibility.
   B. Most people can be creative in solving problems.
   C. People prefer security above all else.
   D. Commitment is the most important factor in motivating people.

7. The one of the following objectives which would be LEAST appropriate as a major goal of research in the field of human resources management is to 7.____
   A. predict future conditions, events, and manpower needs
   B. evaluate established policies, programs, and practices
   C. evaluate proposed policies, programs, and practices
   D. identify deficient organizational units and apply suitable penalties

8. Of the following general interviewing methods or techniques, the one that is USUALLY considered to be effective in counseling, grievances, and appraisal interviews is the _____ interview. 8.____
   A. directed B. non-directed C. panel D. patterned

9. The ESSENTIAL first phase of decision-making is 9.____
   A. finding alternative solutions
   B. making a diagnosis of the problem
   C. selecting the plan to follow
   D. analyzing and comparing alternative solutions

10. Assume that, in a certain organization, a situation has developed in which there is little difference in status or authority between individuals. 10.____
    Which of the following would be the MOST likely result with regard to communication in this organization?
    A. Both the accuracy and flow of communication will be improved.
    B. Both the accuracy and flow of communication will substantially decrease.
    C. Employees will seek more formal lines of communication.
    D. Neither the flow nor the accuracy of communication will be improved over the former hierarchical structure.

11. The main function of many agency administrative offices is *information management*. Information that is received by an administrative officer may be classified as active or passive, depending upon whether or not it requires the recipient to take some action. 11.____

Of the following, the item received which is clearly the MOST active information is
A. an appointment of a new staff member
B. a payment voucher for a new desk
C. a press release concerning a past city event
D. the minutes of a staff meeting

12. Which one of the following sets BEST describes the general order in which to teach an operation to a new employee? 12.____
A. Prepare, present, tryout, follow-up
B. Prepare, test, tryout, re-test
C. Present, test, tryout, follow-up
D. Test, present, follow-up, re-test

13. Of the following, public employees may be separated from public service 13.____
A. for the same reasons which are generally acceptable for discharging employees in private industry
B. only under the most trying circumstances
C. under procedures that are neither formalized nor subject to review
D. solely in extreme cases involving offenses of gravest character

14. Of the following, the one LEAST considered to be a communication barrier is 14.____
A. group feedback
B. charged words
C. selective perception
D. symbolic meanings

15. Of the following ways for a manager to handle his appointments, the BEST way, according to experts in administration, generally is to 15.____
A. schedule his own appointments and inform his secretary not to reserve his time without his approval
B. encourage everyone to make appointments through his secretary and tell her when he makes his own appointments
C. see no one who has not made a previous appointment
D. permit anyone to see him without an appointment

16. Assume that a manager decides to examine closely one of five units under his supervision to uncover problems common to all five. 16.____
His research technique is MOST closely related to the method called
A. experimentation
B. simulation
C. linear analysis
D. sampling

17. If one views the process of management as a dynamic process, which one of the following functions is NOT a legitimate part of that process? 17.____
A. Communication
B. Decision-making
C. Organizational slack
D. Motivation

18. Which of the following would be the BEST statement of a budget-oriented purpose for a government administrator? To 18.____
    A. provide 200 hours of instruction in basic reading for 3,500 adult illiterates at a cost of $1 million in the next fiscal year
    B. inform the public of adult educational programs
    C. facilitate the transfer to a city agency of certain functions of a federally-funded program which is being phased out
    D. improve the reading skills of the adult citizens in the city

19. Modern management philosophy and practices are changing to accommodate the expectations and motivations of organization personnel. 19.____
    Which of the following terms INCORRECTLY describes these newer managerial approaches?
    A. Rational management
    B. Participative management
    C. Decentralization
    D. Democratic supervision

20. Management studies support the hypothesis that, in spite of the tendency of employees to censor the information communicated to their supervisor, subordinates are MORE likely to communicate problem-oriented information upward when they have 20.____
    A. a long period of service in the organization
    B. a high degree of trust in the supervisor
    C. a high educational level
    D. low status on the organizational ladder

## KEY (CORRECT ANSWERS)

| | | | |
|---|---|---|---|
| 1. | C | 11. | A |
| 2. | B | 12. | A |
| 3. | A | 13. | A |
| 4. | B | 14. | A |
| 5. | A | 15. | B |
| 6. | C | 16. | D |
| 7. | D | 17. | C |
| 8. | B | 18. | A |
| 9. | B | 19. | A |
| 10. | D | 20. | B |

# EXAMINATION SECTION

## TEST 1

DIRECTIONS: Each question or incomplete statement is followed by several suggested answers or completions. Select the one that BEST answers the question or completes the statement. *PRINT THE LETTER OF THE CORRECT ANSWER IN THE SPACE AT THE RIGHT.*

1. A management approach widely used today is based on the belief that decisions should be made and actions should be taken by managers closest to the organization's problems. 1.____
   This style of management is MOST appropriately called _____ management.
   A. scientific
   B. means-end
   C. decentralized
   D. internal process

2. As contrasted with tall organization structures with narrow spans of control, flat organization structures with wide spans of control MOST usually provide 2.____
   A. fast communication and information flows
   B. more levels in the organizational hierarchy
   C. fewer workers reporting to supervisors
   D. lower motivation because of tighter control standards

3. Use of the systems approach is MOST likely to lead to 3.____
   A. consideration of the impact on the whole organization of actions taken in any part of that organization
   B. the placing of restrictions on departmental activity
   C. use of mathematical models to suboptimize production
   D. consideration of the activities of each unit of an organization as a totality without regard to the remainder of the organization

4. An administrator, with overall responsibility for all administrative operations in a large operating agency, is considering organizing the agency's personnel office around either of the following two alternative concepts: 4.____
   Alternative I: A corps of specialists for each branch of personnel subject matter, whose skills, counsel, or work products are coordinated only by the agency personnel officer
   Alternative II: A crew of so-called *personnel generalists*, who individually work with particular segments of the organization but deal with all subspecialties of the personnel function
   The one of the following which MOST tends to be a DRAWBACK of Alternative I, as compared with Alternative II, is that
   A. training and employee relations work call for education, interests, and talents that differ from those required for classification and compensation work
   B. personnel office staff may develop only superficial familiarity with the specialized areas to which they have been assigned

C. supervisors may fail to get continuing overall personnel advice on an integrated basis
D. the personnel specialists are likely to become so interested in and identified with the operating view as to particular cases that they lose their professional objectivity and become merely advocates of what some supervisor wants

5. The matrix summary or decision matrix is a useful tool for making choices. Its effectiveness is MOST dependent upon the user's ability to 5.____
A. write a computer program (Fortran or Cobol)
B. assign weights representing the relative importance of the objectives
C. solve a set of two equations with two unknowns
D. work with matrix algebra

6. An organizational form which is set up only on an *ad hoc* basis to meet specific goals is said PRIMARILY to use 6.____
A. clean break departmentation
B. matrix or task force organization
C. scalar specialization
D. geographic or area-wide decentralization

7. The concept of job enlargement would LEAST properly be implemented by 7.____
A. permitting workers to follow through on tasks or projects from start to finish
B. delegating the maximum authority possible for decision-making to lower levels in the hierarchy
C. maximizing the number of professional classes in the classification plan
D. training employees to grow beyond whatever tasks they have been performing

8. As used in the area of admission, the principle of *unity of command* MOST specifically means that 8.____
A. an individual should report to only one superior for any single activity
B. individuals make better decisions than do committees
C. in large organizations, chains of command are normally too long
D. an individual should not supervise over five subordinates

9. The method of operations research, statistical decision-making, and linear programming have been referred to as the tool kit of the manager. Utilization of these tools is LEAST useful in the performance of which of the following functions? 9.____
A. Elimination of the need for using judgment when making decisions
B. Facilitation of decision-making without the need for sub-optimization
C. Quantifying problems for management study
D. Research and analysis of management operations

10. When acting in their respective managerial capacities, the chief executive officer and the office supervisor both perform the fundamental functions of management. 10.____
Of the following differences between the two, the one which is generally considered to be the LEAST significant is the
   A. breadth of the objectives
   B. complexity of measuring actual efficiency of performance
   C. number of decisions made
   D. organizational relationships affected by actions taken

11. The ability of operations researchers to solve complicated problems rests on their use of models. 11.____
These models can BEST be described as
   A. mathematical statements of the problem
   B. physical constructs that simulate a work layout
   C. toy-like representations of employees in work environments
   D. role-playing simulations

12. Of the following, it is MOST likely to be proper for the agency head to allow the agency personnel officer to make final selection of appointees from certified eligible lists where there are 12.____
   A. *small* numbers of employees to be hired in newly-developed professional fields
   B. *large* numbers of persons to be hired for key managerial positions
   C. *large* numbers of persons to be hired in very routine occupations where the individual discretion of operating officials is not vital
   D. *small* numbers of persons to be hired in highly specialized professional occupations which are vital to the agency's operations

13. Of the following, an operating agency personnel office is LEAST likely to be able to exert strong influence or control within the operating agency by 13.____
   A. interpreting to the operating agency head what is intended by the directives and rules emanating from the central personnel agency
   B. establishing the key objectives of those line divisions of the operating agency employing large numbers of staff and operating under the management-by-objectives approach
   C. formulating and proposing to the agency head the internal policies and procedures on personnel matters required within the operating agency
   D. exercising certain discretionary authority in the application of the agency head's general personnel policies to actual specific situations

14. PERT is a recently developed system used PRIMARILY to 14.____
   A. evaluate the quality of applicants' background
   B. analyze and control the timing aspects of a major project
   C. control the total expenditure of agency funds within a monthly or quarterly time period
   D. analyze and control the differential effect on costs of purchasing different quantities

15. Assume that an operating agency has among its vacant positions two positions, each of which encompasses mixed duties. Both require appointees to have considerable education and experience, but these requirements are essential only for the more difficult duties of these positions. In the place of these positions, an administrator creates two new positions, one in which the higher duties are concentrated and the other with the lesser functions requiring only minimum preparation. 15.____
Of the following, it is generally MOST appropriate to characterize the administrator's action as a(n)
   A. *undesirable* example of deliberate downgrading of standards and requirements
   B. *undesirable* manipulation of the classification system for non-merit purposes
   C. *desirable* broadening of the definition of a class of positions
   D. *desirable* example of job redesign

16. Of the following, the LEAST important stumbling block to the development of personnel mobility among governmental jurisdictions is the 16.____
   A. limitations on lateral entry above junior levels in many jurisdictions
   B. continued collection of filing fees for civil service tests by many governmental jurisdictions
   C. absence of reciprocal exchange of retirement benefit eligibility between governments
   D. disparities in salary scales between governments

17. Of the following, the MAJOR disadvantage of a personnel system that features the *selection out* (forced retirement) of those who have been passed over a number of times for promotion is that such a system 17.____
   A. wastes manpower which is perfectly competent at one level but unable to rise above that level
   B. wastes funds by requiring review boards
   C. leads to excessive recruiting of newcomers from outside the system
   D. may not be utilized in *closed* career systems with low maximum age limits for entrance

18. Of the following, the fields in which operating agency personnel offices generally exercise the MOST stringent controls over first line supervisors in the agency are 18.____
   A. methods analysis and work simplification
   B. selection and position classification
   C. vestibule training and Gantt chart
   D. suggestion systems and staff development

19. Of the following, computers are normally MOST effective in handling 19.____
   A. large masses of data requiring simple processing
   B. small amounts of data requiring constantly changing complex processing
   C. data for which reported values are often subject to inaccuracies
   D. large amounts of data requiring continual programming and reprocessing

20. Contingency planning, which has long been used by the military and is assuming increasing importance in other organizations, may BEST be described as a process which utilizes 20.____
    A. alternative plans based on varying assumptions
    B. *crash programs* by organizations departmentalized along process lines
    C. plans which mandate substitution of equipment for manpower at predetermined operational levels
    D. plans that individually and accurately predict future events

21. In the management of inventory, two kinds of costs normally determine when to order and in what amounts. 21.____
    The one of the following choices which includes BOTH of these kinds of costs is _____ costs and _____ costs.
    A. carrying; storage
    B. personnel; order
    C. computer; order
    D. personnel; computer

22. At top management levels, the one of the following which is generally the MOST important executive skill is skill in 22.____
    A. budgeting procedures
    B. a technical discipline
    C. controlling actions in accordance with previously approved plans
    D. seeing the organization as a whole

23. Of the following, the BEST way to facilitate the successful operation of a committee is to set guidelines establishing its 23.____
    A. budget exclusive of personnel costs
    B. location
    C. schedule of meetings or conferences
    D. scope of purpose

24. Executive training programs that single out particular managers and groom them for promotion create the so-called organizational *crown princes*. 24.____
    Of the following, the MOST serious problem that arises in connection with this practice is that
    A. the managers chosen for promotion seldom turn out to be the best managers since the future potential of persons cannot be predicted
    B. not enough effort is made to remove organizational obstacles in the way of their development and achievement
    C. the resentment of the managers not selected for the program has an adverse effect on the motivation of those managers not selected
    D. performance appraisal and review are not carried out systematically enough

25. Of the following, the LEAST likely result of the use of the concept of job enlargement is that 25.____
    A. coordination will be simplified
    B. the individual's job will become less challenging
    C. worker satisfaction will increase
    D. fewer people will have to give attention to each piece of work

# KEY (CORRECT ANSWERS)

| | | | |
|---|---|---|---|
| 1. | C | 11. | A |
| 2. | A | 12. | C |
| 3. | A | 13. | B |
| 4. | C | 14. | B |
| 5. | B | 15. | D |
| 6. | B | 16. | B |
| 7. | C | 17. | A |
| 8. | A | 18. | B |
| 9. | A | 19. | A |
| 10. | C | 20. | A |

| | |
|---|---|
| 21. | A |
| 22. | D |
| 23. | D |
| 24. | C |
| 25. | B |

# TEST 2

DIRECTIONS: Each question or incomplete statement is followed by several suggested answers or completions. Select the one that BEST answers the question or completes the statement. *PRINT THE LETTER OF THE CORRECT ANSWER IN THE SPACE AT THE RIGHT.*

1. The one of the following which is MOST likely to be emphasized in the use of the brainstorming technique is the 1.____
   A. early consideration of cost factors of all ideas which may be suggested
   B. avoidance of impractical suggestions
   C. separation of the generation of ideas from their evaluation
   D. appraisal of suggestions concurrently with their initial presentation

2. Of the following, the BEST method for assessing managerial performance is generally to 2.____
   A. compare the manager's accomplishments against clear, specific, agreed-upon goals
   B. compare the manager's traits with those of his peers on a predetermined objective
   C. measure the manager's behavior against a listing of itemized personal traits
   D. measure the manager's success according to the enumeration of the *satisfaction* principle

3. As compared with recruitment from outside, selection from within the service must generally show GREATER concern for the 3.____
   A. prestige in which the public service as a whole is held by the public
   B. morale of the candidate group compromising the recruitment field
   C. cost of examining per candidate
   D. benefits of the use of standardized and validated tests

4. Performance budgeting focuses PRIMARY attention upon which one of the following? The 4.____
   A. things to be acquired, such as supplies and equipment
   B. general character and relative importance of the work to be done or the service to be rendered
   C. list of personnel to be employed, by specific title
   D. separation of employee performance evaluations from employee compensation

5. Of the following, the FIRST step in the installation and operation of a performance budgeting system generally should be the 5.____
   A. identification of program costs in relationship to the accounting system and operating structure
   B. identification of the specific end results of past programs in other jurisdictions

C. identification of work programs that are meaningful for management purposes
D. establishment of organizational structures each containing only one work program

6. Of the following, the MOST important purpose of a system of quarterly allotments of appropriated funds generally is to enable the 6.____
   A. head of the judicial branch to determine the legality of agency requests for budget increases
   B. operating agencies of government to upgrade the quality of their services without increasing costs
   C. head of the executive branch to control the rate at which the operating agencies obligate and expend funds
   D. operating agencies of government to avoid payment for services which have not been properly rendered by employees

7. In the preparation of the agency's budget, the agency's central budget office has two responsibilities: program review and management improvement. Which one of the following questions concerning an operating agency's program is MOST closely related to the agency budget officer's program review responsibility? 7.____
   A. Can expenditures for supplies, materials, or equipment be reduced?
   B. Will improved work methods contribute to a more effective program?
   C. What is the relative importance of this program as compared to a higher level of program performance?
   D. Will a realignment of responsibilities contribute to a higher level of program performance?

8. Of the following, the method of evaluating relative rates of return normally and generally thought to be MOST useful in evaluating government operations is _____ analysis. 8.____
   A. cost-benefit
   B. budget variance
   C. investment capital
   D. budget planning program

9. The one of the following assumptions that is LEAST likely to be made by a democratic or permissive type of leader is that 9.____
   A. commitment to goals is seldom a result of monetary rewards alone
   B. people can learn not only to accept, but also to seek, responsibility
   C. the average person prefers security over advancement
   D. creativity may be found in most segments of the population

10. In attempting to motivate subordinates, a manager should PRINCIPALLY be aware of the fact that 10.____
   A. the psychological qualities of people, in general, are easily predictable
   B. fear, as a traditional form of motivation, has lost much of its former power to motivate people in our modern industrial society
   C. fear is still the most potent force in motivating the behavior of subordinates in the public service
   D. the worker has very little control over the quality and quantity of his output

11. Assume that the following figures represent the number of work-unit that were produced during a week by each of sixteen employees in a division: 11.____

| | | | |
|---|---|---|---|
| 12 | 16 | 13 | 18 |
| 21 | 12 | 16 | 13 |
| 16 | 13 | 17 | 21 |
| 13 | 15 | 18 | 20 |

If all of the employees of the division who produced thirteen work-units during the week had instead produced fifteen work-units during that same week, then for that week the
   A. mean, median, and mode would all change
   B. mean and mode would change, but the median would remain the same
   C. mode and median would change, but the mean would remain the same
   D. mode, mean, and median would all still remain unchanged in value

12. An important law in motivation theory is called the *law of effect*. This law says that behavior which satisfies a person's needs tends to be repeated; behavior which does not satisfy a person's needs tends to be eliminated. 12.____
The one of the following which is the BEST interpretation of this law is that
   A. productivity depends on personality traits
   B. diversity of goals leads to instability and motivation
   C. the greater the satisfaction, the more likely it is that the behavior will be reinforced
   D. extrinsic satisfaction is more important than intrinsic reward

13. Of the following, the MOST acceptable reason an administrator can give for taking advice from other employees in the organization only when he asks for it is that he wants to 13.____
   A. encourage creativity and high morale
   B. keep dysfunctional pressures and inconsistent recommendations to a minimum
   C. show his superiors and peers who is in charge
   D. show his subordinates who is in charge

14. A complete picture of the communication channels in an organization can BEST be revealed by 14.____
   A. observing the planned paperwork system
   B. recording the highly intermittent patterns of communication
   C. plotting the entire flow of information over a period of time
   D. monitoring the *grapevine*

Questions 15-16.

DIRECTIONS: Questions 15 and 16 are to be answered SOLELY on the basis of the following passage.

Management by objectives (MBO) may be defined as the process by which the superior and the subordinate managers of an organization jointly define its common goals, define each individual's major areas of responsibility in terms of the results expected of him and use these measures as guides for operating the unit and assessing the contribution of each of its members.

The MBO approach requires that after organizational goals are established and communicated, targets must be set for each individual position which are congruent with organizational goals. Periodic performance reviews and a final review using the objectives set as criteria are also basic to this approach.

Recent studies have shown that MBO programs are influenced by attitudes and perceptions of the boss, the company, the reward-punishment system, and the program itself. In addition, the manner in which the MBO program is carried out can influence the success of the program. A study done in the late sixties indicates that the best results are obtained when the manager sets goals which deal with significant problem areas in the organizational unit, or with the subordinate's personal deficiencies. These goals must be clear with regard to what is expected of the subordinate. The frequency of feedback is also important in the success of a management-by-objectives program. Generally, the greater the amount of feedback, the more successful the MBO program.

15. According to the above passage, the expected output for individual employees should be determined 15.____
    A. after a number of reviews of work performance
    B. after common organizational goals are defined
    C. before common organizational goals are defined
    D. on the basis of an employee's personal qualities

16. According to the above passage, the management-by-objectives approach requires 16.____
    A. less feedback than other types of management programs
    B. little review of on-the-job performance after the initial setting of goals
    C. general conformance between individual goals and organizational goals
    D. the setting of goals which deal with minor problem area in the organization

Questions 17-19.

DIRECTIONS: Questions 17 through 19 are to be answered SOLELY on the basis of the following passage.

During the last decade, a great deal of interest has been generated around the phenomenon of organizational development, or the process of developing human resources through conscious organization effort. Organizational development (OD) stresses improving interpersonal relationships and organizational skills, such as communication, to a much greater degree than individual training ever did.

The kind of training that an organization should emphasize depends upon the present and future structure of the organization. If future organizations are to be unstable, shifting coalitions, then individual skills and abilities, particularly those emphasizing innovativeness, creativity, flexibility, and the latest technological knowledge, are crucial, and individual training is most appropriate.

But if there is to be little change in organizational structure, then the main thrust of training should be group-oriented or organizational development. This approach seems better designed for overcoming hierarchical barriers, for developing a degree of interpersonal relationships which make communication along the chain of command possible, and for retaining a modicum of innovation and/or flexibility.

17. According to the above passage, group-oriented training is MOST useful in 17.____
    A. developing a communications system that will facilitate understanding through the chain of command
    B. highly flexible and mobile organizations
    C. preventing the crossing of hierarchical barriers within an organization
    D. saving energy otherwise wasted on developing methods of dealing with rigid hierarchies

18. The one of the following conclusions which can be drawn MOST appropriately from the above passage is that 18.____
    A. behavioral research supports the use of organizational development training method rather than individualized training
    B. it is easier to provide individualized training in specific skills than to set up sensitivity training programs
    C. organizational development eliminates innovative or flexible activity
    D. the nature of an organization greatly influences which training methods will be most effective

19. According to the above passage, the one of the following which is LEAST important for large-scale organizations geared to rapid and abrupt change is 19.____
    A. current technological information
    B. development of a high degree of interpersonal relationships
    C. development of individual skills and abilities
    D. emphasis on creativity

Questions 20-25.

DIRECTIONS: Each of Questions 20 through 25 consist of a statement which contains one word that is incorrectly used because it is not in keeping with the meaning that the quotation is evidently intended to convey. Determine which word is INCORRECTLY used. Select from the choices lettered A, B, C, and D the word which, when substituted for the incorrectly used word, would BEST help to convey the meaning of the statement.

20. One of the considerations likely to affect the currency of classification, particularly in professional and managerial occupations, is the impact of the incumbent's capacities on the job. Some work is highly susceptible to change as the result of the special talents or interests of the classifier. Organization should never be so rigid as not to capitalize on the innovative or unusual proclivities of its key employees. While a machine operator may not be able, even subtly, to change the character or level of his job, the design engineer, the attorney, or the organization and methods analyst might readily do so. Reliance on his judgment and the scope of his assignments may both grow as the result of his skill, insight, and capacity. 20.____
   A. unlikely B. incumbent C. directly D. scope

21. The supply of services by the state is not governed by market price. The aim is to supply such services to all who need them and to treat all consumers equally. This objective especially compels the civil servant to maintain a role f strict impartiality, based on the principle of equality of individual citizens vis-à-vis their government. However, there is a clear difference between being neutral and impartial. If the requirement is construed to mean that all civil servants should be political eunuchs, devoid of the drive and motivation essential to dynamic administration, then the concept of impartiality is being seriously utilized. Modern governments should not be stopped from demanding that their hirelings have not only the technical but the emotional qualifications necessary for whole-hearted effort. 21.____
   A. determined B. rule C. stable D. misapplied

22. The manager was barely listening. Recently, at the divisional level, several new fronts of troubles had erupted, including a requirement to increase production yet hold down operating costs and somehow raise quality standards. Though the three objectives were basically obsolete, top departmental management was insisting on the simultaneous attainment of them, an insistence not helping the manager's ulcer, an old enemy within. Thus, the manager could not find time for interest in individuals—only in statistics which regiment of individuals, like unconsidered Army privates, added up to. 22.____
   A. quantity B. battalion C. incompatible D. quiet

23. When a large volume of data flows directly between operators and first-line supervisors, senior executives tend to be out of the mainstream of work. Summary reports can increase their remoteness. An executive needs to know the volume, quality, and cost of completed work, and exceptional problems. In addition, he may desire information on key operating conditions. Summary reports on these matters are, therefore, essential features of a communications network and make delegation without loss of control possible. 23.____
   A. unimportant B. quantity C. offset D. incomplete

24. Of major significance in management is harmony between the overall objectives of the organization and the managerial objectives within that organization. In addition, harmony among goals of managers is impossible; they should not be at cross-purposes. Each manager's goal should supplement and assist the goals of his colleagues. Likewise, the objectives of individuals or non-management members should be harmonized with those of the manager. When this is accomplished, genuine teamwork is the result, and human relations are aided materially. The integration of managers' and individuals' goals aids in achieving greater work satisfaction at all levels. 24.____
A. competition B. dominate C. incremental D. vital

25. Change constantly challenges the manager. Some of this change is evolutionary, some revolutionary, some recognizable, some non-recognizable. Both forces within an enterprise and forces outside the enterprise cause managers to act and react in initiating changes in their immediate working environment. Change invalidates existing operations. Goals are not being accomplished in the best manner, problems develop, and frequently because of the lack of time, only patched-up solutions are followed. The result is that the mode of management is profound in nature and temporary in effectiveness. A complete overhaul of managerial operations should take place. It appears quite likely that we are just beginning to see the real effects of change in our society; the pace probably will accelerate in ways that few really understand or know how to handle. 25.____
A. confirms B. decline C. instituting D. superficial

---

## KEY (CORRECT ANSWERS)

| | | | |
|---|---|---|---|
| 1. | C | 11. | B |
| 2. | A | 12. | C |
| 3. | B | 13. | B |
| 4. | B | 14. | C |
| 5. | C | 15. | B |
| 6. | C | 16. | C |
| 7. | C | 17. | A |
| 8. | A | 18. | D |
| 9. | C | 19. | B |
| 10. | B | 20. | B |

| | |
|---|---|
| 21. | D |
| 22. | C |
| 23. | C |
| 24. | D |
| 25. | D |

# EXAMINATION SECTION

## TEST 1

DIRECTIONS: Each question or incomplete statement is followed by several suggested answers or completions. Select the one that BEST answers the question or completes the statement. *PRINT THE LETTER OF THE CORRECT ANSWER IN THE SPACE AT THE RIGHT.*

1. The one of the following which has had GREATEST effect upon size of the budget of large cities in the last twenty years is 1.____
   A. change in the organization of the city resulting from new charters
   B. increase in services rendered by the city
   C. development of independent authorities
   D. increase in the city's ability to borrow money
   E. increase in the size of the city

2. The one of the following services for which cities receive the LEAST amount of direct financial assistance from state governments is 2.____
   A. education B. welfare C. housing
   D. roads E. museums

3. Major problems which face most large cities, including New York, arise from the vertical sandwiching of governments in a single area and from the many independent governments that crowd the boundaries of the central city. 3.____
   Of the following methods of solving these problems, the one which has been MOST successful in the past has been to
   A. decentralize the administration of the central city
   B. create various supra-municipal authorities which tend to integrate the activities of the metropolitan area
   C. bring the metropolitan population under a single local government
   D. set up intermunicipal coordinating agencies to solve area administrative and economic problems
   E. allow each government element in the metropolitan area to work out its own solution

4. By means of the *debt limit*, the states regulate many facets of the debt of the cities. 4.____
   The one of the following factors which is NOT regulated in this manner is the
   A. purpose for which the debt is incurred
   B. amount of debt which may be incurred
   C. terms of the notes or bonds issued by the city
   D. forms of debts which may be incurred
   E. source from which the money may be borrowed

5. The one of the following which is a characteristic of NEITHER the state nor the federal governments, but which is a characteristic of the government of cities is that the latter 5.____
   A. is not sovereign but an agent
   B. does not have the power to raise taxes
   C. cannot enter into contracts
   D. may not make treaties with foreign countries
   E. may not coin money

Questions 6-8.

DIRECTIONS: Questions 6 through 8 are to be answered on the basis of the following paragraph.

The regressive uses of discipline is ubiquitous. Administrative architects who seek the optimum balance between structure and morale must accordingly look toward the identification and isolation of disciplinary elements. The whole range of disciplinary sanctions, from the reprimand to the dismissal presents opportunities for reciprocity and accommodation of institutional interests. When rightly seized upon, these opportunities may provide the moment and the means for fruitful exercise of leadership and collaboration.

6. The one of the following ways of reworking the ideas presented in this paragraph in order to be BEST suited for presentation in an in-service training course in supervision is: 6.____
   A. When one of your men does something wrong, talk it over with him. Tell him what he should have done. This is a chance for you to show the man that you are on his side and that you would welcome him on your side.
   B. It is not necessary to reprimand or to dismiss an employee because he needs disciplining. The alert foreman will lead and collaborate with his subordinates making discipline unnecessary.
   C. A good way to lead the men you supervise is to take those opportunities which present themselves to use the whole range of disciplinary sanctions from reprimand to dismissal as a means for enforcing collaboration.
   D. Chances to punish a man in your squad should be welcomed as opportunities to show that you are a "*good guy*" who does not bear a grudge.
   E. Before you talk to a man or have him report to the office for something he has done wrong, attempt to lead him and get him to work with you. Tell him that his actions were wrong, that you expect him not to repeat the same wrong act, and that you will take a firmer stand if the act is repeated.

7. Of the following, the PRINCIPAL point made in the paragraph is that 7.____
   A. discipline is frequently used improperly
   B. it is possible to isolate the factors entering into a disciplinary situation
   C. identification of the disciplinary elements is desirable

D. disciplinary situations may be used to the advantage of the organization
E. obtaining the best relationship between organizational form and spirit, depend upon the ability to label disciplinary elements

8. The MOST novel idea presented in the paragraph is that 8.____
A. discipline is rarely necessary
B. discipline may be a joint action of man and supervisor
C. there are disciplinary elements which may be identified
D. a range of disciplinary sanctions exist
E. it is desirable to seek for balance between structure and morale

9. When, in the process of developing a classification plan, it has been decided that certain positions all have distinguishing characteristics sufficiently similar to justify treating them alike in the process of selecting appointees and establishing pay rates or scales, then the kind of employment represented by such positions will be called a "class." 9.____
According to this paragraph, a group of positions is called a class if they
A. have distinguishing characteristics
B. represent a kind of employment
C. can be treated in the same manner for some functions
D. all have the same pay rates
E. are treated in the same manner in the development of a classification plan

Questions 10-12.

DIRECTIONS: Questions 10 through 12 are to be answered on the basis of the following paragraph.

The fundamental characteristic of the type of remote control which management needs to bridge the gap between itself and actual operations is the more effective use of records and reports—more specifically, the gathering and interpretation of the facts contained in records and reports. Facts, for management purposes, are those data (narrative and quantitative) which express in simple terms the current standing of the agency's program, work and resources in relation to the plans and policies formulated by management. They are those facts or measures (1) which permit management to compare current status with past performance and with its forecasts for the immediate future, and (2) which provide management with a reliable basis for long-range forecasting.

10. According to the above statement, a characteristic of a type of management control 10.____
A. is the kind of facts contained in records and reports
B. is narrative and quantitative data
C. is its remoteness from actual operations
D. is the use of records
E. which expresses in simple terms the current standing of the agency's program, provides management with a reliable basis for long-range forecasting

11. For management purposes, facts are, according to the paragraph, 11.____
    A. forecasts which can be compared to current status
    B. data which can be used for certain control purposes
    C. a fundamental characteristic of a type of remote control
    D. the data contained in records and reports
    E. data (narrative and quantitative) which describe the plans and policies formulated by management

12. An inference which can be drawn from this statement is that 12.____
    A. management which has a reliable basis for long-range forecasting has at its disposal a type of remote control which is needed to bridge the gap between itself and actual operations
    B. data which do not express in simple terms the current standing of the agency's program, work and resources in relationship to the plans and policies formulated by management, may still be facts for management purposes
    C. data which express relationships among the agency's program, work, and resources are management facts
    D. the gap between management and actual operations can only be bridged by characteristics which are fundamentally a type of remote control
    E. management compares current status with past performance in order to obtain a reliable basis for long-range forecasting

Questions 13-14.

DIRECTIONS: Questions 13 and 14 are to be answered on the basis of the following paragraph.

People must be selected to do the tasks involved and must be placed on a payroll in jobs fairly priced. Each of these people must be assigned those tasks which he can perform best: the work of each must be appraised, and good and poor work singled out appropriately. Skill in performing assigned tasks must be developed, and the total work situation must be conducive to sustained high performance. Finally, employees must be separated from the work force either voluntarily or involuntarily because of inefficient or unsatisfactory performance or because of curtailment of organizational activities.

13. A personnel function which is NOT included in the above description is 13.____
    A. classification B. training C. placement
    D. severance E. service rating

14. The underlying implied purpose of the policy enunciated in the above paragraph is 14.____
    A. to plan for the curtailment of the organizational program when it becomes necessary
    B. to single out appropriate skill in performing assigned tasks
    C. to develop and maintain a high level of performance by employees

D. that training employees in relation to the total work situation is essential if good and poor work are to be singled out
E. that equal money for equal work results in a total work situation which insures proper appraisal

15. Changes in program must be quickly and effectively translated into organizational adjustments if the administrative machinery is to be fully adapted to current operating needs. Continuous administrative planning is indispensable to the successful and expeditious accomplishment of such organization changes. 15.____
According to this statement,
   A. the absence of continuous administrative planning must result in out-moded administrative machinery
   B. continuous administrative planning is necessary for changes in program
   C. if changes in program are quickly and effectively translated into organizational adjustments, the administrative machinery is fully adapted to current operating needs
   D. continuous administrative planning results in successful and expeditious accomplishment of organization changes
   E. if administrative machinery is not fully adapted to current operating needs, then continuous administrative planning is absent

16. The first-line supervisor executes policy as elsewhere formulated. He does not make policy. He is the element of the administrative structure closest to the employee group. 16.____
From this point of view, it follows that a MAJOR function of the first-line supervisor is to
   A. suggest desirable changes in procedure to top management
   B. prepare time schedules showing when his unit will complete a piece of work so that it will dovetail with the requirements of other units
   C. humanize policy so as to respect employee needs and interests
   D. report danger points to top management in order to forestall possible bottlenecks
   E. discipline employees who continuously break departmental rules

17. During a supervisory staff meeting, the department head said to the first-line supervisors, "*The most important job you have is to get across to the employees in your units the desirability of achieving our department's aims and the importance of the jobs they are performing toward reaching our goals.*" 17.____
In general, adoption of this point of view would tend to result in an organization
   A. in which supervisors would be faced by many disciplinary problems caused by employee reaction to the program
   B. in which less supervision is required of the work of the average employee
   C. having more clearly defined avenues of communication
   D. lacking definition; supervisors would tend to forget their primary mission of getting the assigned work completed as efficiently as possible
   E. in which most employees would be capable of taking over a supervisory position when necessary

18. A supervisor, in assigning a man to a job, generally followed the policy of fitting the man to the job. 18.____
This procedure is
A. *undesirable*; the job should be fitted to the man
B. *desirable*; primary emphasis should be on the work to be accomplished
C. *undesirable*; the policy does not consider human values
D. *desirable*; setting up a definite policy and following it permits careful analysis
E. *undesirable*; it is not always possible to fit the available man to the job

19. Assume that one of the units under your jurisdiction has 40 typists. Their skill range from 15 to 80 words a minute. 19.____
The MOST feasible of the following methods to increase the typing output of this unit is to
A. study the various typing jobs to determine the skill requirements for each type of work and assign to each typist tasks commensurate with her skill
B. assign the slow typists to clerical work and hire new typists
C. assign such tasks as typing straight copy to the slower typists
D. reduce the skill requirements necessary to produce a satisfactory quantity of work
E. simplify procedures and keep records, memoranda, and letters short and concise

20. In a division of a department, private secretaries were assigned to members of the technical staff since each required a secretary who was familiar with his particular field and who could handle various routine matters without referring to anyone. Other members of the staff depended for their dictation and typing work upon a small pool consisting of two stenographers and two typists. Because of turnover and the difficulty of recruiting new stenographers and typists, the pool had to be discontinued. 20.____
Of the following, the MOST satisfactory way to provide stenographic and typing service for the division is to
A. organize the private secretaries into a decentralized pool under the direction of a supervisor to whom nontechnical staff members would send requests for stenographic and typing assistance
B. organize the private secretaries into a central pool under the direction of a supervisor to whom all staff members would send requests for stenographic and typing assistance
C. train clerks as typists and typists as stenographers
D. relieve stenographers and typists of jobs that can be done by messengers or clerks
E. conserve time by using such devices as indicating minor corrections on a final draft in such a way that they can be erased and by using duplicating machines to eliminate typing many copies

21. Even under perfect organizational conditions, the relationships between the line units and the units charged with budget planning and personnel management may be precarious at times. 21.____
The one of the following which is a MAJOR reason for this is that
   A. service units assist the head of the agency in formulating and executing policies
   B. line units frequently find lines of communication to the agency head blocked by service units
   C. there is a natural antagonism between planners and doers
   D. service units tend to become line in attitude and emphasis, and to conflict with operating units
   E. service units tend to function apart from the operating units

22. The one of the following which is the CHIEF reason for training supervisors is that 22.____
   A. untrained supervisors find it difficult to train their subordinates
   B. most persons do not start as supervisors and consequently are in need of supervisory training
   C. training permits a higher degree of decentralization of the decision-making process
   D. training permits a higher degree of centralization of the decision-making process
   E. coordinated actions on the part of many persons pre-supposes familiarity with the procedures to be employed

23. The problem of determining the type of organization which should exist is inextricably interwoven with the problem of recruitment. 23.____
In general, this statement is
   A. *correct*; since organizations are man-made, they can be changed
   B. *incorrect*; the organizational form which is most desirable is independent of the persons involved
   C. *correct*; the problem of organization cannot be considered apart from employee qualifications
   D. *incorrect*; organizational problems can be separated into many parts and recruitment is important in only few of these
   E. *correct*; a good recruitment program will reduce the problems of organization

24. The conference as an administrative tool is MOST valuable for solving problems which 24.____
   A. are simple and within a familiar frame of reference
   B. are of long standing
   C. are novel and complex
   D. are not solvable
   E. require immediate solution

25. Of the following, a recognized procedure for avoiding conflicts in the delegation of authority is to 25.____
   A. delegate authority so as to preserve control by top management
   B. provide for a workable span of control
   C. preview all assignments periodically
   D. assign all related work to the same control
   E. use the linear method of assignment

---

# KEY (CORRECT ANSWERS)

| | | | |
|---|---|---|---|
| 1. | B | 11. | B |
| 2. | E | 12. | A |
| 3. | C | 13. | A |
| 4. | E | 14. | C |
| 5. | A | 15. | A |
| 6. | A | 16. | C |
| 7. | D | 17. | B |
| 8. | B | 18. | B |
| 9. | C | 19. | A |
| 10. | D | 20. | A |

| | |
|---|---|
| 21. | D |
| 22. | C |
| 23. | C |
| 24. | C |
| 25. | D |

# TEST 2

DIRECTIONS: Each question or incomplete statement is followed by several suggested answers or completions. Select the one that BEST answers the question or completes the statement. *PRINT THE LETTER OF THE CORRECT ANSWER IN THE SPACE AT THE RIGHT.*

1. A danger which exists in any organization as complex as that required for administration of a large city is that each department comes to believe that it exists for its own sake. 1.____
The one of the following which has been attempted in some organizations as a cure for this condition is to
   A. build up the departmental esprit de corps
   B. expand the functions and jurisdictions of the various departments so that better integration is possible
   C. develop a body of specialists in the various subject matter fields which cut across departmental lines
   D. delegate authority to the lowest possible echelon
   E. systematically transfer administrative personnel from one department to another

2. At best, the organization chart is ordinarily and necessarily an idealized picture of the intent of top management, a reflection of hopes and aims rather than a photograph of the operating facts within an organization. 2.____
The one of the following which is the BASIC reason for this is that the organization chart
   A. does not show the flow of work within the organization
   B. speaks in terms of positions rather than of live employees
   C. frequently contains unresolved internal ambiguities
   D. is a record of past organization or of proposed future organization and never a photograph of the living organization
   E. does not label the jurisdiction assigned to each component unit

3. The drag of inadequacy is always downward. The need in administration is always for the reverse; for a department head to project his thinking to the city level, for the unit chief to try to see the problems of the department. 3.____
The inability of a city administration to recruit administrators who can satisfy this need usually results in departments characterized by
   A. disorganization
   B. poor supervision
   C. circumscribed viewpoints
   D. poor public relations
   E. a lack of programs

4. When, as a result of a shift in public sentiment, the elective officers of a city are changed, is it desirable for career administrators to shift ground without performing any illegal or dishonest act in order to conform to the policies of the new elective officers? 4.____
   A. *No*; the opinions and beliefs of the career officials are the result of long experience in administration and are more reliable than those of politicians.

B. *Yes*; only in this way can citizens, political officials, and career administrators alike have confidence in the performance of their respective functions.
C. *No*; a top career official who is so spineless as to change his views or procedures as a result of public opinion is of little value to the public service.
D. *Yes*; legal or illegal, it is necessary that a city employee carry out the orders of his superior officers
E. *No*; shifting ground with every change in administration will preclude the use of a constant overall policy.

5. Participation in developing plans which will affect levels in the organization in addition to his own, will contribute to an individual's understanding of the entire system. When possible, this should be encouraged. 5.____
This policy is, in general,
A. *desirable*; the maintenance of any organization depends upon individual understanding
B. *undesirable*; employees should participate only in those activities which affect their own level, otherwise conflicts in authority may arise
C. *desirable*; an employee's will to contribute to the maintenance of an organization depends to a great extent on the level which he occupies
D. *undesirable*; employees can be trained more efficiently and economically in an organized training program than by participating in plan development
E. *desirable*; it will enable the employee to make intelligent suggestions for adjustment of the plan in the future

6. Constant study should be made of the information contained in reports to isolate those elements of experience which are static, those which are variable and repetitive, and those which are variable and due to chance. 6.____
Knowledge of those elements of experience in his organization which are static or constant will enable the operating official to
A. fix responsibility for their supervision at a lower level
B. revise the procedure in order to make the elements variable
C. arrange for follow-up and periodic adjustment
D. bring related data together
E. provide a frame of reference within which detailed standards for measure-meant can be installed

7. A chief staff officer, serving as one of the immediate advisors to the department head, has demonstrated a special capacity for achieving internal agreements and for sound judgment. As a result he has been used more and more as a source of counsel and assistance by the department head. Other staff officers and line officials as well have discovered that it is wise for them to check with this colleague in advance on all problematical matters handed up to the department head. 7.____
Developments such as this are
A. *undesirable*; they disrupt the normal lines for flow of work in an organization

B. *desirable*; they allow an organization to make the most of its strength wherever such strength resides
C. *undesirable*; they tend to undermine the authority of the department head and put it in the hands of a staff officer who does not have the responsibility
D. *desirable*; they tend to resolve internal ambiguities in organization
E. *undesirable*; they make for bad morale by causing *cut throat* competition

8. A common difference among executives is that some are not content unless they are out in front of everything that concerns their organization, while others prefer to run things by pulling strings, by putting others out in front and by stepping into the breach only when necessary. 8.____
Generally speaking, an advantage this latter method of operation has over the former is that it
A. results in a higher level of morale over a sustained period of time
B. gets results by exhortation and direct stimulus
C. makes it necessary to calculate integrated moves
D. makes the personality of the executive felt further down the line
E. results in the executive getting the reputation for being a good fellow

9. Administrators frequently have to get facts by interviewing people. Although the interview is a legitimate fact-gathering technique, it has definite limitations which should not be overlooked. 9.____
The one of the following which is an important limitation is that
A. people who are interviewed frequently answer questions with guesses rather than admit their ignorance
B. it is a poor way to discover the general attitude and thinking of supervisors interviewed
C. people sometimes hesitate to give information during an interview which they will submit in written form
D. it is a poor way to discover how well employees understand departmental policies
E. the material obtained from the interview can usually be obtained at lower cost from existing records

10. It is desirable and advantageous to leave a maximum measure of planning responsibility to operating agencies or units, rather than to remove the responsibility to a central planning staff agency. 10.____
Adoption of the former policy (decentralized planning) would lead to
A. *less effective* planning; operating personnel do not have the time to make long-term plans
B. *more effective* planning; operating units are usually better equipped technically than any staff agency and consequently are in a better position to set up valid plans
C. *less effective* planning; a central planning agency has a more objective point of view than any operating agency can achieve
D. *more effective* planning; plans are conceived in terms of the existing situation and their execution is carried out with the will to succeed

E. *less effective* planning; there is little or no opportunity to check deviation from plans in the proposed set-up

Questions 11-15.

DIRECTIONS: The following sections appeared in a report on the work production of two bureaus of a department. Questions 10 through 12 are to be answered on the basis of the following information. Throughout the report, assume that each month has 4 weeks.

Each of the two bureaus maintains a chronological file. In Bureau A, every 9 months on the average, this material fills a standard legal size file cabinet sufficient for 12,000 work units. In Bureau B, the same type of cabinet is filled in 18 months. Each bureau maintains three complete years of information plus a current file. When the current file cabinet is filled, the cabinet containing the oldest material is emptied, the contents disposed of and the cabinet used for current material. The similarity of these operations makes it possible to consolidate these files with little effort.

Study of the practice of using typists as filing clerks for periods when there is no typing work showed (1) Bureau A has for the past 6 months completed a total of 1,500 filing work units a week using on the average 200 man-hours of trained file clerk time and 20 man-hours of typist time, (2) Bureau B has in the same period completed a total of 2,000 filing work units a week using on the average 125 man-hours of trained file clerk time and 60 hours of typist time. This includes all work in chronological files. Assuming that all clerks work at the same speed and that all typists work at the same speed, this indicates that work other than filing should be found for typists or that they should be given some training in the filing procedures used. It should be noted that Bureau A has not been producing the 1,600 units of technical (not filing) work per 30 day period required by Schedule K, but is at present 200 units behind. The Bureau should be allowed 3 working days to get on schedule.

11. What percentage (approximate) of the total number of filing work units completed in both units consists of the work involved in the maintenance of the chronological files? 11.____

A. 5% B. 10% C. 15% D. 20% E. 25%

12. If the two chronological files are consolidated, the number of months which should be allowed for filling a cabinet is 12.____

A. 2 B. 4 C. 6 D. 8 E. 14

13. The MAXIMUM number of file cabinets which can be released for other uses as a result of the consolidation recommended is 13.____

A. 0
B. 1
C. 2
D. 3
E. not determinable on the basis of the data given

14. If all the filing work for both units is consolidated without any diminution in the amount to be done and all filing work is done by trained file clerks, the number of clerks required (35-hour work week) is 14.____
   A. 4 B. 5 C. 6 D. 7 E. 8

15. In order to comply with the recommendation with respect to Schedule K, the present work production of Bureau A must be increased by 15.____
   A. 50%
   B. 100%
   C. 150%
   D. 200%
   E. an amount which is not determinable on the basis of the data given

16. A certain training program during World War II resulted in training of thousands of supervisors in industry. The methods of this program were later successfully applied in various governmental agencies. The program was based upon the assumption that there is an irreducible minimum of three supervisory skills. The one of these skills among the following is 16.____
   A. to know how to perform the job at hand well
   B. to be able to deal personally with workers, especially face-to-face
   C. to be able to imbue workers with the will to perform the job well
   D. to know the kind of work that is done by one's unit and the policies and procedures of one's agency
   E. the "know-how" of administrative and supervisory processes

17. A comment made by an employee about a training course was, *We never have any idea how we are getting along in that course."* 17.____
   The fundamental error in training methods to which this criticism points is
   A. insufficient student participation
   B. failure to develop a feeling of need or active want for the material being presented
   C. the training sessions may be too long
   D. no attempt may have been made to connect the new material with what was already known
   E. no goals have been set for the students

18. Assume that you are attending a departmental conference on efficiency ratings at which it is proposed that a man-to-man rating scale be introduced. 18.____
   You should point out that, of the following, the CHIEF weakness of the man-to-man rating scale is that
   A. it involves abstract numbers rather than concrete employee characteristics
   B. judges are unable to select their own standards for comparison
   C. the standard for comparison shifts from man to man for each person rated
   D. not every person rated is given the opportunity to serve as a standard for comparison
   E. standards for comparison will vary from judge to judge

19. Assume that you are conferring with a supervisor who has assigned to his subordinates efficiency ratings which you believe to be generally too low. The supervisor argues that his ratings are generally low because his subordinates are generally inferior. 19.____
Of the following, the evidence MOST relevant to the point at issue can be secured by comparing efficiency ratings assigned by this supervisor
   A. with ratings assigned by other supervisors in the same agency
   B. this year with ratings assigned by him in previous years
   C. to men recently transferred to his unit with ratings previously earned by these men
   D. with the general city average of ratings assigned by all supervisors to all employees
   E. with the relative order of merit of his employees as determined independently by promotion test marks

20. The one of the following which is NOT among the most common of the compensable factors used in wage evaluation studies is 20.____
   A. initiative and ingenuity required
   B. physical demand
   C. responsibility for the safety of others
   D. working conditions
   E. presence of avoidable hazards

21. If independent functions are separated, there is an immediate gain in conserving special skills. If we are to make optimum use of the abilities of our employees, these skills must be conserved. 21.____
Assuming the correctness of this statement, it follows that
   A. if we are not making optimum use of employee abilities, independent functions have not been separated
   B. we are making optimum use of employee abilities if we conserve special skills
   C. we are making optimum use of employee abilities if independent functions have been separated
   D. we are not making optimum use of employee abilities if we do not conserve special skills
   E. if special skills are being conserved, independent functions need not be separated

22. A reorganization of the bureau to provide for a stenographic pool instead of individual unit stenographer will result in more stenographic help being available too each unit when it is required, and consequently will result in greater productivity for each unit. An analysis of the space requirements shows that setting up a stenographic pool will require a minimum of 400 square feet of good space. In order to obtain this space, it will be necessary to reduce the space available for technical personnel, resulting in lesser productivity for each unit. 22.____
On the basis of the above discussion, it can be stated that in order to obtain greater productivity for each unit,

A. a stenographic pool should be set up
B. further analysis of the space requirement should be made
C. it is not certain as to whether or not a stenographic pool should be set up
D. the space available for each technician should be increased in order to compensate for the absence of a stenographic pool
E. a stenographic pool should not be set up

23. The adoption of a single consolidated form will mean that most of the form will not be used in any one operation. This would create waste and confusion. This conclusion is based upon the unstated hypothesis that 23.____
A. if waste and confusion are to be avoided, a single consolidated form should be used
B. if a single consolidated form is constructed, most of it can be used in each operation
C. if waste and confusion are to be avoided, most of the form employed should be used
D. most of a single consolidated form is not used
E. a single consolidated form should not be used

24. Assume that you are studying the results of mechanizing several hand operations. 24.____
The type of data which would be MOST useful in proving that an increase in mechanization is followed by a lower cost of operation is data which show that in
A. some cases a lower cost of operation was not preceded by an increase in mechanization
B. no case was a higher cost of operation preceded by a decrease in mechanization
C. some cases a lower cost of operation was preceded by a decrease in mechanization
D no case was a higher cost of operation preceded by an increase in mechanization
E. some cases an increase in mechanization was followed by a decrease in cost of operation

25. The type of data which would be MOST useful in determining if an increase in the length of rest periods is followed by an increased rate of production is data which would indicate that _____ in the length of the rest period. 25.____

A. *decrease* in the total production never follows an increase in
B. *increase* in the total production never follows an increase
C. *increase* in the rate of production never follows a decrease
D. *decrease* in the total production may follow a decrease
E. *increase* in the total production sometimes follows an increase

# KEY (CORRECT ANSWERS)

| | | | |
|---|---|---|---|
| 1. | E | 11. | C |
| 2. | B | 12. | C |
| 3. | C | 13. | B |
| 4. | B | 14. | D |
| 5. | E | 15. | E |
| 6. | A | 16. | B |
| 7. | B | 17. | E |
| 8. | A | 18. | E |
| 9. | A | 19. | C |
| 10. | D | 20. | E |

| | |
|---|---|
| 21. | D |
| 22. | C |
| 23. | C |
| 24. | D |
| 25. | A |

# TEST 3

DIRECTIONS: Each question or incomplete statement is followed by several suggested answers or completions. Select the one that BEST answers the question or completes the statement. *PRINT THE LETTER OF THE CORRECT ANSWER IN THE SPACE AT THE RIGHT.*

1. You have been asked to answer a request from a citizen of the city. After giving the request careful consideration, you find that it cannot be granted. In answering the letter, you should begin by 1.____
   A. saying that the request cannot be granted
   B. discussing in detail the consideration you have to the request
   C. quoting the laws relating to the request
   D. explaining in detail why the request cannot be granted
   E. indicating an alternative method of achieving the end desired

2. Reports submitted to the department head should be complete to the last detail. A far as possible, summaries should be avoided. This statement is, in general, 2.____
   A. *correct*; only on the basis of complete information can a proper decision be reached
   B. *incorrect*; if all reports submitted were of this character, a department head would never complete his work
   C. *correct*; the decision as to what is important and what is not can only be made by the person who is responsible for the action
   D. *incorrect*; preliminary reports, obviously, cannot be complete to the last detail
   E. *correct*; summaries tend to conceal the actual state of affairs and to encourage generalizations which would not be made if the details were known; consequently, they should be avoided if possible

3. The supervisor of a large bureau, who was required in the course of business to answer a large number of letters from the public, completely formalized his responses, that is, the form and vocabulary of every letter he prepared were the same as far as possible. This method of solving the problem of how to handle correspondence is, in general 3.____
   A. *good*; it reduces the time and thought necessary for a response
   B. *bad*; the time required to develop a satisfactory standard form and vocabulary is usually not available in an active organization
   C. *good*; the use of standard forms causes similar requests to be answered in a similar way
   D. *bad*; the use of standard forms and vocabulary to the extent indicated results in letters in *officialese* hindering unambiguous explanation and clear understanding
   E. *good*; if this method were applied to an entire department, the answering of letters could be left to clerks and the administrators would be free for more constructive work

4. Of the following systems of designating the pages in a looseleaf manual subject to constant revision and addition, the MOST practicable one is to use _____ for main divisions and _____ for subdivisions. 4._____
   A. decimals; integers
   B. integers; letters
   C. integers; decimals
   D. letters; integers
   E. integers; integers

5. A subordinate submits a proposed draft of a form which is being revised to facilitate filling in the form on a typewriter. The draft shows that the captions for each space will be printed below the space to be filled in. 5._____
   This proposal is
   A. *undesirable*; it decreases visibility
   B. *desirable*; it makes the form easy to understand
   C. *undesirable*; it makes the form more difficult to understand
   D. *desirable*; it increases visibility
   E. *undesirable*; it is less compact than other layouts

6. The one of the following which is NOT an essential element of an integrated reporting system for work-measurement is a 6._____
   A. uniform record form for accumulating data and instructions for its maintenance
   B. procedure for routing reports upward through the organization and routing summaries downward
   C. standard report form for summarizing basic records and instructions for its preparation
   D. method for summarizing, analyzing and presenting data from several reports
   E. looseleaf revisable manual which contains all procedural materials that are reasonably permanent and have a substantial reference value

7. Forms control only accomplishes the elimination, consolidation, and simplification of forms. It contributes little to the elimination, consolidation, and simplification of procedures. 7._____
   This statement is
   A. *correct*; the form is static while the procedure is dynamic; consequently, control of one does not necessarily result in control of the other
   B. *incorrect*; forms frequently dictate the way work is laid out; consequently, control of one frequently results in control of the other
   C. *correct*; the procedure is primary and the form secondary; consequently, control of procedure will also control form
   D. *incorrect*; the form and procedure are identical from the viewpoint of work control; consequently, control of one means control of the other
   E. *correct*; the assurance that forms are produced and distributed economically has little relationship to the consolidation and simplification of procedures

8. Governmental agencies frequently attempt to avoid special interest group pressures by referring them to the predetermined legislative policy, or to the necessity for rules and regulations applying generally to all groups and situations. 8.____
Of the following, the MOST important weakness of this formally correct position is that
   A. it is not tenable in the face of determined opposition
   B. it tends to legalize and formalize the informal relationships between citizen groups and the government
   C. the achievement of an agency's aims is in large measure dependent upon its ability to secure the cooperation and support of special interest groups
   D. independent groups which participate in the formulation of policy in their sphere of interest tend to criticize openly and to press for changes in the direction of their policy
   E. agencies following this policy find it difficult to decentralize their public relation activities as subdivisions can only refer to the agency's overall policy

9. One of the primary purposes of the performance budget is to improve the ability to examine budgetary requirement by groups who have not been engaged in the construction of the budget. 9.____
This is accomplished by
   A. making line by line appropriations
   B. making lump sum appropriations by department
   C. enumerating authorization for all expenditures
   D. standardizing the language used and the kinds of authorizations permitted
   E. permitting examination on the level of accomplishment

10. When engaged in budget construction or budget analysis, there is no point in trying to determine the total or average benefits to be obtained from total expenditures for a particular commodity or function. 10.____
The validity of this argument is USUALLY based upon the
   A. viewpoint that it is not possible to construct a functional budget
   B. theory (or phenomenon) of diminishing utility
   C. hypothesis that as governmental budgets provide in theory for minimum requirements, there is no need to determine total benefits
   D. assumption that such determinations are not possible
   E. false hypothesis that a comparison between expected and achieved results does not aid in budget construction

Questions 11-12.

DIRECTIONS: Questions 11 and 12 are to be answered on the basis of the following paragraph.

Production planning is mainly a process of synthesis. As a basis for the positive act of bringing complex production elements properly together, however, analysis is necessary, especially if improvement is to be made in an existing organization. The necessary analysis requires customary means of orientation and preliminary fact gathering with emphasis, however, on the recognition of administrative goals and of the relationship among work steps.

11. The entire process described is PRIMARILY one of 11.____
    A. taking apart, examining, and recombining
    B. deciding what changes are necessary, making the changes and checking on their value
    C. fact finding so as to provide the necessary orientation
    D. discovering just where the emphasis in production should be placed and then modifying the existing procedure so that it is placed properly
    E. recognizing administrative goals and the relationship among work steps

12. In production planning according to the above paragraph, analysis is used PRIMARILY as 12.____
    A. a means of making important changes in an organization
    B. the customary means of orientation and preliminary fact finding
    C. a development of the relationship among work steps
    D. a means for holding the entire process intact by providing a logical basis
    E. a method to obtain the facts upon which a theory can be built

Questions 13-15.

DIRECTIONS: Questions 13 through 15 are to be answered on the basis of the following paragraph.

Public administration is policy-making. But it is not autonomous, exclusive or isolated policy-making. It is policy-making on a field where mighty forces contend, forces engendered in and by society. It is policy-making subject to still other and various policy makers. Public administration is one of a number of basic political processes by which these people achieves and controls government.

13. From the point of view expressed in the above paragraph, public administration is 13.____
    A. becoming a technical field with completely objective processes
    B. the primary force in modern society
    C. a technical field which should be divorced from the actual decision-making function
    D. basically anti-democratic
    E. intimately related to politics

14. According to the above paragraph, public administration is NOT entirely 14.____
    A. a force generated in and by society
    B. subject at times to controlling influences
    C. a social process
    D. policy-making relating to administrative practices
    E. related to policy-making at lower levels

15. The above paragraph asserts that public administration 15.____
    A. develops the basic and controlling policies
    B. is the result of policies made by many different forces
    C. should attempt to break through its isolated policy-making and engage on a broader field
    D. is a means of directing government
    E. is subject to the political processes by which acts are controlled

Questions 16-18.

DIRECTIONS: Questions 16 through 18 are to be answered on the basis of the following chart.

In order to understand completely the source of an employee's insecurity on his job, it is necessary to understand how he came to be, who he is and what kind of person he is away from his job. This would necessitate an understanding of those personal assets and liabilities which the employee brings to the job situation. These arise from his individual characteristics and his past experiences and established patterns of interpersonal relations. This whole area is of tremendous scope, encompassing everything included within the study of psychiatry and interpersonal relations. Therefore, it has been impracticable to consider it in detail. Attention has been focused on the relatively circumscribed area of the actual occupational situation. The factors considered those which the employee brings to the job situation and which arise from his individual characteristics and his past experience and established patterns of interpersonal relations are: intellectual-level or capacity, specific aptitudes, education, work experience, health, social and economic background, patterns of interpersonal relations and resultant personality characteristics.

16. According to the above paragraph, the one of the following fields of study which would be of LEAST importance in the study of the problem is the 16.____
    A. relationships existing among employees
    B. causes of employee insecurity in the job situation
    C. conflict, if it exists, between intellectual level and work experience
    D. distribution of intellectual achievement
    E. relationship between employee characteristics and the established pattern of interpersonal relations in the work situation

17. According to the above paragraph, in order to make a thoroughgoing and comprehensive study of the sources of employee insecurity, the field of study should include 17.____
    A. only such circumscribed areas as are involved in extra-occupational situations
    B. a study of the dominant mores of the period
    C. all branches of the science of psychology
    D. a determination of the characteristics, such as intellectual capacity, which an employee should bring to the job situation
    E. employee personality characteristics arising from previous relationships with other people

18. It is implied by this paragraph that it would be of GREATEST advantage to bring to this problem a comprehensive knowledge of 18.____
    A. all established patterns of interpersonal relations
    B. the milieu in which the employee group is located
    C. what assets and liabilities are presented in the job situation
    D. methods of focusing attention on relatively circumscribed regions
    E. the sources of an employee's insecurity on his job

Questions 19-20.

DIRECTIONS: Questions 19 and 20 are to be answered on the basis of the following paragraph.

If, during a study, some hundreds of values of a variable (such as annual number of latenesses for each employee in a department) have been noted merely in the arbitrary order in which they happen to occur, the mind cannot properly grasp the significance of the record, the observations must be ranked or classified in some way before the characteristics of the series can be comprehended, and those comparisons, on which arguments as to causation depend, can be made with other series. A dichotomous classification is too crude; if the values are merely classified according to whether they exceed or fall short of some fixed value, a large part of the information given by the original record is lost. Numerical measurements lend themselves with peculiar readiness to a manifold classification.

19. According to the above paragraph, if the values of a variable which are gathered during a study are classified in a few subdivisions, the MOST likely result will be 19.____
    A. an inability to grasp the signification of the record
    B. an inability to relate the series with other series
    C. a loss of much of the information in the original data
    D. a loss of the readiness with which numerical measurements lend themselves to a manifold classification
    E. that the order in which they happen to occur will be arbitrary

20. The above paragraph advocates, with respect to numerical data, the use of 20.____
    A. arbitrary order
    B. comparisons with other series
    C. a two-value classification
    D. a many value classification
    E. all values of a variable

Questions 21-25.

DIRECTIONS: Questions 21 through 25 are to be answered on the basis of the following chart.

DEPARTMENT X
WORKLOAD AND LABOR FORCE
2011 - 2020

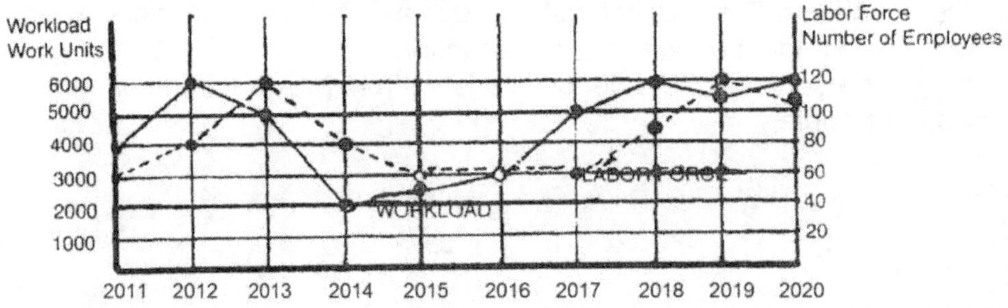

21. The one of the following years for which average employee production was LOWEST was 21.____
    A. 2012 B. 2014 C. 2016 D. 2018 E. 2020

22. The average annual employee production for the ten-year period was, in terms of work units, MOST NEARLY 22.____
    A. 30 B. 50 C. 70 D. 80 E. 90

23. On the basis of the chart, it can be deduced that personnel needs for the coming year are budgeted on the basis of 23.____
    A. workload for the current year
    B. expected workload for the coming year
    C. no set plan
    D. average workload over the five years immediately preceding the period
    E. expected workload for the five coming years

24. The chart indicates that the operation is carefully programmed and that the labor force has been used properly. 24.____
    This opinion is
    A. *supported* by the chart; the organization has been able to meet emergency situations requiring much additional work without commensurate increase in staff
    B. *not supported* by the chart; the irregular workload shows a complete absence of planning
    C. *supported* by the chart; the similar shapes of the workload and labor force curves show that these important factors are closely related
    D. *not supported* by the chart; poor planning with respect to labor requirements is obvious from the chart
    E. *supported* by the chart; the average number of units of work performed in any 5-year period during the 10 years shows sufficient regularity to indicate a definite trend

25. The chart indicates that the department may be organized in such a way as to require a permanent minimum staff which is too large for the type of operation indicated. 25.____
    This opinion is
    A. *supported* by the chart; there is indication that the operation calls for an irreducible minimum number of employees and application of the most favorable work production records shows this to be too high for normal operation
    B. *not supported* by the chart; the absence of any sort of regularity makes it impossible to express any opinion with any degree of certainty
    C. *supported* by the chart; the expected close relationship between workload and labor force is displaced somewhat, a phenomenon which usually occurs as a result of a fixed minimum requirement
    D. *not supported* by the chart; the violent movement of the labor force curve makes it evident that no minimum requirements are in effect

E. *supported* by the chart; calculation shows that the average number of employees was 84 with an average variation of 17.8, thus indicating that the minimum number of 60 persons was too high for efficient operation

## KEY (CORRECT ANSWERS)

1. A
2. B
3. D
4. C
5. A

6. E
7. B
8. C
9. E
10. B

11. A
12. E
13. E
14. D
15. D

16. D
17. E
18. B
19. C
20. D

21. B
22. B
23. A
24. D
25. A

# EXAMINATION SECTION

## TEST 1

DIRECTIONS: Each question or incomplete statement is followed by several suggested answers or completions. Select the one that BEST answers the question or completes the statement. *PRINT THE LETTER OF THE CORRECT ANSWER IN THE SPACE AT THE RIGHT.*

1. An executive assigns A, the head of a staff unit, to devise plans for reducing the delay in submittal of reports by a local agency headed by C. The reports are under the supervision of C's subordinate line official B with whom A is to deal directly. In his investigation, A finds: (1) the reasons for the delay; and (2) poor practices which have either been overlooked or condoned by line official B. 1.____

   Of the following courses of action A could take, the BEST one would be to
   A. develop recommendations with line official B with regard to reducing the delay and correcting the poor practice and then report fully to his own executive
   B. discuss the findings with C in an attempt to correct the situation before making any formal report on the poor practices
   C. report both findings to his executive, attaching the explanation offered by C
   D. report to his executive on the first finding and discuss the second in a friendly way with line official B
   E. report the first finding to his executive, ignoring the second until his opinion is requested

2. Drafts of a proposed policy, prepared by a staff committee, are circulated to ten member of the field staff of the organization by route slips with a request for comments within two weeks. Two members of the field staff make extensive comments, four offer editorial suggestions, and the remainder make minor favorable comments. Shortly after, it found that the statement needs considerable revision by the field staff. 2.____

   Of the following possible reasons for the original failure of the field staff to identify difficulties, the MOST likely is that the
   A. field staff did not take sufficient time to review the manual
   B. field staff had not been advised of the type of contribution expected
   C. low morale of the field staff prevented their showing interest
   D. policy statement was too advanced for the staff
   E. staff committee was not sufficiently representative

3. Operator participation in management improvement work is LEAST likely to 3.____
   A. assure the use of best available management technique
   B. overcome the stigma of the outside expert
   C. place responsibility for improvement in the person who knows the job best
   D. simplify installation
   E. take advantage of the desire of most operators to seek self-improvement

4. In general, the morale of workers in an agency is MOST frequently and MOST significantly affected by the 4.____
   A. agency policies of organizational structure and operational procedures
   B. distance of the employee's job from his home community
   C. fringe benefits
   D. number of opportunities for advancement
   E. relationship with supervisors

5. Of the following, the PRIMARY function of a work distribution chart is to 5.____
   A. analyze the soundness of existing divisions of labor
   B. eliminate the unnecessary clerical detail
   C. establish better supervisory techniques
   D. simplify work methods
   E. weed out core functions

6. In analyzing a process chart, which one of the following should be asked FIRST? 6.____
   A. How B. When C. Where D. Who E. Why

7. Which one of the following is NOT an advantage of the interview method of collecting data? It 7.____
   A. enables interviewer to judge the person interviewed on such matters as general attitude, knowledge, etc.
   B. helps build up personal relations for later installation of changes
   C. is a flexible method that can be adjusted to changing circumstances
   D. permits the obtaining of *off the record* information
   E. produces more accurate information than other methods

8. Which one of the following may be defined as a *regularly recurring appraisal of the manner in which all elements of agency management are being carried out*? 8.____
   A. Functional survey
   B. Operations audit
   C. Organization survey
   D. Over-all survey
   E. Reconnaissance survey

9. An analysis of the flow of work in a department should begin with the _____ work. 9.____
   A. major routine
   B. minor routine
   C. supervisory
   D. technical
   E. unusual

10. Which method would MOST likely be used to get first-hand information on complaints from the public? 10.____
   A. Study of correspondence
   B. Study of work volume
   C. Tracing specific transactions through a series of steps
   D. Tracing use of forms
   E. Worker desk audit

11. People will generally produce the MOST if 11.____
   A. management exercises close supervision over the work
   B. there is strict discipline in the group
   C. they are happy in their work
   D. they feel involved in their work
   E. they follow *the one best way*

12. The normal analysis of which chart listed below is MOST closely related to organizational analysis? _____ chart. 12.____
   A. Layout
   B. Operation
   C. Process
   D. Work count
   E. Work distribution

13. The work count would be LEAST helpful in accomplishing which one of the following? 13.____
   A. Demonstrating personnel needs
   B. Improving the sequence of steps
   C. Measuring the value of a step
   D. Spotting bottlenecks
   E. Stimulating interest in work

14. Which one of the following seems LEAST useful as a guide in interviewing an employee in a procedure and methods survey? 14.____
   A. Explaining who you are and the purpose of your visit
   B. Having a general plan of what you intend to get from the interview
   C. Listening carefully and not interrupting
   D. Trying out his reactions to your ideas for improvements
   E. Trying to analyze his reasons for saying what he says

15. Which one of the following is an advantage of the questionnaire method of gathering facts as compared with the interview method? 15.____
   A. Different people may interpret the questions differently
   B. Less *off the record* information is given
   C. More time may be taken in order to give exact answers
   D. Personal relationships with the people involved are not established
   E. There is less need for follow-up

16. Which one of the following is generally NOT an advantage of the personal observation method of gathering facts? It 16.____
   A. enables staff to use *off the record* information if personally observed
   B. helps in developing valid recommendations
   C. helps the person making the observation acquire *know how* valuable for later installation and follow-up
   D. is economical in time and money
   E. may turn up other problems in need of solution

17. Which of the following would MOST often be the best way to minimize resistance to change? 17.____
   A. Break the news about the change gently to the people affected
   B. Increase the salary of the people affected by the change
   C. Let the people concerned participate at the decision to change

D. Notify all people concerned with the change, both orally and in writing
E. Stress the advantages of the new system

18. The functional organization chart 18.____
A. does not require periodic revision
B. includes a description of the duties of each organization segment
C. includes positions and titles for each organization segment
D. is the simplest type of organization chart
E. is used primarily by newly established agencies

19. The principle of span of control has frequently been said to be in conflict with the 19.____
A. principle of unity of command
B. principle that authority should be commensurate with responsibility
C. principle that like functions should be grouped into one unit
D. principle that the number of levels between the top of an organization and the bottom should be small
E. scalar principle

20. If an executive delegates to his subordinates authority to handle problems of a routine nature for which standard solutions have been established, he may expect that 20.____
A. fewer complaint will be received
B. he has made it more difficult for his subordinates to solve these problems
C. he has opened the way for confusion in his organization
D. there will be a lack of consistency in the methods applied to the solution of these problems
E. these routine problems will be handled efficiently and he will have more time for other non-routine work

21. Which of the following would MOST likely be achieved by a change in the basic organization structure from the *process* or *functional* type to the *purpose* or *product* type? 21.____
A. Easier recruitment of personnel in a tight labor market
B. Fixing responsibility at a lower level in the organization
C. Greater centralization
D. Greater economy
E. Greater professional development

22. Usually the MOST difficult problem in connection with a major reorganization is 22.____
A. adopting a pay plan to fit the new structure
B. bringing the organization manual up-to-date
C. determining the new organization structure
D. gaining acceptance of the new plan by the higher level employees
E. gaining acceptance of the new plan by the lower level employees

23. Which of the following statements MOST accurately describes the work of the chiefs of MOST staff divisions in departments? 23.____
Chiefs
    A. focus more on getting the job done than on how it is done
    B. are mostly interested in short-range results
    C. nearly always advise but rarely advise
    D. usually command or control but rarely advise
    E. provide service to the rest of the organization and/or assist the chief executive in planning and controlling operations

24. In determining the type of organization structure of an enterprise, the one factor that might be given relatively greater weight in a small organization than in a larger organization of the same nature is the 24.____
    A. geographical location of the enterprise
    B. individual capabilities of incumbents
    C. method of financing to be employed
    D. size of the area served
    E. type of activity engaged in

25. Functional foremanship differs MOST markedly from generally accepted principle of administration in that it advocates 25.____
    A. an unlimited span of control
    B. less delegation of responsibility
    C. more than one supervisor for an employee
    D. nonfunctional organization
    E. substitution of execution for planning

# KEY (CORRECT ANSWERS)

| | | | |
|---|---|---|---|
| 1. | A | 11. | D |
| 2. | B | 12. | E |
| 3. | A | 13. | B |
| 4. | E | 14. | D |
| 5. | A | 15. | C |
| 6. | E | 16. | D |
| 7. | E | 17. | C |
| 8. | B | 18. | B |
| 9. | A | 19. | D |
| 10. | A | 20. | E |

| | |
|---|---|
| 21. | B |
| 22. | D |
| 23. | E |
| 24. | B |
| 25. | C |

# TEST 2

DIRECTIONS: Each question or incomplete statement is followed by several suggested answers or completions. Select the one that BEST answers the question or completes the statement. *PRINT THE LETTER OF THE CORRECT ANSWER IN THE SPACE AT THE RIGHT.*

1. Decentralization of the authority to make decisions is a necessary result of increased complexity in an organization, but for the sake of efficiency and coordination of operations, such decentralization must be planned carefully. A good general rule is that 1.____
   A. any decision should be made at the lowest possible point in the organization where all the information and competence necessary for a sound decision are available
   B. any decision should be made at the highest possible point in the organization, thus guaranteeing the best decision
   C. any decision should be made at the lowest possible point in the organization, but always approved by management
   D. any decision should be made by management and referred to the proper subordinate for comment
   E. no decision should be made by any individual in the organization without approval by a superior

2. One drawback of converting a conventional consecutive filing system to a terminal digit filing system for a large installation is that 2.____
   A. conversion would be expensive in time and manpower
   B. conversion would prevent the proper use of recognized numeric classification systems, such as the Dewey decimal, in classifying files material
   C. responsibility for proper filing cannot be pinpointed in the terminal digit system
   D. the terminal digit system requires considerably more space than a normal filing system

3. The basic filing system that would ordinarily be employed in a large administrative headquarters unit is the _____ file system. 3.____
   A alphabetic
   B. chronological
   C. mnemonic
   D. retention
   E. subject classification

4. A records center is of benefit in a records management program PRIMARILY because 4.____
   A. all the records of the organization are kept in one place
   B. inactive records can be stored economically in less expense storage areas
   C. it provides a place where useless records can be housed at little or no cost to the organization

D. obsolete filing and storage equipment can be utilized out of view of the public
E. records analysts can examine an organization's files without affecting the unit's operation or upsetting the supervisors

5. In examining a number of different forms to see whether any could be combined or eliminated, which of the following would one be MOST likely to use? 5.____
A. Forms analysis sheet of recurring data
B. Forms control log
C. Forms design and approval request
D. Forms design and guide sheet
E. Numerical file

6. The MOST important reason for control of *bootleg* forms is that 6.____
A. they are more expensive than authorized forms
B. they are usually poorly designed
C. they can lead to unnecessary procedures
D. they cannot be reordered as easily as authorized terms
E. violation of rules and regulations should not be allowed

7. With a box design of a form, the caption title or question to be answered should be located in the _____ of the box. 7.____
A. center at the bottom
B. center at the top
C. lower left corner
D. lower right corner
E. upper left corner

8. A two-part snapout form would be MOST properly justified if 8.____
A. it is a cleaner operation
B. it is prepared ten times a week
C. it saves time in preparation
D. it is to be filled out by hand rather than by typewriter
E. proper registration is critical

9. When deciding whether or not to approve a request for a new form, which reference is normally MOST pertinent? 9.____
A. Alphabetical Forms File
B. Functional Forms File
C. Numerical Forms File
D. Project Completion Report
E. Records Retention Data

10. Which of the following statements BEST explains the significance of the famed Hawthorne Plant experiments? 10.____
They showed that
A. a large span of control leads to more production than a small span of control
B. morale has no relationship to production
C. personnel counseling is of relatively little importance in a going organization

D. the special attention received by a group in an experimental situation has a greater impact on production than changes in working conditions
E. there is a direct relationship between the amount of illumination and production

11. Which of the following would most often NOT result from a highly efficient management control system? 11.____
A. Facilitation of delegation
B. Highlighting of problem areas
C. Increase in willingness of people to experiment or to take calculated risks
D. Provision of an objective test of new ideas or new methods and procedures
E. Provision of information useful for revising objectives, programs, and operations

12. The PERT system is a 12.____
A. method for laying out office space on a modular basis utilizing prefabricated partitions
B. method of motivating personnel to be continuously alert and to improve their appearance
C. method of program planning and control using a network or flow plan
D. plan for expanding reporting techniques
E. simplified method of cost accounting

13. The term *management control* is MOST frequently used to mean 13.____
A. an objective and unemotional approach by management
B. coordinating the efforts of all parts of the organization
C. evaluation of results in relation to plan
D. giving clear, precise orders to subordinates
E. keeping unions from making managerial decisions

14. Which one of the following factors has the MOST bearing on the frequency with which a control report should be made? 14.____
A. Degree of specialization of the work
B. Degree of variability in activities
C. Expense of the report
D. Number of levels of supervision
E. Number of personnel involved

15. The value of statistical records is MAINLY dependent upon the 15.____
A. method of presenting the material
B. number of items used
C. range of cases sampled
D. reliability of the information used
E. time devoted to compiling the material

16. When a supervisor delegates an assignment, he should 16.____
    A. delegate his responsibility for the assignment
    B. make certain that the assignment is properly performed
    C. participate in the beginning and final stages of the assignment
    D. retail all authority needed to complete the assignment
    E oversee all stages of the assignment

17. Assume that the department in which you are employed has never given official sanction to a mid-afternoon coffee break. Some bureaus have it and others do not. In the latter case, some individuals merely absent themselves for about 15 minutes at 3 P.M. while others remain on the job despite the fatigue which seems to be common among all employees in this department at that time. 17.____
    The course of action which you should recommend, if possible, is to
    A. arrange a schedule of mid-afternoon coffee breaks for all employees
    B. forbid all employees to take a mid-afternoon coffee break
    C. permit each bureau to decide for itself whether or not it will have a coffee break
    D. require all employees who wish a coffee break to take a shorter lunch period
    E. arrange a poll to discover the consensus of the department

18. The one of the following which is LEAST important in the management of a suggestion program is 18.____
    A. giving awards which are of sufficient value to encourage competition
    B. securing full support from the department's officers and executives
    C. publicizing the program and the awards given
    D. holding special conferences to analyze and evaluate some of the suggestions needed
    E. providing suggestion boxes in numerous locations

19. The one of the following which is MOST likely to decrease morale is 19.____
    A. insistence on strict adherence to safety rules
    B. making each employee responsible for the tidiness of his work area
    C. overlooking evidence of hostility between groups of employees
    D. strong, aggressive leadership
    E. allocating work on the basis of personal knowledge of the abilities and interests of the member of the department

20. Assume that a certain office procedure has been standard practice for many years. 20.____
    When a new employee asks why this particular procedure is followed, the supervisor should FIRST
    A. explain that everyone does it that way
    B. explain the reason for the procedure
    C. inform him that it has always been done that way in that particular office
    D. tell him to try it for a while before asking questions
    E. tell him he has never thought about it that way

21. Several employees complain informally to their supervisor regarding some new procedures which have been instituted. 21.____
The supervisor should IMMEDIATELY
    A. explain that management is responsible
    B. state frankly that he had nothing to do with it
    C. refer the matter to the methods analyst
    D. tell the employees to submit their complaint as a formal grievance
    E. investigate the complaint

22. A new employee asks his supervisor how he is doing. Actually, he is not doing well in some phases of the job, but it is felt that he will learn in time. 22.____
The BEST response for the supervisor to make is:
    A. Some things you are doing well, and in others I am sure you will improve.
    B. Wait until the end of your probation period when we will discuss this matter.
    C. You are not doing too well.
    D. You are doing very well.
    E. I'll be able to tell you when I go over your record.

23. The PRINCIPAL aim of a supervisor is to 23.____
    A. act as liaison between employee and management
    B. get the work done
    C. keep up morale
    D. train his subordinates
    E. become chief of the department

24. When the work of two bureaus must be coordinated, direct contact between the subordinates in each bureau who are working on the problem is 24.____
    A. *bad*, because it violates the chain of command
    B. *bad*, because they do not have authority to make decisions
    C. *good*, because it enable quicker results
    D. *good*, because it relieves their superiors of any responsibilities
    E. *bad*, because they may work at cross purposes

25. Of the following, the organization defect which can be ascertained MOST readily merely by analyzing an accurate and well-drawn organization chart is 25.____
    A. ineffectiveness of an activity
    B. improper span of control
    C. inappropriate assignment of functions
    D. poor supervision
    E. unlawful delegation of authority

# KEY (CORRECT ANSWERS)

| | | | |
|---|---|---|---|
| 1. | A | 11. | C |
| 2. | A | 12. | C |
| 3. | E | 13. | C |
| 4. | B | 14. | B |
| 5. | A | 15. | D |
| 6. | C | 16. | B |
| 7. | E | 17. | A |
| 8. | E | 18. | E |
| 9. | B | 19. | C |
| 10. | D | 20. | B |

| | |
|---|---|
| 21. | E |
| 22. | A |
| 23. | B |
| 24. | C |
| 25. | B |

# SUPERVISION, ADMINISTRATION, MANAGEMENT, AND ORGANIZATION

## EXAMINATION SECTION

## TEST 1

DIRECTIONS: Each question or incomplete statement is followed by several suggested answers or completions. Select the one that BEST answers the question or completes the statement. *PRINT THE LETTER OF THE CORRECT ANSWER IN THE SPACE AT THE RIGHT.*

1. In coaching a subordinate on the nature of decision-making, an executive would be right if he stated that the one of the following which is general the BEST definition of decision-making is: 1.____
   A. Choosing between alternatives
   B. Making diagnoses of feasible ends
   C. Making diagnoses of feasible means
   D. Comparing alternatives

2. Of the following, which one would be LEAST valid as a purpose of an organizational policy statement? 2.____
   To
   A. keep personnel from performing improper actions and functions on routine matters
   B. prevent the mishandling of non-routine matters
   C. provide management personnel with a tool that precludes the need for their use of judgment
   D. provide standard decisions and approaches in handling problems of a recurrent nature

3. Much has been written criticizing bureaucratic organizations. Current thinking on the subject is GENERALLY that 3.____
   A. bureaucracy is on the way out
   B. bureaucracy, though not perfect, is unlikely to be replaced
   C. bureaucratic organizations are most effective in dealing with constant change
   D. bureaucratic organizations are most effective when dealing with sophisticated customers or clients

4. The development of alternate plans as a major step in planning will normally result in the planner having several possible courses of action available. 4.____
   GENERALLY, this is
   A. *desirable*, since such development helps to determine the most suitable alternative and to provide for the unexpected
   B. *desirable*, since such development makes the use of planning premises and constraints unnecessary

C. *undesirable*, since the planners should formulate only one way of achieving given goals at a given time
D. *undesirable*, since such action restricts efforts to modify the planning to take advantage of opportunities

5. The technique of departmentation by task force includes the assigning of a team or task force to a definite project or block of work which extends from the beginning to the completing of a wanted and definite type and quantity of work. Of the following, the MOST important actor aiding the successful use of this technique *normally* is 5.____
A. having the task force relatively large, at least one hundred members
B. having a definite project termination date established
C. telling each task force member what his next assignment will be only after the current project ends
D. utilizing it only for projects that are regularly recurring

6. With respect to communication in small group settings such as may occur in business, government, and the military, it is generally TRUE that people usually derive more satisfaction and are usually more productive under conditions which 6.____
A. permit communication only with superiors
B. permit the minimum intragroup communication possible
C. are generally restricted by management
D. allow open communication among all group members

7. If an executive were asked to list some outstanding features of decentralization, which one of the following would NOT be such a feature? 7.____
Decentralization
A. provides decision-making experience for lower level managers
B. promotes uniformity of policy
C. is a relatively new concept in management
D. is similar to the belief in encouragement of free enterprise

8. Modern management experts have emphasized the importance of the informal organization in motivating employees to increase productivity. 8.____
Of the following, the characteristic which would have the MOST direct influence on employee motivation is the tendency of members of the informal organization to
A. resist change
B. establish their own norms
C. have similar outside interests
D. set substantially higher goals than those of management

9. According to leading management experts, the decision-making process contains separate and distinct steps that must be taken in an orderly sequence. 9.____
Of the following arrangements, which one is in CORRECT order?

A. I. Search for alternatives; II. diagnosis; III. comparison; IV. choice
B. I. Diagnose; II. comparison; III. search for alternatives; IV. choice
C. I. Diagnose; II. search for alternatives; III. comparison; IV. choice
D. I. Diagnose; II. search for alternatives; III. choice; IV. comparison

10. Of the following, the growth of professionalism in large organizations can PRIMARILY be expected to result in 10.____
A. greater equalization of power
B. increased authoritarianism
C. greater organizational disloyalty
D. increased promotion opportunities

11. Assume an executive carries out his responsibilities to his staff according to what is now known about managerial leadership. 11.____
Which of the following statements would MOST accurately reflect his assumptions about proper management?
A. Efficiency in operations results from allowing the human element to participate in a minimal way.
B. Efficient operation result from balancing work considerations with personnel considerations.
C. Efficient operation results from a workforce committed to its self-interest.
D. Efficient operation results from staff relationships that produce a friendly work climate.

12. Assume that an executive is called upon to conduct a management audit. To do this properly, he would have to take certain steps in a specific sequence. 12.____
Of the following steps, which step should this manager take FIRST?
A. Managerial performance must be surveyed.
B. A method of reporting must be established.
C. Management auditing procedures and documentation must be developed.
D. Criteria for the audit must be considered.

13. If a manager is required to conduct a scientific investigation of an organizational problem, the FIRST step he should take is to 13.____
A. state his assumptions about the problem
B. carry out a search for background information
C. choose the right approach to investigate the validity of his assumptions
D. define and state the problem

14. An executive would be right to assert that the principle of delegation states that decisions should be made PRIMARILY 14.____
A. by persons in an executive capacity qualified to make them
B. by persons in a non-executive capacity
C. at as low an organization level of authority as practicable
D. by the next lower level of authority

15. Of the following, which one is NOT regarded by management authorities as a FUNDAMENTAL characteristic of an *ideal* bureaucracy? 15.____
    A. Division of labor and specialization
    B. An established hierarchy
    C. Decentralization of authority
    D. A set of operating rules and regulations

16. As the number of subordinates in a manager's span of control increases, the ACTUAL number of possible relationships 16.____
    A. increases disproportionately to the number of subordinates
    B. increases in equal number to the number of subordinates
    C. reaches a stable level
    D. will first increase then slowly decrease

17. An executive's approach to controlling the activities of his subordinates concentrated on ends rather than means, and was diagnostic rather than punitive. 17.____
    This manager may MOST properly be characterized as using the managerial technique of management-by-
    A. exception B. objectives C. crisis D. default

18. In conducting a training session on the administrative control process, which of the following statements would be LEAST valid for an executive to make? 18.____
    Controlling
    A. requires checking upon assignments to see what is being done
    B. involves comparing what is being done to what ought to be done
    C. requires corrective action when what is being done does not meet expectations
    D. occurs after all the other managerial processes have been performed

19. The "brainstorming" technique for creative solutions of management problems MOST generally consists of 19.____
    A. bringing staff together in an exchange of a quantity of freewheeling ideas
    B. isolating individual staff members to encourage thought
    C. developing improved office procedures
    D. preparation of written reports on complex problems

20. Computer systems hardware MOST often operates in relation to which one of the following steps in solving a data-processing problem? 20.____
    A. Determining the problem
    B. Defining and stating the problem
    C. Implementing the programmed solution
    D. Completing the documentation of every unexplored solution

21. There is a tendency in management to upgrade objectives. 21.____
    This trend is generally regarded as
    A. *desirable*; the urge to improve is demonstrated by adopting objectives that have been adjusted to provide improved service

B. *undesirable*; the typical manager searches for problems which obstruct his objectives
C. *desirable*; it is common for a manager to find that the details of an immediate operation have occupied so much of his time that he has lost sight of the basic overall objective
D. *undesirable*; efforts are wasted when they are expended on a mass of uncertain objectives, since the primary need of most organizations is a single target or several major ones

22. Of the following, it is generally LEAST effective for an executive to delegate authority where working conditions involve 22.____
A. rules establishing normal operating procedures
B. consistent methods of operation
C. rapidly changing work standards
D. complex technology

23. If an executive was explaining the difficulty of making decisions under *risk* conditions, he would be MOST accurate if he said that such decisions would be difficult to make when the decision maker has _____ information and experience and can expect _____ outcomes for each action. 23.____
A. limited; many
B. much; many
C. much; few
D. limited; few

24. If an executive were asked to list some outstanding features of centralized organization, which one of the following would be INCORRECT? 24.____
Centralized organization
A. lessens risks of errors by unskilled subordinates
B. utilizes the skills of specialized experts at a central location
C. produces uniformity of policy and non-uniformity of action
D. enables closer control of operations than a decentralized set-up

25. It is possible for an organization's management to test whether or not the organization has a sound structure. 25.____
Of the following, which one is NOT a test of soundness in an organization's structure?
The
A. ability to replace key personnel with minimum loss of effectiveness
B. ability of information and decisions to flow more freely through the *grapevine* than through formal channels
C. provision for orderly organizational growth with the ability to handle change as the need arises.

# KEY (CORRECT ANSWERS)

| | | | |
|---|---|---|---|
| 1. | A | 11. | B |
| 2. | C | 12. | D |
| 3. | B | 13. | D |
| 4. | A | 14. | C |
| 5. | B | 15. | C |
| 6. | D | 16. | A |
| 7. | B | 17. | B |
| 8. | B | 18. | D |
| 9. | C | 19. | A |
| 10. | A | 20. | C |

| | |
|---|---|
| 21. | A |
| 22. | C |
| 23. | A |
| 24. | C |
| 25. | B |

# TEST 2

DIRECTIONS: Each question or incomplete statement is followed by several suggested answers or completions. Select the one that BEST answers the question or completes the statement. *PRINT THE LETTER OF THE CORRECT ANSWER IN THE SPACE AT THE RIGHT.*

1. Management experts generally believe that computer-based management information systems (MIS) have greater potential for improving the process of management than any other development in recent decades. 1.____
   The one of the following which MOST accurately describes the objectives of MIS is to
   A. provide information for decision-making on planning, initiating, and controlling the operations of the various units of the organization
   B. establish mechanization of routine functions such as clerical records, payroll, inventory, and accounts receivable in order to promote economy and efficiency
   C. computerize decision-making on planning, initiative, organizing, and controlling the operations of an organization
   D. provide accurate facts and figures on the various programs of the organization to be used for purposes of planning and research

2. The one of the following which is the BEST application on the *management-by-exception* principle is that this principle 2.____
   A. stimulates communication and aids in management of crisis situations, thus reducing the frequency of decision-making
   B. saves time and reserves top-management decisions only for crisis situations, thus reducing the frequency of decision-making
   C. stimulates communication, saves time, and reduces the frequency of decision-making
   D. is limited to crisis-management situations

3. It is generally recognized that each organization is dependent upon availability of qualified personnel. 3.____
   Of the following, the MOST important factor affecting the availability of qualified people to each organization is
   A. innovations in technology and science
   B. the general decline in the educational levels of our population
   C. the rise of sentiment against racial discrimination
   D. pressure by organized community groups

4. A fundamental responsibility of all managers is to decide what physical facilities and equipment are needed to help attain basic goals. 4.____
   Good planning for the purchase and use of equipment is seldom easy to do and is complicated MOST by the fact that
   A. organizations rarely have stable sources of supply
   B. nearly all managers tend to be better at personnel planning than at equipment planning

C. decisions concerning physical resources are made too often on a *crash basis* rather than under carefully prepared policies
D. legal rulings relative to depreciation fluctuate very frequently

5. In attempting to reconcile managerial objectives and an individual employee's goals, it is generally LEAST desirable for management to 5.____
A. recognize the capacity of the individual to contribute toward realization of managerial goals
B. encourage self-development of the employee to exceed minimum job performance
C. consider an individual employee's work separately from other employees
D. demonstrate that an employee advances only to the extent that he contributes directly to the accomplishment of stated goals

6. As a management tool for discovering individual training needs a job analysis would generally be of LEAST assistance in determining 6.____
A. the performance requirements of individual jobs
B. actual employee performance on the job
C. acceptable standards of performance
D. training needs for individual jobs

7. One of the major concerns of organizational managers today is how the spread of automation will affect them and the status of their positions. Realistically speaking, one can say that the MOST likely effect of our newer forms of highly automated technology on managers will be to 7.____
A. make most top-level positions superfluous or obsolete
B. reduce the importance of managerial work in general
C. replace the work of managers with the work of technicians
D. increase the importance of and demand for top managerial personnel

8. Which one of the following is LEAST likely to be an area or cause of trouble in the use of staff people (e.g., assistants to the administrator)? 8.____
A. Misunderstanding of the role the staff people are supposed to play, as a result of vagueness of definition of their duties and authority
B. Tendency of staff personnel almost always to be older than line personnel at comparable salary levels with who they must deal
C. Selection of staff personnel who fail to have simultaneously both competence in their specialties and skill in staff work
D. The staff person fails to understand mixed staff and operating duties

9. The one of the following which is the BEST measure of decentralization in an agency is the 9.____
A. amount of checking required on decisions made at lower levels in the chain of command
B. amount of checking required on decisions made at lower levels of the chain of command and the number of functions affected thereby
C. number of functions affected by decisions made at higher levels
D. number of functions affected by middle echelon decision-making

10. Which of the following is generally NOT a valid statement with respect to the supervisory process? 10.____
    A. General supervision is more effective than close supervision.
    B. Employee-centered supervisors lead more effectively than do production-centered supervisors.
    C. Employee satisfaction is directly related to productivity.
    D. Low-producing supervisors use techniques that are different from high-producing supervisors.

11. The one of the following which is the MOST essential element for proper evaluation of the performance of subordinate supervisors is a 11.____
    A. careful definition of each supervisor's specific job responsibilities and of his progress in meeting mutually agreed upon work goals
    B. system of rewards and penalties based on each supervisor's progress in meeting clearly defined performance standards
    C. definition of personality traits, such as industry, initiative, dependability, and cooperativeness, required for effective job performance
    D. breakdown of each supervisor's job into separate components and a rating of his performance on each individual task

12. The one of the following which is the PRINCIPAL advantage of specialization for the operating efficiency of a public service agency is that specialization 12.____
    A. reduces the amount of red tape in coordinating the activities of mutually dependent departments
    B. simplifies the problem of developing adequate job controls
    C. provides employees with a clear understanding of the relationship of their activities to the overall objectives of the agency
    D. reduces destructive competition for power between departments

13. Of the following, the group which generally benefits MOST from supervisory training programs in public service agencies are those supervisors who have 13.____
    A. accumulated a long period of total service to the agency
    B. responsibility for a large number of subordinate personnel
    C. been in the supervisory ranks for a long period of time
    D. a high level of formalized academic training

14. A list of conditions which encourages good morale inside a work group would NOT include a 14.____
    A. high rate of agreement among group members on values and objectives
    B. tight control system to minimize the risk of individual error
    C. good possibility that joint action will accomplish goals
    D. past history of successful group accomplishment

15. Of the following, the MOST important factor to be considered in selecting a training strategy or program is the 15.____
    A. requirements of the job to be performed by the trainees
    B. educational level or prior training of the trainees
    C. size of the training group
    D. quality and competence of available training specialists

16. Of the following, the one which is considered to be LEAST characteristic of the higher ranks of management is 16.____
    A. that higher levels of management benefit from modern technology
    B. that success is measured by the extent to which objectives are achieved
    C. the number of subordinates that directly report to an executive
    D. the de-emphasis of individual and specialized performance

17. Assume that an executive is preparing a training syllabus to be used in training members of his staff. 17.____
    Which of the following would NOT be a valid principle of the learning process for this manager to keep in mind in the preparation of the training syllabus?
    A. When a person has thoroughly learned a task, it takes a lot of effort to create a little more improvement.
    B. In complicated learning situations, there is a period in which an additional period of practice produces an equal amount of improvement in learning.
    C. The less a person knows about the task, the slower the initial progress.
    D. The more the person knows about the risk, the slower the initial progress.

18. Of the following, which statement BEST illustrates when collective bargaining agreements are working well? 18.____
    A. Executives strongly support subordinate managers.
    B. The management rights clause in the contract is clear and enforced.
    C. Contract provisions are competently interpreted.
    D. The provisions of the agreement are properly interpreted, communicated, and observed.

19. An executive who wishes to encourage subordinates to communicate freely with him about a job-related problem should FIRST 19.____
    A. state his own position on the problem before listening to the subordinates' ideas
    B. invite subordinates to give their own opinions on the problem
    C. ask subordinates for their reactions to his own ideas about the problem
    D. guard the confidentiality of management information about the problem

20. The ability to deal constructively with intra-organizational conflict is an essential attribute of the successful manager. 20.____
    The one of the following types of conflict which would be LEAST difficult to handle constructively is a situation in which there is
    A. agreement on objectives, but disagreement as to the probable results of adopting the various alternatives
    B. agreement on objectives, disagreement on alternative courses of action, and relative certainty as to the outcome of one of the alternatives
    C. disagreement on objectives and on alternate courses of action, but relative certainty as to the outcome of the alternatives
    D. disagreement on objectives and on alternative course of action, but uncertainty as to the outcome of the alternatives

21. Which of the following statements is LEAST accurate in describing formal job evaluation and wage and salary classification plans? 21.____
    A. Parties that disagree on wage matters can examine an established system rather than unsupported opinions.
    B. The use of such plans tends to overlook the effect of age and seniority of employees on job values in the plan.
    C. Such plans can eliminate salary controversies in organizations designing and using them properly.
    D. These plans are not particularly useful in checking on executive compensation.

22. In carrying out disciplinary action, the MOST important procedure for all managers to follow is to 22.____
    A. sell all levels of management on the need for discipline from the organization's viewpoint
    B. follow up on a disciplinary action and not assume that the action has been effective
    C. convince all executives that proper discipline is a legitimate tool for their use
    D. convince all executives that they need to display confidence in the organization's rules

Questions 23-25.

DIRECTIONS: Questions 23 through 25 are to be answered on the basis of the following situation. Richard Ford, a top administrator, is responsible for output in his organization. Because productivity had been lagging for two periods in a row, Ford decided to establish a committee of his subordinate managers to investigate the reasons for the poor performance and to make recommendations for improvements. After two meetings, the committee came to the conclusions and made the recommendations that follow:

Output forecasts had been handed down from the top without prior consultation with middle management and first level supervision. Lines of authority and responsibility had been unclear. The planning and control process should be decentralized.

After receiving the committee's recommendations, Ford proceeded to take the following actions:

Ford decided he would retain final authority to establish quotas but would delegate to the middle managers the responsibility for meeting quotas.

After receiving Ford's decision, the middle managers proceeded to delegate to the first-line supervisors the authority to establish their own quotas. The middle managers eventually received and combined the first-line supervisors' quotas so that these conformed with Ford's.

23. Ford's decision to delegate responsibility for meeting quotas to the middle managers is INCONSISTENT with sound management principles because of which one of the following? 23.____
    A. Ford shouldn't have involved himself in the first place.
    B. Middle managers do not have the necessary skills.

C. Quotas should be established by the chief executive.
D. Responsibility should not be delegated.

24. The principle of co-extensiveness of responsibility and authority bears on Ford's decision. 24.____
In this case, it IMPLIES that
A. authority should exceed responsibility
B. authority should be delegated to match the degree of responsibility
C. both authority and responsibility should be retained and not delegated
D. responsibility should be delegated but authority should be retained

25. The middle manager's decision to delegate to the first-line supervisors the authority to establish quotas was INCORRECTLY reasoned because 25.____
A. delegation and control must go together
B. first-line supervisors are in no position to establish quotas
C. one cannot delegate authority that one does not possess
D. the meeting of quotas should not be delegated

## KEY (CORRECT ANSWERS)

1. A
2. C
3. A
4. C
5. C

6. B
7. D
8. B
9. B
10. C

11. A
12. B
13. D
14. B
15. A

16. C
17. D
18. D
19. B
20. B

21. C
22. B
23. D
24. B
25. C

# TEST 3

DIRECTIONS: Each question or incomplete statement is followed by several suggested answers or completions. Select the one that BEST answers the question or completes the statement. *PRINT THE LETTER OF THE CORRECT ANSWER IN THE SPACE AT THE RIGHT.*

1. A danger which exists in any organization as complex as that required for administration of a large public agency is that each department comes to believe that it exists for its own sake. 1.____
   The one of the following which has been attempted in some organizations as a cure for this condition is to
   A. build up the departmental esprit de corps
   B. expand the functions and jurisdictions of the various departments so that better integration is possible
   C. develop a body of specialists in the various subject matter fields which cut across departmental lines
   D. delegate authority to the lowest possible echelon
   E. systematically transfer administrative personnel from one department to another

2. At best, the organization chart is ordinarily and necessarily an idealized picture of the intent of top management, a reflection of hopes and aims rather than a photograph of the operating facts within the organization. 2.____
   The one of the following which is the basic reason for this is that the organization chart
   A. does not show the flow of work within the organization
   B. speaks in terms of positions rather than of live employees
   C. frequently contains unresolved internal ambiguities
   D. is a record of past organization or proposed future organization and never a photograph of the living organization
   E. does not label the jurisdiction assigned to each component unit

3. The drag of inadequacy is always downward. The need in administration is always for the reverse; for a department head to project his thinking to the city level, for the unit chief to try to see the problems of the department. 3.____
   The inability of a city administration to recruit administrators who can satisfy this need usually results in departments characterized by
   A. disorganization
   B. poor supervision
   C. circumscribed viewpoints
   D. poor public relations
   E. a lack of programs

4. When, as a result of a shift in public sentiment, the elective officers of a city are changed, is it desirable for career administrators to shift ground without performing any illegal or dishonest act in order to conform to the policies of the new elective officers? 4.____
   A. *No*; the opinions and beliefs of the career officials are the result of long experience in administration and are more reliable than those of politicians

B. *Yes*; only in this way can citizens, political officials, and career administrators alike have confidence in the performance of their respective functions
C. *No*; a top career official who is so spineless as to change his views or procedures as a result of public opinion is of little value to the public service
D. *Yes*; legal or illegal, it is necessary that a city employee carry out the orders of his superior officers
E. *No*; shifting ground with every change in administration will preclude the use of a constant overall policy

5. Participation in developing plans which will affect levels in the organization in addition to his own, will contribute to an individual's understanding of the entire system. When possible, this should be encouraged. 5.____
This policy is, in general,
A. *desirable*; the maintenance of any organization depends upon individual understanding
B. *undesirable*; employees should participate only in these activities which affect their own level, otherwise conflicts in authority may arise
C. *desirable*; an employee's will to contribute to the maintenance of an organization depends to a great extent on the level which he occupies
D. *undesirable*; employees can be trained more efficiently and economically in an organized training program than by participating in plan development
E. *desirable*; it will enable the employee to make intelligent suggestions for adjustment of the plan in the future

6. Constant study should be made of the information contained in reports to isolate those elements of experience which are static, those which are variable and repetitive, and those which are variable and due to chance. 6.____
Knowledge of those elements of experience in his organization which are static or constant will enable the operating official to
A. fix responsibility for their supervisor at a lower level
B. revise the procedure in order to make the elements variable
C. arrange for follow-up and periodic adjustment
D. bring related data together
E. provide a frame of reference within which detailed standards for measurement can be installed

7. A chief staff officer, serving as one of the immediate advisors to the department head, has demonstrated a special capacity for achieving internal agreements and for sound judgment. As a result he has been used more and more as a source of counsel and assistance by the department head. Other staff officers and line officials as well have discovered that it is wise for them to check with this colleague in advance on all problematical matters handed up to the department head. 7.____

Developments such as this are
- A. *undesirable*; they disrupt the normal lines for flow of work in an organization
- B. *desirable*; they allow an organization to make the most of its strength wherever such strength resides
- C. *undesirable*; they tend to undermine the authority of the department head and put it in the hands of a staff officer who does not have the responsibility
- D. *desirable*; they tend to resolve internal ambiguities in organization
- E. *undesirable*; they make for bad morale by causing *cutthroat* competition

8. A common difference among executives is that some are not content unless they are out in front of everything that concerns their organization, while others prefer to run things by pulling strings, by putting others out in front and by stepping into the breach only when necessary. 8.____
Generally speaking, an advantage this latter method of operation has over the former is that it
- A. results in a higher level of morale over a sustained period of time
- B. gets results by exhortation and direct stimulus
- C. makes it unnecessary to calculate integrated moves
- D. makes the personality of the executive felt further down the line
- E. results in the executive getting the reputation for being a good fellow

9. Administrators frequently have to get facts by interviewing people. Although the interview is a legitimate fact gathering technique, it has definite limitations which should not be overlooked. 9.____
The one of the following which is an important limitation is that
- A. people who are interviewed frequently answer questions with guesses rather than admit their ignorance
- B. it is a poor way to discover the general attitude and thinking of supervisors interviewed
- C. people sometimes hesitate to give information during an interview which they will submit in written form
- D. it is a poor way to discover how well employees understand departmental policies
- E. the material obtained from the interview can usually be obtained at lower cost from existing records

10. It is desirable and advantageous to leave a maximum measure of planning responsibility to operating agencies or units, rather than to remove the responsibility to a central planning staff agency. 10.____
Adoption of the former policy (decentralized planning) would lead to
- A. *less effective planning*; operating personnel do not have the time to make long-term plans
- B. *more effective planning*; operating units are usually better equipped technically than any staff agency and consequently are in a better position to set up valid plans
- C. *less effective planning*; a central planning agency has a more objective point of view than any operating agency can achieve

D. *more effective planning*; plans are conceived in terms of the existing situation and their execution is carried out with the will to succeed
E. *less effective planning*; there is little or no opportunity to check deviation from plans in the proposed set-up

Questions 11-15.

DIRECTIONS: The following sections appeared in a report on the work production of two bureaus of a department. Base your answers to Questions 11 through 15 on this information. Throughout the report, assume that each month has 4 weeks.

Each of the two bureaus maintains a chronological file. In Bureau A, every 9 months on the average, this material fills a standard legal size cabinet sufficient for 12,000 work units. In Bureau B the same type of cabinet is filled in 18 months. Each bureau maintains three complete years of information plus a current file. When the current file cabinet is filled, the cabinet containing the oldest material is emptied, the contents disposed of, and the cabinet used for current material. The similarity of these operations makes it possible to consolidate these files with little effort.

Study of the practice of using typists as filing clerks for periods when there is no typing work showed: (1) Bureau A has for the past 6 months completed a total of 1,500 filing work units a week using on the average 100 man-hours of trained file clerk time and 20 man-hours of typist time; (2) Bureau B has in the same period completed a total of 2,000 filing work units a week using on the average 125 man-hours of trained file clerk time and 60 hours of typist time. This includes all work in chronological files. Assuming that all clerks work at the same speed and that all typists work at the same speed, this indicates that work other than filing should be found for typists or that they should be given some training in the filing procedures used. It should be noted that Bureau A has not been producing the 1,600 units of technical (not filing) work per 30-day period required by Schedule K, but is at present 200 units behind. The Bureau should be allowed 3 working days to get on schedule.

11. What percentage (approximate) of the total number of filing work units completed in both units consists of the work involved in the maintenance of the chronological files? 11.____
A. 5% B. 10% C. 15% D. 20% E. 25%

12. If the two chronological files are consolidated, the number of months which should be allowed for filling a cabinet is 12.____
A. 2 B. 4 C. 6 D. 8 E. 14

13. The MAXIMUM number of file cabinets which can be released for other uses as a result of the consolidation recommended is 13.____
A. 0
B. 1
C. 2
D. 3
E. not determinable on the basis of the data given

14. If all the filing work for both units is consolidated without diminution in the amount to be done and all filing work is done by trained file clerks, the number of clerks required (35-hour work week) is 14.____
    A. 4 B. 5 C. 6 D. 7 E. 8

15. In order to comply with the recommendation with respect to Schedule K, the present work production of Bureau A must be increased by 15.____
    A. 50%
    B. 100%
    C. 150%
    D. 200%
    E. an amount which is not determinable

16. A certain training program during World War II resulted in the training of thousands of supervisors in industry. The methods of this program were later successfully applied in various government agencies. The program was based upon the assumption that there is an irreducible minimum of three supervisory skills. 16.____
    The one of these skills among the following is
    A. to know how to perform the job at hand well
    B. to be able to deal personally with workers, especially face-to-face
    C. to be able to imbue workers with the will to perform the job well
    D. to know the kind of work that is done by one's unit and the policies and procedures of one's agency
    E. the *know-how* of administrative and supervisory processes

17. A comment made by an employee about a training course was, "*We never have any idea how we ae getting along in that course.*" 17.____
    The fundamental error in training methods to which this criticism points is
    A. insufficient student participation
    B. failure to develop a feeling of need or active want for the material being presented
    C. the training sessions may be too long
    D. no attempt may have been made to connect the new material with what was already known
    E. no goals have been set for the students

18. Assume that you are attending a departmental conference on efficiency ratings at which it is proposed that a man-to-man rating scale be introduced. 18.____
    You should point out that, of the following, the CHIEF weakness of the man-to-man rating scale is that
    A. it involves abstract numbers rather than concrete employee characteristics
    B. judges are unable to select their own standards for comparison
    C. the standard for comparison shifts from man-to-man for each person rated
    D. not every person rated is given the opportunity to serve as a standard for comparison
    E. standards for comparison will vary from judge to judge

19. Assume that you are conferring with a supervisor who has assigned to his subordinates efficiency ratings which you believe to be generally too low. The supervisor argues that his ratings are generally low because his subordinates are generally inferior. 19.____
Of the following, the evidence MOST relevant to the point at issue can be secured by comparing efficiency ratings assigned by the supervisor
   A. with ratings assigned by other supervisors in the same agency
   B. this year with ratings assigned by him in previous years
   C. to men recently transferred to his unit with ratings previously earned by these men
   D. with the general city average of ratings assigned by all supervisors to all employees
   E. with the relative order of merit of his employees as determined independently by promotion test marks

20. The one of the following which is NOT among the most common of the compensable factors used in wage evaluation studies is 20.____
   A. initiative and ingenuity required
   B. physical demand
   C. responsibility for the safety of others
   D. working conditions
   E. presence of avoidable hazards

21. If independent functions are separated, there is an immediate gain in conserving special skills. If we are to make optimum use of the abilities of our employees, these skills must be conserved. 21.____
Assuming the correctness of this statement, it follows that
   A. if we are not making optimum use of employee abilities, independent functions have not been separated
   B. we are making optimum uses of employee abilities if we conserve special skills
   C. we are making optimum use of employee abilities if independent functions have been separated
   D. we are not making optimum use of employee abilities if we do not conserve special skills
   E. if special skills are being conserved, independent functions need not be separated

22. A reorganization of the bureau to provide for a stenographic pool instead of individual unit stenographers will result in more stenographic help being available to each unit when it is required, and consequently will result in greater productivity for each unit. An analysis of the space requirements shows that setting up a stenographic pool will require a minimum of 400 square feet of good space. In order to obtain this space, it will be necessary to reduce the space available for technical personnel, resulting in lesser productivity for each unit. 22.____

On the basis of the above discussion, it can be stated that, in order to obtain greater productivity for each unit,
A. a stenographic pool should be set up
B. further analysis of the space requirement should be made
C. it is not certain as to whether or not a stenographic pool should be set up
D. the space available for each technician should be increased in order to compensate for the absence of a stenographic pool
E. a stenographic pool should not be set up

23. The adoption of single consolidated form will mean that most of the form will not be used in any one operation. This would create waste and confusion. This conclusion is based upon the unstated hypothesis that 23.____
A. if waste and confusion are to be avoided, a single consolidated form should be used
B. if a single consolidated form is constructed, most of it can be used in each operation
C. if waste and confusion are to be avoided, most of the form employed should be used
D. most of a single consolidation form is not used
E. a single consolidated form should not be used

# KEY (CORRECT ANSWERS)

| | | | |
|---|---|---|---|
| 1. | E | 11. | C |
| 2. | B | 12. | C |
| 3. | C | 13. | B |
| 4. | B | 14. | D |
| 5. | E | 15. | E |
| 6. | A | 16. | B |
| 7. | B | 17. | E |
| 8. | A | 18. | E |
| 9. | A | 19. | C |
| 10. | D | 20. | E |

21. D
22. C
23. C

# EVALUATING CONCLUSIONS BASED ON FACTUAL INFORMATION

Test material will be presented in a multiple-choice question format.

Test Task: You will be given a set of statements and a conclusion based on the statements. You are to assume the statements are true. The conclusion is reached from these statements *only* not on what you may happen to know about the subject discussed. Each question has three possible answers. You must then select the correct answer in the following manner:

Select A, if the statements prove that the conclusion is true.
Select B, if the statements prove that the conclusion is false.
Select C, if the statements are inadequate to prove the conclusion either true or false.

**SAMPLE QUESTION #1:**

**STATEMENTS:** All uniforms are cleaned by the Conroy Company. Blue uniforms are cleaned on Mondays or Fridays; green or brown uniforms are cleaned on Wednesdays. Alan and Jean have blue uniforms, Gary has green uniforms, and Ryan has brown uniforms.

**CONCLUSION:** Jean's uniforms are cleaned on Wednesdays.
A statements prove the conclusion TRUE
B statements prove the conclusion FALSE
C statements are INADEQUATE to prove the conclusion

The correct answer to this sample question is Choice B.

**SOLUTION:** The last sentence of the statements says that Jean has blue uniforms. The second sentence of the statements says that blue uniforms are cleaned on Monday or Friday. The conclusion says Jean's uniforms are cleaned on Wednesday. Wednesday is neither Monday nor Friday. Therefore, the conclusion must be false (choice B).

**SAMPLE QUESTION #2**

**STATEMENTS:** If Beth works overtime, the assignment will be completed. If the assignment is completed, then all unit employees will receive a bonus. Beth works overtime.

**CONCLUSION:** A bonus will be given to all employees in the unit.
A. statements prove the conclusion TRUE.
B. statements prove the conclusion FALSE.
C. statements are INADEQUATE to prove the conclusion

The correct answer to this sample question is Choice A.

**SOLUTION:** The conclusion follows necessarily from the statements. Beth works overtime. The assignment is completed. Therefore, all unit employees will receive a bonus.

**SAMPLE QUESTION #3**

**STATEMENTS:** Bill is older than Wanda. Edna is older than Bill. Sarah is twice as old as Wanda.

**CONCLUSION:** Sarah is older than Edna.

A. statements prove the conclusion TRUE
B. statements prove the conclusion FALSE
C. statements are INADEQUATE to prove the conclusion

The correct answer to this sample question is Choice C.

**SOLUTION:** We know from the statements that both Sarah and Edna are older than Wanda. We do not have any other information about Sarah and Edna. Therefore, no conclusion about whether or not Sarah is older than Edna can be made.

# EVALUATING CONCLUSIONS IN LIGHT OF KNOWN FACTS

## EXAMINATION SECTION

## TEST 1

DIRECTIONS: Each question or incomplete statement is followed by several suggested answers or completions. Select the one that BEST answers the question or completes the statement. *PRINT THE LETTER OF THE CORRECT ANSWER IN THE SPACE AT THE RIGHT.*

Questions 1-9.

DIRECTIONS: In Questions 1 through 9, you will read a set of facts and a conclusion drawn from them. The conclusion may be valid or invalid, based on the facts—it's your task to determine the validity of the conclusion.

For each question, select the letter before the statement that BEST expresses the relationship between the given facts and the conclusion that has been drawn from them. Your choices are:

A. The facts prove the conclusion;
B. The facts disprove the conclusion; or
C. The facts neither prove nor disprove the conclusion.

1. FACTS: If the supervisor retires, James, the assistant supervisor, will not be transferred to another department. James will be promoted to supervisor if he is not transferred. The supervisor retired. 1.____

   CONCLUSION: James will be promoted to supervisor.
   A. The facts prove the conclusion.
   B. The facts disprove the conclusion.
   C. The facts neither prove nor disprove the conclusion.

2. FACTS: In the town of Luray, every player on the softball team works at Luray National Bank. In addition, every player on the Luray softball team wear glasses. 2.____

   CONCLUSIONS: At least some of the people who work at Luray National Bank wear glasses.
   A. The facts prove the conclusion.
   B. The facts disprove the conclusion.
   C. The facts neither prove nor disprove the conclusion.

3. FACTS: The only time Henry and June go out to dinner is on an evening when they have childbirth classes. Their childbirth classes meet on Tuesdays and Thursdays. 3.____

CONCLUSION: Henry and June never go out to dinner on Friday or Saturday.
A. The facts prove the conclusion.
B. The facts disprove the conclusion.
C. The facts neither prove nor disprove the conclusion.

4. FACTS: Every player on the field hockey team has at least one bruise. Everyone on the field hockey team also has scarred knees. 4.____

CONCLUSION: Most people with both bruises and scarred knees are field hockey players.
A. The facts prove the conclusion.
B. The facts disprove the conclusion.
C. The facts neither prove nor disprove the conclusion.

5. FACTS: In the chess tournament, Lance will win his match against Jane if Jane wins her match against Mathias. If Lance wins his match against Jane, Christine will not win her match against Jane. 5.____

CONCLUSION: Christine will not win her match against Jane if Jane wins her match against Mathias.
A. The facts prove the conclusion.
B. The facts disprove the conclusion.
C. The facts neither prove nor disprove the conclusion.

6. FACTS: No green lights on the machine are indicators for the belt drive status. Not all of the lights on the machine's upper panel are green. Some lights on the machine's lower panel are green. 6.____

CONCLUSION: The green lights on the machine's lower panel may be indicators for the belt drive status.
A. The facts prove the conclusion.
B. The facts disprove the conclusion.
C. The facts neither prove nor disprove the conclusion.

7. FACTS: At a small, one-room country school, there are eight students: Amy, Ben, Carla, Dan, Elliot, Francine, Greg, and Hannah. Each student is in either the 6$^{th}$, 7$^{th}$, or 8$^{th}$ grade. Either two or three students are in each grade. Amy, Dan, and Francine are all in different grades. Ben and Elliot are both in the 7$^{th}$ grade. Hannah and Carl are in the same grade. 7.____

CONCLUSION: Exactly three students are in the 7$^{th}$ grade.
A. The facts prove the conclusion.
B. The facts disprove the conclusion.
C. The facts neither prove nor disprove the conclusion.

8. FACTS: Two married couples are having lunch together. Two of the four people are German and two are Russian, but in each couple the nationality of the spouse is not necessarily the same as the other's. One person in the group is a teacher, the other a lawyer, one an engineer, and the other a writer. The teacher is a Russian man. The writer is Russian, and her husband is an engineer. One of the people, Mr. Stern, is German. 8.____

CONCLUSION: Mr. Stern's wife is a writer.
- A. The facts prove the conclusion.
- B. The facts disprove the conclusion.
- C. The facts neither prove nor disprove the conclusion.

9. FACTS: The flume ride at the county fair is open only to children who are at least 36 inches tall. Lisa is 30 inches tall. John is shorter than Henry, but more than 10 inches taller than Lisa. 9.____

CONCLUSION: Lisa is the only one who can't ride the flume ride.
- A. The facts prove the conclusion.
- B. The facts disprove the conclusion.
- C. The facts neither prove nor disprove the conclusion.

Questions 10-17.

DIRECTIONS: Questions 10 through 17 are based on the following reading passage. It is not your knowledge of the particular topic that is being tested, but your ability to reason based on what you have read. The passage is likely to detail several proposed courses of action and factors affecting these proposals. The reading passage is followed by a conclusion or outcome based on the facts in the passage, or a description of a decision taken regarding the situation. The conclusion is followed by a number of statements that have a possible connection to the conclusion. For each statement, you are to determine whether:
- A. The statement proves the conclusion.
- B. The statement supports the conclusion but does not prove it.
- C. The statement disproves the conclusion.
- D. The statement weakens the conclusion but does not disprove it.
- E. The statement has no relevance to the conclusion.

Remember that the conclusion after the passage is to be accepted as the outcome of what actually happened, and that you are being asked to evaluate the impact each statement would have had on the conclusion.

PASSAGE:

The Grand Army of Foreign Wars, a national veteran's organization, is struggling to maintain its National Home, where the widowed spouses and orphans of deceased members are housed together in a small village-like community. The Home is open to spouses and children who are bereaved for any reason, regardless of whether the member's death was related to military service, but a new global conflict has led to a dramatic surge in the number of members' deaths: many veterans who re-enlisted for the conflict have been killed in action.

The Grand Army of Foreign Wars is considering several options for handling the increased number of applications for housing at the National Home, which has been traditionally supported by membership due. At its national convention, it will choose only one of the following:

The first idea is a one-time $50 tax on all members, above and beyond the dues they pay already. Since the organization has more than a million member, this tax should be sufficient for the construction and maintenance of new housing for applicants on the existing grounds of the National Home. The idea is opposed, however, by some older members who live on fixed incomes. These members object in principle to the taxation of Grand Army members. The Grand Army has never imposed a tax on its members.

The second idea is to launch a national fundraising drive the public relations campaign that will attract donations for the National Home. Several national celebrities are members of the organization, and other celebrities could be attracted to the cause. Many Grand Army members are wary of this approach, however: in the past, the net receipts of some fundraising efforts have been relatively insignificant, given the costs of staging them.

A third approach, suggested by many of the younger members, is to have new applicants share some of the costs of construction and maintenance. The spouses and children would pay an up-front "enrollment" fee, based on a sliding scale proportionate to their income and assets, and then a monthly fee adjusted similarly to contribute to maintenance costs. Many older members are strongly opposed to this idea, as it is in direct contradiction to the principles on which the organization was founded more than a century ago.

The fourth option is simply to maintain the status quo, focus the organization's efforts on supporting the families who already live at the National Home, and wait to accept new applicants based on attrition.

CONCLUSION: At its annual national convention, the Grand Army of Foreign Wars votes to impose a one-time tax of $10 on each member for the purpose of expanding and supporting the National Home to welcome a larger number of applicants. The tax is considered to be the solution most likely to produce the funds needed to accommodate the growing number of applicants.

10. Actuarial studies have shown that because the Grand Army's membership consists mostly of older veterans from earlier wars, the organization's membership will suffer a precipitous decline in numbers in about five years. 10.____
    A. The statement proves the conclusion.
    B. The statement supports the conclusion but does not prove it.
    C. The statement disproves the conclusion.
    D. The statement weakens the conclusion but does not disprove it.
    E. The statement has no relevance to the conclusion.

11. After passage of the funding measure, a splinter group of older members appeals for the "sliding scale" provision to be applied to the tax, so that some members may be allowed to contribute less based on their income. 11.____
    A. The statement proves the conclusion.
    B. The statement supports the conclusion but does not prove it.
    C. The statement disproves the conclusion.
    D. The statement weakens the conclusion but does not disprove it.
    E. The statement has no relevance to the conclusion.

12. The original charter of the Grand Army of Foreign Wars specifically states that the organization will not levy taxes or duties on its members beyond its modest annual dues. It takes a super-majority of attending delegates at the national convention to make alterations to the charter. 12.____
    A. The statement proves the conclusion.
    B. The statement supports the conclusion but does not prove it.
    C. The statement disproves the conclusion.
    D. The statement weakens the conclusion but does not disprove it.
    E. The statement has no relevance to the conclusion.

13. Six months before Grand Army of Foreign Wars' national convention, the Internal Revenue Service rules that because it is an organization that engages in political lobbying, the Grand Army must no longer enjoy its own federal tax-exempt status. 13.____
    A. The statement proves the conclusion.
    B. The statement supports the conclusion but does not prove it.
    C. The statement disproves the conclusion.
    D. The statement weakens the conclusion but does not disprove it.
    E. The statement has no relevance to the conclusion.

14. Two months before the national convention, Dirk Rockwell, arguably the country's most famous film actor, announces in a nationally televised interview that he has been saddened to learn of the plight of the National Home, and that he is going to make it his own personal crusade to see that it is able to house and support a greater number of widowed spouses and orphans in the future. 14.____
    A. The statement proves the conclusion.
    B. The statement supports the conclusion but does not prove it.
    C. The statement disproves the conclusion.
    D. The statement weakens the conclusion but does not disprove it.
    E. The statement has no relevance to the conclusion.

15. The Grand Army's final estimate is that the cost of expanding the National Home to accommodate the increased number of applicants will be about $61 million. 15.____
    A. The statement proves the conclusion.
    B. The statement supports the conclusion but does not prove it.
    C. The statement disproves the conclusion.
    D. The statement weakens the conclusion but does not disprove it.
    E. The statement has no relevance to the conclusion.

16. Just before the national convention, the Federal Department of Veterans Affairs announces steep cuts in the benefits package that is currently offered to the widowed spouses and orphans of veterans. 16.____
    A. The statement proves the conclusion.
    B. The statement supports the conclusion but does not prove it.
    C. The statement disproves the conclusion.
    D. The statement weakens the conclusion but does not disprove it.
    E. The statement has no relevance to the conclusion.

17. After the national convention, the Grand Army of Foreign Wars begins charging a modest "start-up" fee to all families who apply for residence at the national home. 17.____
   A. The statement proves the conclusion.
   B. The statement supports the conclusion but does not prove it.
   C. The statement disproves the conclusion.
   D. The statement weakens the conclusion but does not disprove it.
   E. The statement has no relevance to the conclusion.

Questions 18-25.

DIRECTIONS: Questions 18 through 25 each provide four factual statements and a conclusion based on these statements. After reading the entire question, you will decide whether:
   A. The conclusion is proved by statements I-IV;
   B. The conclusion is disproved by statements I-IV.
   C. The facts are not sufficient to prove or disprove the conclusion.

18. FACTUAL STATEMENTS: 18.____
   I. In the Field Day high jump competition, Martha jumped higher than Frank.
   II. Carl jumped higher than Ignacio.
   III. Ignacio jumped higher than Frank.
   IV. Dan jumped higher than Carl.

   CONCLUSION: Frank finished last in the high jump competition.
   A. The conclusion is proved by statements I-IV;
   B. The conclusion is disproved by statements I-IV.
   C. The facts are not sufficient to prove or disprove the conclusion.

19. FACTUAL STATEMENTS: 19.____
   I. The door to the hammer mill chamber is locked if light 6 is red.
   II. The door to the hammer mill chamber is locked only when the mill is operating.
   III. If the mill is not operating, light 6 is blue.
   IV. Light 6 is blue.

   CONCLUSION: The door to the hammer mill chamber is locked.
   A. The conclusion is proved by statements I-IV;
   B. The conclusion is disproved by statements I-IV.
   C. The facts are not sufficient to prove or disprove the conclusion.

20. FACTUAL STATEMENTS: 20.____
   I. Ziegfried, the lion tamer at the circus, has demanded ten additional minutes of performance time during each show.
   II. If Ziegfried is allowed his ten additional minutes per show, he will attempt to teach Kimba the tiger to shoot a basketball.
   III. If Kimba learns how to shoot a basketball, then Ziegfried was not given his ten additional minutes.
   IV. Ziegfried was given his ten additional minutes.

CONCLUSION: Despite Ziegfried's efforts, Kimba did not learn how to shoot a basketball.
A. The conclusion is proved by statements I-IV;
B. The conclusion is disproved by statements I-IV.
C. The facts are not sufficient to prove or disprove the conclusion.

21. FACTUAL STATEMENTS: 21.____
I. If Stan goes to counseling, Sara won't divorce him.
II. If Sara divorces Stan, she'll move back to Texas.
III. If Sara doesn't divorce Stan, Irene will be disappointed.
IV. Stan goes to counseling.

CONCLUSION: Irene will be disappointed.
A. The conclusion is proved by statements I-IV;
B. The conclusion is disproved by statements I-IV.
C. The facts are not sufficient to prove or disprove the conclusion.

22. FACTUAL STATEMENTS: 22.____
I. If Delia is promoted to district manager, Claudia will have to be promoted to team leader.
II. Delia will be promoted to district manager unless she misses her fourth-quarter sales quota.
III. If Claudia is promoted to team leader, Thomas will be promoted to assistant team leader.
IV. Delia meets her fourth-quarter sales quota.

CONCLUSION: Thomas is promoted to assistant team leader.
A. The conclusion is proved by statements I-IV;
B. The conclusion is disproved by statements I-IV.
C. The facts are not sufficient to prove or disprove the conclusion.

23. FACTUAL STATEMENTS: 23.____
I. Clone D is identical to Clone B.
II. Clone B is not identical to Clone A.
III. Clone D is not identical to Clone C.
IV. Clone E is not identical to the clones that are identical to Clone B.

CONCLUSION: Clone E is identical to Clone D.
A. The conclusion is proved by statements I-IV;
B. The conclusion is disproved by statements I-IV.
C. The facts are not sufficient to prove or disprove the conclusion.

24. FACTUAL STATEMENTS: 24.____
I. In the Stafford Tower, each floor is occupied by a single business.
II. Big G Staffing is on a floor between CyberGraphics and MainEvent.
III. Gasco is on the floor directly below CyberGraphics and three floors above Treehorn Audio.
IV. MainEvent is five floors below EZ Tax and four floors below Treehorn Audio.

CONCLUSION: EZ Tax is on a floor between Gasco and MainEvent.
A. The conclusion is proved by statements I-IV;
B. The conclusion is disproved by statements I-IV.
C. The facts are not sufficient to prove or disprove the conclusion.

25. FACTUAL STATEMENTS: 25.____
I. Only county roads lead to Nicodemus.
II. All the roads from Hill City to Graham County are federal highways.
III. Some of the roads from Plainville lead to Nicodemus.
IV. Some of the roads running from Hill City lead to Strong City.

CONCLUSION: Some of the roads from Plainville are county roads.
A. The conclusion is proved by statements I-IV;
B. The conclusion is disproved by statements I-IV.
C. The facts are not sufficient to prove or disprove the conclusion.

# KEY (CORRECT ANSWERS)

1. A
2. A
3. A
4. C
5. A

6. B
7. A
8. A
9. A
10. E

11. A
12. D
13. E
14. D
15. B

16. B
17. C
18. A
19. B
20. A

21. A
22. A
23. B
24. A
25. A

## SOLUTIONS TO PROBLEMS

1. CORRECT ANSWER: A
Given Statement 3, we deduce that James will not be transferred to another department. By Statement 2, we can conclude that James will be promoted.

2. CORRECT ANSWER: A
Since every player on the softball team wears glasses, these individuals compose some of the people who work at the bank. Although not every person who works at the bank plays softball, those bank employees who do play softball wear glasses.

3. CORRECT ANSWER: A
If Henry and June go out to dinner, we conclude that it must be on Tuesday or Thursday, which are the only two days when they have childbirth classes. This implies that if it is not Tuesday or Thursday, then this couple does not go out to dinner.

4. CORRECT ANSWER: C
We can only conclude that if a person plays on the field hockey team, then he or she has both bruises and scarred knees. But there are probably a great number of people who have both bruises and scarred knees but do not play on the field hockey team. The given conclusion can neither be proven or disproven.

5. CORRECT ANSWER: A
From statement 1, if Jane beats Mathias, then Lance will beat Jane. Using statement 2, we can then conclude that Christine will not win her match against Jane.

6. CORRECT ANSWER: B
Statement 1 tells us that no green light can be an indicator of the belt drive status. Thus, the given conclusion must be false.

7. CORRECT ANSWER: A
We already know that Ben and Elliot are in the $7^{th}$ grade. Even though Hannah and Carl are in the same grade, it cannot be the $7^{th}$ grade because we would then have at least four students in this $7^{th}$ grade. This would contradict the third statement, which states that either two or three students are in each grade. Since Amy, Dan, and Francine are in different grade, exactly one of them must be in the $7^{th}$ grade. Thus, Ben, Elliot, and exactly one of Amy, Dan, and Francine are the three students in the $7^{th}$ grade.

8. CORRECT ANSWER: A
One man is a teacher, who is Russian. We know that the writer is female and is Russian. Since her husband is an engineer, he cannot be the Russian teacher. Thus, her husband is of German descent, namely Mr. Stern. This means that Mr. Stern's wife is the writer. Note that one couple consists of a male Russian teacher and a female German lawyer. The other couple consists of a male German engineer and a female Russian writer.

9. CORRECT ANSWER: A
Since John is more than 10 inches taller than Lisa, his height is at least 46 inches. Also, John is shorter than Henry, so Henry's height must be greater than 46 inches. Thus, Lisa is the only one whose height is less than 36 inches. Therefore, she is the only one who is not allowed on the flume ride.

18. CORRECT ANSWER: A
Dan jumped higher than Carl, who jumped higher than Ignacio, who jumped higher than Frank. Since Martha jumped higher than Frank, every person jumped higher than Frank. Thus, Frank finished last.

19. CORRECT ANSWER: B
If the light is red, then the door is locked. If the door is locked, then the mill is operating. Reversing the logical sequence of these statements, if the mill is not operating, then the door is not locked, which means that the light is blue. Thus, the given conclusion is disproved.

20. CORRECT ANSWER: A
Using the contrapositive of statement III, Ziegfried was given his ten additional minutes, then Kimba did not learn how to shoot a basketball. Since statement IV is factual, the conclusion is proved.

21. CORRECT ANSWER: A
From Statements IV and I, we conclude that Sara doesn't divorce Stan. Then statement III reveals that Irene will be disappointed. Thus, the conclusion is proved.

22. CORRECT ANSWER: A
Statement II can be rewritten as "Delia is promoted to district manager or she misses her sales quota." Furthermore, this statement is equivalent to "If Delia makes her sales quota, then she is promoted to district manager." From statement I, we conclude that Claudia is promoted to team leader. Finally, by statement III, Thomas is promoted to assistant team leader.

23. CORRECT ANSWER: B
By statement IV, Clone E is not identical to any clones identical to Clone B. Statement I tells us that Clones B and D are identical. Therefore, Clone E cannot be identical to Clone D. The conclusion is disproved.

24. CORRECT ANSWER: A
Based on all four statements, CyberGraphics is somewhere below MainEvent. Gasco is one floor below CyberGraphics. EZ Tax is two floors below Gasco. Treehorn Audio is one floor below EZ Tax. MainEvent is four floors below Treehorn Audio. Thus, EZ Tax is two floors below Gasco and five floors above MainEvent. The conclusion is proved.

25. CORRECT ANSWER: A
From statement III, we know that some of the roads from Plainville lead to Nicodemus. But statement I tells us that only county roads lead to Nicodemus. Therefore, some of the roads from Plainville must be county roads. The conclusion is proved.

# TEST 2

DIRECTIONS: Each question or incomplete statement is followed by several suggested answers or completions. Select the one that BEST answers the question or completes the statement. *PRINT THE LETTER OF THE CORRECT ANSWER IN THE SPACE AT THE RIGHT.*

Questions 1-9.

DIRECTIONS: In Questions 1 through 9, you will read a set of facts and a conclusion drawn from them. The conclusion may be valid or invalid, based on the facts—it's your task to determine the validity of the conclusion.

For each question, select the letter before the statement that BEST expresses the relationship between the given facts and the conclusion that has been drawn from them. Your choices are:

A. The facts prove the conclusion;
B. The facts disprove the conclusion; or
C. The facts neither prove nor disprove the conclusion.

1. FACTS: Some employees in the testing department are statisticians. Most of the statisticians who work in the testing department are projection specialists. Tom Wilks works in the testing department. 1.____

   CONCLUSION: Tom Wilks is a statistician.
   A. The facts prove the conclusion.
   B. The facts disprove the conclusion.
   C. The facts neither prove nor disprove the conclusion.

2. FACTS: Ten coins are split among Hank, Lawrence, and Gail. If Lawrence gives his coins to Hank, then Hank will have more coins than Gail. If Gail gives her coins to Lawrence, then Lawrence will have more coins than Hank. 2.____

   CONCLUSION: Hank has six coins.
   A. The facts prove the conclusion.
   B. The facts disprove the conclusion.
   C. The facts neither prove nor disprove the conclusion.

3. FACTS: Nobody loves everybody. Janet loves Ken. Ken loves everybody who loves Janet. 3.____

   CONCLUSION: Everybody loves Janet.
   A. The facts prove the conclusion.
   B. The facts disprove the conclusion.
   C. The facts neither prove nor disprove the conclusion.

4. <u>FACTS:</u> Most of the Torres family lives in East Los Angeles. Many people in East Los Angeles celebrate Cinco de Mayo. Joe is a member of the Torres family. 4.____

<u>CONCLUSION:</u> Joe lives in East Los Angeles.
A. The facts prove the conclusion.
B. The facts disprove the conclusion.
C. The facts neither prove nor disprove the conclusion.

5. <u>FACTS:</u> Five professionals each occupy one story of a five-story office building. Dr. Kane's office is above Dr. Assad's. Dr. Johnson's office is between Dr. Kane's and Dr. Conlon's. Dr. Steen's office is between Dr. Conlon's and Dr. Assad's. Dr. Johnson is on the fourth story. 5.____

<u>CONCLUSION:</u> Dr. Kane occupies the top story.
A. The facts prove the conclusion.
B. The facts disprove the conclusion.
C. The facts neither prove nor disprove the conclusion.

6. <u>FACTS:</u> To be eligible for membership in the Yukon Society, a person must be able to either tunnel through a snowbank while wearing only a T-shirt and short, or hold his breath for two minutes under water that is 50°F. Ray can only hold his breath for a minute and a half. 6.____

<u>CONCLUSION:</u> Ray can still become a member of the Yukon Society by tunneling through a snowbank while wearing a T-shirt and shorts.
A. The facts prove the conclusion.
B. The facts disprove the conclusion.
C. The facts neither prove nor disprove the conclusion.

7. <u>FACTS:</u> A mark is worth five plunks. You can exchange four sharps for a tinplot. It takes eight marks to buy a sharp. 7.____

<u>CONCLUSION:</u> A sharp is the most valuable.
A. The facts prove the conclusion.
B. The facts disprove the conclusion.
C. The facts neither prove nor disprove the conclusion.

8. <u>FACTS:</u> There are gibbons, as well as lemurs, who like to play in the trees at the monkey house. All those who like to play in the trees at the monkey house are fed lettuce and bananas. 8.____

<u>CONCLUSION:</u> Lemurs and gibbons are types of monkeys.
A. The facts prove the conclusion.
B. The facts disprove the conclusion.
C. The facts neither prove nor disprove the conclusion.

9. FACTS: None of the Blackfoot tribes is a Salishan Indian tribe. Salishan Indians came from the northern Pacific Coast. All Salishan Indians live each of the Continental Divide. 9.____

CONCLUSION: No Blackfoot tribes live east of the Continental Divide.
A. The facts prove the conclusion.
B. The facts disprove the conclusion.
C. The facts neither prove nor disprove the conclusion.

Questions 10-17.

DIRECTIONS: Questions 10 through 17 are based on the following reading passage. It is not your knowledge of the particular topic that is being tested, but your ability to reason based on what you have read. The passage is likely to detail several proposed courses of action and factors affecting these proposals. The reading passage is followed by a conclusion or outcome based on the facts in the passage, or a description of a decision taken regarding the situation. The conclusion is followed by a number of statements that have a possible connection to the conclusion. For each statement, you are to determine whether:
A. The statement proves the conclusion.
B. The statement supports the conclusion but does not prove it.
C. The statement disproves the conclusion.
D. The statement weakens the conclusion but does not disprove it.
E. The statement has no relevance to the conclusion.

Remember that the conclusion after the passage is to be accepted as the outcome of what actually happened, and that you are being asked to evaluate the impact each statement would have had on the conclusion.

PASSAGE:

On August 12, Beverly Willey reported that she was in the elevator late on the previous evening after leaving her office on the 16$^{th}$ floor of a large office building. In her report, she states that a man got on the elevator at the 11$^{th}$ floor, pulled her off the elevator, assaulted her, and stole her purse. Ms. Willey reported that she had seen the man in the elevators and hallways of the building before. She believes that the man works in the building. Her description of him is as follows: he is tall, unshaven, with wavy brown hair and a scar on his left cheek. He walks with a pronounced limp, often dragging his left foot behind his right.

CONCLUSION: After Beverly Willey makes her report, the police arrest a 43-year-old man, Barton Black, and charge him with her assault.

10. Barton Black is a former Marine who served in Vietnam, where he sustained shrapnel wounds to the left side of his face and suffered nerve damage in his left leg. 10.____
   A. The statement proves the conclusion.
   B. The statement supports the conclusion but does not prove it.
   C. The statement disproves the conclusion.
   D. The statement weakens the conclusion but does not disprove it.
   E. The statement has no relevance to the conclusion.

11. When they arrived at his residence to question him, detectives were greeted at the door by Barton Black, who was tall and clean-shaven. 11.____
   A. The statement proves the conclusion.
   B. The statement supports the conclusion but does not prove it.
   C. The statement disproves the conclusion.
   D. The statement weakens the conclusion but does not disprove it.
   E. The statement has no relevance to the conclusion.

12. Barton Black was booked into the county jail several days after Beverly Willey's assault. 12.____
   A. The statement proves the conclusion.
   B. The statement supports the conclusion but does not prove it.
   C. The statement disproves the conclusion.
   D. The statement weakens the conclusion but does not disprove it.
   E. The statement has no relevance to the conclusion.

13. Upon further investigation, detectives discover that Beverly Willey does not work at the office building. 13.____
   A. The statement proves the conclusion.
   B. The statement supports the conclusion but does not prove it.
   C. The statement disproves the conclusion.
   D. The statement weakens the conclusion but does not disprove it.
   E. The statement has no relevance to the conclusion.

14. Upon further investigation, detectives discover that Barton Black does not work at the office building. 14.____
   A. The statement proves the conclusion.
   B. The statement supports the conclusion but does not prove it.
   C. The statement disproves the conclusion.
   D. The statement weakens the conclusion but does not disprove it.
   E. The statement has no relevance to the conclusion.

15. In the spring of the following year, Barton Black is convicted of assaulting Beverly Willey on August 11. 15.____
   A. The statement proves the conclusion.
   B. The statement supports the conclusion but does not prove it.
   C. The statement disproves the conclusion.
   D. The statement weakens the conclusion but does not disprove it.
   E. The statement has no relevance to the conclusion.

16. During their investigation of the assault, detectives determine that Beverly Willey was assaulted on the 12th floor of the office building. 16.____
    A. The statement proves the conclusion.
    B. The statement supports the conclusion but does not prove it.
    C. The statement disproves the conclusion.
    D. The statement weakens the conclusion but does not disprove it.
    E. The statement has no relevance to the conclusion.

17. The day after Beverly Willey's assault, Barton Black fled the area and was never seen again. 17.____
    A. The statement proves the conclusion.
    B. The statement supports the conclusion but does not prove it.
    C. The statement disproves the conclusion.
    D. The statement weakens the conclusion but does not disprove it.
    E. The statement has no relevance to the conclusion.

Questions 18-25.

DIRECTIONS: Questions 18 through 25 each provide four factual statements and a conclusion based on these statements. After reading the entire question, you will decide whether:

A. The conclusion is proved by statements I-IV;
B. The conclusion is disproved by statements I-IV.
C. The facts are not sufficient to prove or disprove the conclusion.

18. FACTUAL STATEMENTS: 18.____
    I. Among five spice jars on the shelf, the sage is to the right of the parsley.
    II. The pepper is to the left of the basil.
    III. The nutmeg is between the sage and the pepper.
    IV. The pepper is the second spice from the left.

    CONCLUSION: The safe is the farthest to the right.
    A. The conclusion is proved by statements I-IV;
    B. The conclusion is disproved by statements I-IV.
    C. The facts are not sufficient to prove or disprove the conclusion.

19. FACTUAL STATEMENTS: 19.____
    I. Gear X rotates in a clockwise direction if Switch C is in the OFF position.
    II. Gear X will rotate in a counter-clockwise direction is Switch C is ON.
    III. If Gear X is rotating in a clockwise direction, then Gear Y will not be rotating at all.
    IV. Switch C is ON.

    CONCLUSION: Gear X is rotating in a counter-clockwise direction.
    A. The conclusion is proved by statements I-IV;
    B. The conclusion is disproved by statements I-IV.
    C. The facts are not sufficient to prove or disprove the conclusion.

20. FACTUAL STATEMENTS: 20.____
I. Lane will leave for the Toronto meeting today only if Terence, Rourke, and Jackson all file their marketing reports by the end of the work day.
II. Rourke will file her report on time only if Ganz submits last quarter's data.
III. If Terence attends the security meeting, he will attend it with Jackson, and they will not file their marketing reports by the end of the work day.

CONCLUSION: Lane will leave for the Toronto meeting today.
A. The conclusion is proved by statements I-IV;
B. The conclusion is disproved by statements I-IV.
C. The facts are not sufficient to prove or disprove the conclusion.

21. FACTUAL STATEMENTS: 21.____
I. Bob is in second place in the Boston Marathon.
II. Gregory is winning the Boston Marathon.
III. There are four miles to go in the race, and Bob is gaining on Gregory at the rate of 100 yards every minute.
IV. There are 1760 yards in a mile and Gregory's usual pace during the Boston Marathon is one mile every six minutes.

CONCLUSION: Bob wins the Boston Marathon.
A. The conclusion is proved by statements I-IV;
B. The conclusion is disproved by statements I-IV.
C. The facts are not sufficient to prove or disprove the conclusion.

22. FACTUAL STATEMENTS: 22.____
I. Four brothers are named Earl, John, Gary, and Pete.
II. Earl and Pete are unmarried.
III. John is shorter than the youngest of the four.
IV. The oldest brother is married, and is also the tallest.

CONCLUSION: Gary is the oldest brother.
A. The conclusion is proved by statements I-IV;
B. The conclusion is disproved by statements I-IV.
C. The facts are not sufficient to prove or disprove the conclusion.

23. FACTUAL STATEMENTS: 23.____
I. Brigade X is ten miles from the demilitarized zone.
II. If General Woundwort gives the order, Brigade X will advance to the demilitarized zone, but not quickly enough to reach the zone before the conflict begins.
III. Brigade Y, five miles behind Brigade X, will not advance unless General Woundwort gives the order.
IV. Brigade Y advances.

CONCLUSION: Brigade X reaches the demilitarized zone before the conflict begins.

A. The conclusion is proved by statements I-IV;
B. The conclusion is disproved by statements I-IV.
C. The facts are not sufficient to prove or disprove the conclusion.

24. FACTUAL STATEMENTS: 24.____

I. Jerry has decided to take a cab from Fullerton to Elverton.
II. Chubby Cab charges $5 plus $3 a mile.
III. Orange Cab charges $7.50 but gives free mileage for the first 5 miles.
IV. After the first 5 miles, Orange Cab charges $2.50 a mile.

CONCLUSION: Orange Cab is the cheaper fare from Fullerton to Elverton.

A. The conclusion is proved by statements I-IV;
B. The conclusion is disproved by statements I-IV.
C. The facts are not sufficient to prove or disprove the conclusion.

25. FACTUAL STATEMENTS: 25.____

I. Dan is never in class when his friend Lucy is absent.
II. Lucy is never absent unless her mother is sick.
III. If Lucy is in class, Sergio is in class also.
IV. Sergio is never in class when Dalton is absent.

CONCLUSION: If Lucy is absent, Dalton may be in class.

A. The conclusion is proved by statements I-IV;
B. The conclusion is disproved by statements I-IV.
C. The facts are not sufficient to prove or disprove the conclusion.

---

# KEY (CORRECT ANSWERS)

| | | | |
|---|---|---|---|
| 1. | C | 11. | E |
| 2. | B | 12. | B |
| 3. | B | 13. | D |
| 4. | C | 14. | E |
| 5. | A | 15. | A |
| 6. | A | 16. | E |
| 7. | B | 17. | C |
| 8. | C | 18. | B |
| 9. | C | 19. | A |
| 10. | B | 20. | C |

| | |
|---|---|
| 21. | C |
| 22. | A |
| 23. | B |
| 24. | A |
| 25. | B |

# SOLUTIONS TO PROBLEMS

1. CORRECT ANSWER: C
   Statement 1 only tells us that some employees who work in the Testing Department are statisticians. This means that we need to allow the possibility that at least one person in this department is not a statistician. Thus, if a person works in the Testing Department, we cannot conclude whether or not this individual is a statistician.

2. CORRECT ANSWER: B
   If Hank had six coins, then the total of Gail's collection and Lawrence's collection would be four. Thus, if Gail gave all her coins to Lawrence, Lawrence would only have four coins. Thus, it would be impossible for Lawrence to have more coins than Hank.

3. CORRECT ANSWER: B
   Statement 1 tells us that nobody loves everybody. If everybody loved Janet, then Statement 3 would imply that Ken loves everybody. This would contradict statement 1. The conclusion is disproved.

4. CORRECT ANSWER: C
   Although most of the Torres family lives in East Los Angeles, we can assume that some members of this family do not live in East Los Angeles. Thus, we cannot prove or disprove that Joe, who is a member of the Torres family, lives in East Los Angeles.

5. CORRECT ANSWER: A
   Since Dr. Johnson is on the 4th floor, either (a) Dr. Kane is on the 5th floor and Dr. Conlon is on the 3rd floor, or (b) Dr. Kane is on the 3rd floor and Dr. Conlon is on the 5th floor. If option (b) were correct, then since Dr. Assad would be on the 1st floor, it would be impossible for Dr. Steen's office to be between Dr. Conlon and Dr. Assad's office. Therefore, Dr. Kane's office must be on the 5th floor. The order of the doctors' offices, from 5th floor down to the 1st floor is: Dr. Kane, Dr. Johnson, Dr. Conlon, Dr. Steen, Dr. Assad.

6. CORRECT ANSWER: A
   Ray does not satisfy the requirement of holding his breath for two minutes under water, since he can only hold is breath for one minute in that setting. But if he tunnels through a snowbank with just a T-shirt and shorts, he will satisfy the eligibility requirement. Note that the eligibility requirement contains the key word "or." So only one of the two clauses separated by "or" need to be fulfilled.

7. CORRECT ANSWER: B
   Statement 2 says that four sharps is equivalent to one tinplot. This means that a tinplot is worth more than a sharp. The conclusion is disproved. We note that the order of these items, from most valuable to least valuable are: tinplot, sharp, mark, plunk.

8. CORRECT ANSWER: C
   We can only conclude that gibbons and lemurs are fed lettuce and bananas. We can neither prove nor disprove that these animals are types of monkeys.

9. CORRECT ANSWER: C
We know that all Salishan Indians live east of the Continental Divide. But some non-members of this tribe of Indians may also live east of the Continental Divide. Since none of the members of the Blackfoot tribe belong to the Salishan Indian tribe, we cannot draw any conclusion about the location of the Blackfoot tribe with respect to the Continental Divide.

18. CORRECT ANSWER: B
Since the pepper is second from the left and the nutmeg is between the sage and the pepper, the positions 2, 3, and 4 (from the left) are pepper, nutmeg, sage. By statement II, the basil must be in position 5, which implies that the parsley is in position 1. Therefore, the basil, not the sage, is farthest to the right. The conclusion disproved.

19. CORRECT ANSWER: A
Statement II assures us that if switch C is ON, then Gear X is rotating in a counterclockwise direction. The conclusion is proved.

20. CORRECT ANSWER: C
Based on Statement IV, followed by Statement II, we conclude that Ganz and Rourke will file their reports on time. Statement III reveals that if Terence and Jackson attend the security meeting, they will fail to file their reports on time. We have no further information if Terence and Jackson attended the security meeting, so we are not able to either confirm or deny that their reports were filed on time. This implies that we cannot know for certain that Lane will leave for his meeting in Toronto.

21. CORRECT ANSWER: C
Although Bob is in second place behind Gregory, we cannot deduce how far behind Gregory he is running. At Gregory's current pace, he will cover four miles in 24 minutes. If Bob were only 100 yards behind Gregory, he would catch up to Gregory in one minute. But if Bob were very far behind Gregory, for example 5 miles, this is the equivalent of (5)(1760) = 8800 yards. Then Bob would need 8800/100 = 88 minutes to catch up to Gregory. Thus, the given facts are not sufficient to draw a conclusion.

22. CORRECT ANSWER: A
Statement II tells us that neither Earl nor Pete could be the oldest; also, either John or Gary is married. Statement IV reveals that the oldest brother is both married and the tallest. By Statement III, John cannot be the tallest. Since John is not the tallest, he is not the oldest. Thus, the oldest brother must be Gary. The conclusion is proved.

23. CORRECT ANSWER: B
By Statements III and IV, General Woundwort must have given the order to advance. Statement II then tells us that Brigade X will advance to the demilitarized zone, but not soon enough before the conflict begins. Thus, the conclusion is disproved.

24. CORRECT ANSWER: A
If the distance is 5 miles or less, then the cost for the Orange Cab is only \$7.50, whereas the cost for the Chubby Cab is \$5 + 3x, where x represents the number of miles traveled. For 1 to 5 miles, the cost of the Chubby Cab is between \$8 and \$20. This means that for a distance of 5 miles, the Orange Cab costs \$7.50, whereas the Chubby Cab costs \$20. After 5 miles, the cost per mile of the Chubby Cab exceeds the cost per mile of the Orange Cab. Thus, regardless of the actual distance between Fullerton and Elverton, the cost for the Orange Cab will be cheaper than that of the Chubby Cab.

25. CORRECT ANSWER: B
It looks like "Dalton" should be replaced by "Dan" in the conclusion. Then by statement I, if Lucy is absent, Dan is never in class. Thus, the conclusion is disproved.

## READING COMPREHENSION
## UNDERSTANDING AND INTERPRETING WRITTEN MATERIAL

# EXAMINATION SECTION

# TEST 1

DIRECTIONS: Each question or incomplete statement is followed by several suggested answers or completions. Select the one that BEST answers the question or completes the statement. *PRINT THE LETTER OF THE CORRECT ANSWER IN THE SPACE AT THE RIGHT.*

Questions 1-3.

DIRECTIONS: Questions 1 through 3 are to be answered SOLELY on the basis of the following passage.

Every organization needs a systematic method of checking its operations as a means to increase efficiency and promote economy. Many successful private firms have instituted a system of audit or internal inspections to accomplish these ends. Law enforcement organizations, which have an extremely important service to *sell*, should be no less zealous in developing efficiency and economy in their operations. Periodic, organized, and systematic inspections are one means of promoting the achievement of these objectives. The necessity of an organized inspection system is perhaps greatest in those law enforcement groups which have grown to such a size that the principal officer can no longer personally supervise or be cognizant of every action taken. Smooth and effective operation demands that the head of the organization have at hand some tool with which he can study and enforce general policies and procedure and also direct compliance with day-to-day orders, most of which are put into execution outside his sight and hearing. A good inspection system can serve as that tool.

1. The central thought of the above passage is that a system of inspections within a police department 1.____
   A. is unnecessary for a department in which the principal officer can personally supervise all official actions taken
   B. should be instituted at the first indication that there is any deterioration in job performance by the force
   C. should be decentralized and administered by first-line supervisory officers
   D. is an important aid to the police administrator in the accomplishment of law enforcement objectives

2. The MOST accurate of the following statements concerning the need for an organized inspection system in a law enforcement organization is: It is 2.____
   A. never needed in an organization of small size where the principal officer can give personal supervision
   B. most needed where the size of the organization prevents direct supervision by the principal officer
   C. more needed in law enforcement organizations than in private firms
   D. especially needed in an organization about to embark upon a needed expansion of services

3. According to the above passage, the head of the police organization utilizes the internal inspection system 3.____
   A. as a tool which must be constantly re-examined in the light of changing demands for police service
   B. as an administrative technique to increase efficiency and promote economy
   C. by personally visiting those areas of police operation which are outside his sight and hearing
   D. to augment the control of local commanders over detailed field operations

Questions 4-10.

DIRECTIONS: Questions 4 through 10 are to be answered SOLELY on the basis of the following passage.

Job evaluation and job rating systems are intended to introduce scientific procedures. Any type of approach, when properly used, will give satisfactory results. The Point System, when properly validated by actual use, is more likely to be suitable for general use than the ranking system. In many aspects, the Factor Comparison Plan is a point system tied to money values. Of course, there may be another system that combines the ranking system with the point system, especially during the initial stages of the development of the program. After the program has been in use for some time, the tendency is to drop off the ranking phase and continue the use of the point system.

In the ranking system of rating of jobs, every job within the plant is arranged in some order, either from the one with the simplest qualifications to the one with maximum requirements, or in the reverse order. This system should be preceded by careful job analysis and the writing of accurate job descriptions before the rating process is undertaken. It is possible, of course, to take the jobs as they are found in the business enterprise and use the names as they are without any attempt at standardization, and merely rank them according to the general overall impression of the raters. Such a procedure is certain to fall short of what may reasonably be expected of job rating. Another procedure that is in reality merely a modification of the simple rating described above is to establish a series of grades or zones and arrange all he jobs in the plant into groups within these grades and zones. The practice in most common use is to arrange all the jobs in the plant according to their requirements by rating them and then to establish the classification or groups.

The actual ranking of jobs may be done by one individual, several individuals, or a committee. If several individuals are working independently on the task, it will usually be found that, in general, they agree but that their rankings vary in certain details. A conference between the individuals, with each person giving his reasons why he rated one way or another, usually produces agreement. The detailed job descriptions are particularly helpful when there is disagreement among raters as to the rating of certain jobs. It is not only possible but desirable to have workers participate in the construction of the job description and in rating the job.

4. The MAIN theme of this passage is 4.____
   A. the elimination of bias in job rating
   B. the rating of jobs by the ranking system
   C. the need or accuracy in allocating points in the point system
   D. pitfalls to avoid in selecting key jobs in the Factor Comparison Plan

5. The ranking system of rating jobs consists MAINLY of 5.____
   A. attaching a point value to each ratable factor of each job prior to establishing an equitable pay scale
   B. arranging every job in the organization in descending order and then following this up with a job analysis of the key jobs
   C. preparing accurate job descriptions after a job analysis and then arranging all jobs either in ascending or descending order based on job requirements
   D. arbitrarily establishing a hierarchy of job classes and grades and then fitting each job into a specific class and grade based on the opinions of unit supervisors

6. The above passage states that the system of classifying jobs MOST used in an organization is to 6.____
   A. organize all jobs in the organization in accordance with their requirements and then create categories or clusters of jobs
   B. classify all jobs in the organization according to the titles and rank by which they are currently known in the organization
   C. establish a pre-arranged series of grades or zones and then fit all jobs into one of the grades or zones
   D. determine the salary currently being paid for each job and then rank the jobs in order according to salary

7. According to the above passage, experience has shown that when a group of raters is assigned to the job evaluation task and each individual rates independently of the others, the raters GENERALLY 7.____
   A. *agree* with respect to all aspects of their rankings
   B. *disagree* with respect to all or nearly all aspects of the rankings
   C. *disagree* on overall ratings, but agree on specific rating factors
   D. *agree* on overall rankings, but have some variance in some details

8. The above passage states that the use of a detailed job description is of special value when 8.____
   A. employees of an organization have participated in the preliminary step involved in actual preparation of the job description
   B. labor representatives are not participating in ranking of the jobs
   C. an individual rater who is unsure of himself is ranking the jobs
   D. a group of raters is having difficulty reaching unanimity with respect to ranking a certain job

9. A comparison of the various rating systems as described in the above passage shows that 9.____
   A. the ranking system is not as appropriate for general use as a properly validated point system
   B. the point system is the same as the Factor Comparison Plan except that it places greater emphasis on money

C. no system is capable of combining the point system and the Factor Comparison Plan
D. the point system will be discontinued last when used in combination with the Factor comparison System

10. The above passage implies that the PRINCIPAL reason for creating job evaluation and rating systems was to help 10.____
A. overcome union opposition to existing salary plans
B. base wage determination on a more objective and orderly foundation
C. eliminate personal bias on the part of the trained scientific job evaluators
D. management determine if it was overpricing the various jobs in the organizational hierarchy

Questions 11-13.

DIRECTIONS: Questions 11 through 13 are to be answered SOLELY on the basis of the following passage.

The common sense character of the merit system seems so natural to most Americans that many people wonder why it should ever have been inoperative. After all, the American economic system, the most phenomenal the world has ever known, is also founded on a rugged selective process which emphasizes the personal qualities of capacity, industriousness, and productivity. The criteria may not have always been appropriate and competition has not always been fair, but competition there was, and the responsibilities and the rewards—with exceptions, of course—have gone to those who could measure up in terms of intelligence, knowledge, or perseverance. This has been true not only in the economic area, in the money-making process, but also in achievement in the professions and other walks of life.

11. According to the above passage, economic rewards in the United State have 11.____
A. always been based on appropriate, fair criteria
B. only recently been based on a competitive system
C. not going to people who compete too ruggedly
D. usually gone to those people with intelligence, knowledge, and perseverance

12. According to the above passage, a merit system is 12.____
A. an unfair criterion on which to base rewards
B. unnatural to anyone who is not American
C. based only on common sense
D. based on the same principles as the American economic system

13. According to the above passage, it is MOST accurate to say that 13.____
A. the United States has always had a civil service merit system
B. civil service employees are very rugged
C. the American economic system has always been based on a merit objective
D. competition is unique to the American way of life

Questions 14-15.

DIRECTIONS: Questions 14 and 15 are to be answered SOLELY on the basis of the following passage.

In-basket tests are often used to assess managerial potential. The exercise consists of a set of papers that would be likely to be found in the in-basket of an administrator or manager at any given time, and requires the individuals participating in the examination to indicate how they would dispose of each item found in the in-basket. In order to handle the in-basket effectively, they must successfully manage their time, refer and assign some work to subordinates, juggle potentially conflicting appointments and meetings, and arrange for follow-up of problems generated by the items in the in-basket. In other words, the in-basket test is attempting to evaluate the participants' abilities to organize their work, set priorities, delegate, control, and make decisions.

14. According to the above passage, to succeed in an in-basket test, an administrator must 14.____
    A. be able to read very quickly
    B. have a great deal of technical knowledge
    C. know when to delegate work
    D. arrange a lot of appointments and meetings

15. According to the above passage, all of the following abilities are indications of managerial potential EXCEPT the ability to 15.____
    A. organize and control
    B. manage time
    C. write effective reports
    D. make appropriate decisions

Questions 16-19.

DIRECTIONS: Questions 16 through 19 are to be answered SOLELY on the basis of the following passage.

A personnel researcher has at his disposal various approaches for obtaining information, analyzing it, and arriving at conclusions that have value in predicting and affecting the behavior of people at work. The type of method to be used depends on such factors as the nature of the research problem, the available data, and the attitudes of those people being studied to the various kinds of approaches. While the experimental approach, with its use of control groups, is the most refined type of study, there are others that are often found useful in personnel research. Surveys, in which the researcher obtains facts on a problem from a variety of sources, are employed in research on wages, fringe benefits, and labor relations. Historical studies are used to trace the development of problems in order to understand them better and to isolate possible causative factors. Case studies are generally developed to explore all the details of a particular problem that is representative of other similar problems. A researcher chooses the most appropriate form of study for the problem he is investigating. He should recognize, however, that the experimental method, commonly referred to as the scientific method, if used validly and reliably, gives the most conclusive results.

16. The above passage discusses several approaches used to obtain information on particular problems. 16.____
Which of the following may be MOST reasonably concluded from the passage?
A(n)
   A. historical study cannot determine causative factors
   B. survey is often used in research on fringe benefits
   C. case study is usually used to explore a problem that is unique and unrelated to other problems
   D. experimental study is used when the scientific approach to a problem fails

17. According to the above passage, all of the following are factors that may determine the type of approach a researcher uses EXCEPT 17.____
   A. the attitudes of people toward being used in control groups
   B. the number of available sources
   C. his desire to isolate possible causative factors
   D. the degree of accuracy he requires

18. The words *scientific method*, as used in the last sentence of the above passage, refer to a type of study which, according to the above passage 18.____
   A. uses a variety of sources
   B. traces the development of problems
   C. uses control groups
   D. analyzes the details of a representative problem

19. Which of the following can be MOST reasonably concluded from the above passage? 19.____
In obtaining and analyzing information on a particular problem, a researcher employs the method which is the
   A. most accurate
   B. most suitable
   C. least expensive
   D. least time-consuming

Questions 20-25.

DIRECTIONS: Questions 20 through 25 are to be answered SOLELY on the basis of the following passage.

The quality of the voice of a worker is an important factor in conveying to clients and co-workers his attitude and, to some degree, his character. The human voice, when not consciously disguised, may reflect a person's mood, temper, and personality. It has been shown in several experiments that certain character traits can be assessed with better than chance accuracy through listening to the voice of an unknown person who cannot be seen.

Since one of the objectives of the worker is to put clients at ease and to present an encouraging and comfortable atmosphere, a harsh, shrill, or loud voice could have a negative effect. A client who displays emotions of anger or resentment would probably be provoked even further by a caustic tone. In a face-to-face situation, an unpleasant voice may be compensated for, to some degree, by a concerned and kind facial expression. However, when one speaks on the telephone, the expression on one's face cannot be seen by the listener. A supervising clerk who wishes to represent himself effectively to clients should try to eliminate as many faults as possible in striving to develop desirable voice qualities.

20. If a worker uses a sarcastic tone while interviewing a resentful client, the client, according to the above passage, would MOST likely — 20.____
    A. avoid the face-to-face problem
    B. be ashamed of his behavior
    C. become more resentful
    D. be provoked to violence

21. According to the passage, experiments comparing voice and character traits have demonstrated that — 21.____
    A. prospects for improving an unpleasant voice through training are better than chance
    B. the voice can be altered to project many different psychological characteristics
    C. the quality of the human voice reveals more about the speaker than his words do
    D. the speaker's voice tells the hearer something about the speaker's personality

22. Which of the following, according to the above passage, is a person's voice MOST likely to reveal? — 22.____
    His
    A. prejudices
    B. intelligence
    C. social awareness
    D. temperament

23. It may be MOST reasonably concluded from the above passage that an interested and sympathetic expression on the face of a worker — 23.____
    A. may induce a client to feel certain he will receive welfare benefits
    B. will eliminate the need for pleasant vocal qualities in the interviewer
    C. may help to make up for an unpleasant voice in the interviewer
    D. is desirable as the interviewer speaks on the telephone to a client

24. Of the following, the MOST reasonable implication of the above paragraph is that a worker should, when speaking to a client, control and use his voice to — 24.____
    A. simulate a feeling of interest in the problems of the client
    B. express his emotions directly and adequately
    C. help produce in the client a sense of comfort and security
    D. reflect his own true personality

25. It may be concluded from the above passage that the PARTICULAR reason for a worker to pay special attention to modulating her voice when talking on the phone to a client is that, during a telephone conversation — 25.____
    A. there is a necessity to compensate for the way in which a telephone distorts the voice
    B. the voice of the worker is a reflection of her mood and character
    C. the client can react only on the basis of the voice and words she hears
    D. the client may have difficulty getting a clear understanding over the telephone

# KEY (CORRECT ANSWERS)

| | | | |
|---|---|---|---|
| 1. | D | 11. | D |
| 2. | B | 12. | D |
| 3. | B | 13. | C |
| 4. | B | 14. | C |
| 5. | C | 15. | C |
| 6. | A | 16. | B |
| 7. | D | 17. | D |
| 8. | D | 18. | C |
| 9. | A | 19. | B |
| 10. | B | 20. | C |

| | |
|---|---|
| 21. | D |
| 22. | D |
| 23. | C |
| 24. | C |
| 25. | C |

# TEST 2

DIRECTIONS: Each question or incomplete statement is followed by several suggested answers or completions. Select the one that BEST answers the question or completes the statement. *PRINT THE LETTER OF THE CORRECT ANSWER IN THE SPACE AT THE RIGHT.*

Questions 1-3.

DIRECTIONS: Questions 1 through 3 are to be answered SOLELY on the basis of the following paragraph.

Suppose you are given the job of printing, collating, and stapling 8,000 copies of a ten-page booklet as soon as possible. You have available one photo-offset machine, a collator with an automatic stapler, and the personnel to operate these machines. All will be available for however long the job takes to complete. The photo-offset machine prints 5,000 impressions an hour, and it takes about 15 minutes to set up a plate. The collator, including time for insertion of pages and stapling, can process about 2,000 booklets an hour. (Answers should be based on the assumption that there are no breakdowns or delays.)

1. Assuming that all the printing is finished before the collating is started, if the job is given to you late Monday and your section can begin work the next day and is able to devote seven hours a day, Monday through Friday, to the job until it is finished, what is the BEST estimate of when the job will be finished? 1.____
   A. Wednesday afternoon of the same week
   B. Thursday morning of the same week
   C. Friday morning of the same week
   D. Monday morning of the next week

2. An operator suggests to you that instead of completing all the printing and then beginning collating and stapling, you first print all the pages for 4,000 booklets, so that they can be collated and stapled while the last 4,000 pages are being printed. 2.____
   If you accepted this suggestion, the job would be completed
   A. sooner but would require more man-hours
   B at the same time using either method
   C. later and would require more man-hours
   D. sooner but there would be more wear and tear on the plates

3. Assume that you have the same assignment and equipment as described above, but 16,000 copies of the booklet are needed instead of 8,000. 3.____
   If you decided to print 8,000 complete booklets, then collate and staple them while you started printing the next 8,000 booklets, which of the following statements would MOST accurately describe the relationship between this new method and your original method of printing all the booklets at one time, and then collating and stapling them? The
   A. job would be completed at the same time regardless of the method used
   B. new method would result in the job's being completed 3½ hours earlier
   C. original method would result in the job's being completed an hour later
   D. new method would result in the job's being completed 1½ hours earlier

Questions 4-6.

DIRECTIONS: Questions 4 through 6 are to be answered SOLELY on the basis of the following passage.

When using words like company, association, council, committee, and board in place of the full official name, the writer should not capitalize these short forms unless he intends them to invoke the full force of the institution's authority. In legal contracts, in minutes, or in formal correspondence where one is speaking formally and officially on behalf of the company, the term Company is usually capitalized, but in ordinary usage, where it is not essential to load the short form with this significance, capitalization would be excessive. (Example: The company will have many good openings for graduates this June.)

The treatment recommended for short forms of place names is essentially the same as that recommended for short forms of organizational names. In general, we capitalize the full form but not the short form. If Park Avenue is referred to in one sentence, then the *avenue* is sufficient in subsequent references. The same is true with words like building, hotel, station, and airport, which are capitalized when part of a proper name changed (Pan Am Building, Hotel Plaza, Union Station, O'Hare Airport), but are simply lower-cased when replacing these specific names.

4. The above passage states that USUALLY the short forms of names of organizations 4.____
   A. and places should not be capitalized
   B. and places should be capitalized
   C. should not be capitalized, but the short forms of names of places should be capitalized
   D. should be capitalized, but the short forms of names of places should not be capitalized

5. The above passage states that in legal contracts, in minutes, and in formal correspondence, the short forms of names of organizations should 5.____
   A. usually not be capitalized
   B. usually be capitalized
   C. usually not be used
   D. never be used

6. It can be inferred from the above passage that decisions regarding when to capitalize certain words 6.____
   A. should be left to the discretion of the writer
   B. should be based on generally accepted rules
   C. depend on the total number of words capitalized
   D. are of minor importance

Questions 7-10.

DIRECTIONS: Questions 7 through 10 are to be answered SOLELY on the basis of the following passage.

Use of the systems and procedures approach to office management is revolutionizing the supervision of office work. This approach views an enterprise as an entity which seeks to fulfill definite objectives. Systems and procedures help to organize repetitive work into a routine, thus reducing the amount of decision making required for its accomplishment. As a result, employees are guided in their efforts and perform only necessary work. Supervisors are relieved of any details of execution and are free to attend to more important work. Establishing work guides which require that identical tasks be performed the same way each time permits standardization of forms, machine operations, work methods, and controls. This approach also reduces the probability of errors. Any error committed is usually discovered quickly because the incorrect work does not meet the requirement of the work guides. Errors are also reduced through work specialization, which allows each employee to become thoroughly proficient in a particular type of work. Such proficiency also tends to improve the morale of the employees.

7. The above passage states that the accuracy of an employee's work is INCREASED by 7.____
   A. using the work specialization approach
   B. employing a probability sample
   C. requiring him to shift at one time into different types of tasks
   D. having his supervisor check each detail of work execution

8. Of the following, which one BEST expresses the main theme of the above passage? The 8.____
   A. advantages and disadvantages of the systems and procedures approach to office management
   B. effectiveness of the systems and procedures approach to office management in developing skills
   C. systems and procedures approach to office management as it relates to office costs
   D. advantages of the systems and procedures approach to office management for supervisors and office workers

9. Work guides are LEAST likely to be used when 9.____
   A. standardized forms are used
   B. a particular office task is distinct and different from all others
   C. identical tasks are to be performed in identical ways
   D. similar work methods are expected from each employee

10. According to the above passage, when an employee makes a work error, it USUALLY 10.____
   A. is quickly corrected by the supervisor
   B. necessitates a change in the work guides
   C. can be detected quickly if work guides are in use
   D. increases the probability of further errors by that employee

Questions 11-12.

DIRECTIONS: Questions 11 and 12 are to be answered SOLELY on the basis of the following passage.

The coordination of the many activities of a large public agency is absolutely essential. Coordination, as an administrative principle, must be distinguished from and is independent of cooperation. Coordination can be of either the horizontal or the vertical type. In large organizations, the objectives of vertical coordination are achieved by the transmission of orders and statements of policy down through the various levels of authority. It is an accepted generalization that the more authoritarian the organization, the more easily may vertical coordination be accomplished. Horizontal coordination is arrived through staff work, administrative management, and conferences of administrators of equal rank. It is obvious that of the two types of coordination, the vertical kind is more important, for at best horizontal coordination only supplements the coordination effected up and down the line,

11. According to the above passage, the ease with which vertical coordination is achieved in a large agency depends upon 11.____
    A. the extent to which control is firmly exercised from above
    B. the objectives that have been established for the agency
    C. the importance attached by employees to the orders and statements of policy transmitted through the agency
    D. the cooperation obtained at the various levels of authority

12. According to the above passage, 12.____
    A. vertical coordination is dependent for its success upon horizontal coordination
    B. one type of coordination may work in opposition to the other
    C. similar methods may be used to achieve both types of coordination
    D. horizontal coordination is at most an addition to vertical coordination

Questions 13-17.

DIRECTIONS: Questions 13 through 17 are to be answered SOLELY on the basis of the following situation.

Assume that you are a newly appointed supervisor in the same unit in which you have been acting as a provisional for some time. You have in your unit the following workers:

WORKER I: He has always been an efficient worker. In a number of his cases, the clients have recently begun to complain that they cannot manage on the departmental budget.

WORKER II: He has been under selective supervision for some time as an experienced, competent worker. He now begins to be late for his supervisory conferences and to stress how much work he has to do.

WORKER III: He has been making considerable improvement in his ability to handle the details of his job. He now tells you, during an individual conference, that he does not need such close supervision and that he wants to operate more independently. He says that Worker II is always available when he needs a little information or help but, in general, he can manage very well by himself.

WORKER IV: He brings you a complex case for decision as to eligibility. Discussion of the case brings out the fact that he has failed to consider all the available resources adequately but has stressed the family's needs to include every extra item in the budget. This is the third case of a similar nature that his worker has brought to you recently. This worker and Worker I work in adjacent territory and are rather friendly.

In the following questions, select the option that describes the method of dealing with these workers that illustrate BEST supervisory practice.

13. With respect to supervision of Worker I, the assistant supervisor should 13.____
    A. discuss with the worker, in an individual conference, any problems that he may be having due to the increase in the cost of living
    B. plan a group conference for the unit around budgeting, as both Workers I and IV seem to be having budgetary difficulties
    C. discuss with Workers I and IV together the meaning of money as acceptance or rejection to the clients
    D. discuss with Worker I the budgetary data in each case in relation to each client's situation

14. With respect to supervision of Worker II, the supervisory should 14.____
    A. move slowly with this worker and give him time to learn that the supervisor's official appointment has not changed his attitudes or methods of supervision
    B. discuss the worker's change of attitude and asks him to analyze the reasons for his change in behavior
    C. take time to show the worker how he is avoiding his responsibility in the supervisor-worker relationship and that he is resisting supervision
    D. hold an evaluatory conference with the worker and show him how he is taking over responsibilities that are not his by providing supervision for Worker III

15. With respect to supervision of Worker III, the supervisor should discuss with this worker 15.____
    A. why he would rather have supervision from Worker II than from the supervisor
    B. the necessity for further improvement before he can go on selective supervision
    C. an analysis of the improvement that has been made and the extent to which the worker is able to handle the total job for which he is responsible
    D. the responsibility of the supervisor to see that clients receive adequate service

16. With respect to supervision of Worker IV, the supervisor should 16.____
    A. show the worker that resources figures are incomplete but that even if they were complete, the family would probably be eligible for assistance
    B. ask the worker why he is so protective of these families since there are three cases so similar

C. discuss with the worker all three cases at the same time so that the worker may see his own role in the three situations
D. discuss with the worker the reasons for departmental policies and procedures around budgeting

17. With respect to supervision of Workers I and IV, since these two workers are friends and would seem to be influencing each other, the supervisor should 17.____
A. hold a joint conference with them both, pointing out how they should clear with the supervisor and not make their own rules together
B. handle the problems of each separately in individual conferences
C. separate them by transferring one to another territory or another unit
D. take up the problem of workers asking help of each other rather than from the supervisor in a group meeting

Questions 18-20.

DIRECTIONS: Questions 18 through 20 are to be answered SOLELY on the basis of the following passage.

One of the key supervisory problems in a large municipal recreation department is that many leaders are assigned to isolated playgrounds or small centers, where it is difficult to observe their work regularly. Often their facilities are extremely limited. In such settings, as well as in larger recreation centers, where many recreation leaders tend to have other jobs as well, there tends to be a low level of morale and incentive. Still, it is the supervisor's task to help recreation personnel to develop pride in their work and to maintain a high level of performance. With isolated leaders, the supervisor may give advice or assistance. Leaders may be assigned to different tasks or settings during the year to maximize their productivity and provide new challenges. When it is clear that leaders are no willing to make a real effort to contribute to the department, the possibility of penalties must be considered, within the scope of departmental policy and the union contract. However, the supervisor should be constructive, encourage and assist workers to take a greater interest in their work, be innovative, and try to raise morale and to improve performance in positive ways.

18. The one of the following that would the MOST appropriate title for the above passage is 18.____
A. Small Community Centers – Pro and Con
B. Planning Better Recreation Programs
C. The Supervisor's Task in Upgrading Personnel Performance
D. The Supervisor and the Municipal Union – Rights and Obligations

19. The above passage makes clear that recreation leadership performance in all recreation playgrounds and centers throughout a large city is 19.____
A. generally above average, with good morale on the part of most recreation leaders
B. beyond description since no one has ever observed or evaluated recreation leaders

C. a key test of the personnel department's effort to develop more effective hiring standards
D. of mixed quality, with many recreation leaders having poor morale and a low level of achievement

20. According to the above passage, the supervisor's role is to 20.____
A. use disciplinary action as his major tool in upgrading performance
B. tolerate the lack of effort of individual employees since they are assigned to isolated playgrounds or small centers
C. employ encouragement, advice, and, when appropriate, disciplinary action to improve performance
D. inform the county supervisor whenever malfeasance or idleness is detected

Questions 21-25.

DIRECTIONS: Questions 21 through 25 are to be answered SOLELY on the basis of the following passage.

EMPLOYEE LEAVE REGULATIONS

Peter Smith, as a full-time permanent city employee under the Career and Salary Plan, earns an *annual leave allowance*. This consists of a certain number of days off a year with pay and may be used for vacation, personal business, and for observing religious holidays. As a newly appointed employee, during his first 8 years of city service, he will earn an annual leave allowance of 20 days off a year (an average of $1^2/_3$ days off a month). After he has finished 8 full years of working for the city, he will begin earning an additional 5 days off a year. His annual leave allowance, therefore, will then be 25 days a year and will remain at this amount for seven full years. He will begin earning an additional two days off a year at this amount for seven full years. He will begin earning an additional two days off a year after he has completed a total of 15 years of city employment. Therefore, in his sixteenth year of working for the city, Mr. Smith will be earning 27 days off a year as his annual leave allowance (an average of 2¼ days off a month).

A *sick leave allowance* of one day a month is also given to Mr. Smith, but it can be used only in cases of actual illness. When Mr. Smith returns to work after using sick leave allowance, he must have a doctor's note if the absence is for a total of more than 3 days, but he may also be required to show a doctor's note for absences of 1, 2, or 3 days.

21. According to the above passage, Mr. Smith's annual leave allowance consists of a certain number of days off a year which he 21.____
A. does not get paid for
B. gets paid for at time and a half
C. may use for personal business
D. may not use for observing religious holidays

22. According to the above passage, after Mr. Smith has been working for the city for 9 years, his annual leave allowance will be _____ days a year. 22.____
A. 20 B. 25 C. 27 D. 37

23. According to the above passage, Mr. Smith will begin earning an average of 2 days off a month as his annual leave allowance after he has worked for the city for _____ full years. 23.____
    A. 7 B. 8 C. 15 D. 17

24. According to the above passage, Mr. Smith is given a sick leave allowance of 24.____
    A. 1 day every 2 months
    B. 1 day per month
    C. $1\frac{2}{3}$ days per month
    D. $2\frac{1}{4}$ days a month

25. According to the above passage, when he uses sick leave allowance, Mr. Smith may be required to show a doctor's note 25.____
    A. even if his absence is for only 1 day
    B. only if his absence is for more than 2 days
    C. only if his absence is for more than 3 days
    D. only if his absence is for 3 days or more

# KEY (CORRECT ANSWERS)

| | | | |
|---|---|---|---|
| 1. | C | 11. | A |
| 2. | C | 12. | D |
| 3. | D | 13. | D |
| 4. | A | 14. | A |
| 5. | B | 15. | C |
| 6. | B | 16. | C |
| 7. | A | 17. | B |
| 8. | D | 18. | C |
| 9. | B | 19. | D |
| 10. | C | 20. | C |

21. C
22. B
23. C
24. B
25. A

# TEST 3

DIRECTIONS: Each question or incomplete statement is followed by several suggested answers or completions. Select the one that BEST answers the question or completes the statement. *PRINT THE LETTER OF THE CORRECT ANSWER IN THE SPACE AT THE RIGHT.*

Questions 1-6.

DIRECTIONS: Questions 1 through 6 are to be answered SOLELY on the basis of the following passage.

A folder is made of a sheet of heavy paper (manila, kraft, pressboard, or red rope stock) that has been folded once so that the back is about one-half inch higher than the front. Folders are larger than the papers they contain in order to protect them. Two standard folder sizes are *letter size* for papers that are 8½" x 11" and *legal cap* for papers that are 8½" x 13".

Folders are cut across the top in two ways: so that the back is straight (straight-cut) or so that the back has a tab that projects above the top of the folder. Such tabs bear captions that identify the contents of each folder. Tabs vary in width and position. The tabs of a set of folders that are *one-half cut* are half the width of the folder and have only two positions.

*One-third cut* folders have three positions, each tab occupying a third of the width of the folder. Another standard tabbing is *one-fifth cut*, which has five positions. There are also folders with *two-fifths cut*, with the tabs in the third and fourth or fourth and fifth positions.

1. Of the following, the BEST title for the above passage is 1.____
   A. Filing Folders
   B. Standard Folder Sizes
   C. The Uses of the Folder
   D. The Use of Tabs

2. According to the above passage, one of the standard folder sizes is called 2.____
   A. Kraft cut
   B. legal cap
   C. one-half cut
   D. straight-cut

3. According to the above passage, tabs are GENERALLY placed along the _____ of the folder. 3.____
   A. back
   B. front
   C. left side
   D. right side

4. According to the above passage, a tab is GENERALLY used to 4.____
   A. distinguish between standard folder sizes
   B. identify the contents of a folder
   C. increase the size of the folder
   D. protect the papers within the folder

5. According to the above passage, a folder that is two-fifths cut has _____ tabs. 5.____
   A. no
   B. two
   C. three
   D. five

6. According to the above passage, one reason for making folders larger than the papers they contain is that 6.____
   A. only a certain size folder can be made from heavy paper
   B. they will protect the papers
   C. they will aid in setting up a tab system
   D. the back of the folder must be higher than the front

Questions 7-15.

DIRECTIONS: Questions 7 through 15 are to be answered SOLELY on the basis of the following passage.

The City University of New York traces its origins to 1847, when the Free Academy, which later became City College, was founded as the first tuition-free municipal college. City and Hunter Colleges were placed under the direction of the Board of Higher Education in 1926, and Brooklyn and Queens Colleges were subsequently added to the system of municipal colleges. In 1955, Staten Island Community College, the first of the two-year colleges sponsored by the Board of Higher Education under the program of the State University of New York, joined the system.

In 1961, the four senior colleges and three community colleges then under the jurisdiction of the Board of Higher Education became the City University of New York, and a University Graduate Division was organized to offer programs leading to the Ph.D. Since then, the university has undergone even more rapid growth. Today, it consists of nine senior colleges, an upper division college which admits students at the junior level, eight community colleges, a graduate division, and an affiliated medical center.

In the summer of 1969, the Board of Higher Education resolved that the time had come to commit the resources of the university to meeting an urgent social need—unrestricted access to higher education for all youths of the City. Determined to prevent the waste of human potential represented by the thousands of high school graduates whose limited educational opportunities left them unable to meet existing admission standards, the Board moved to adopt a policy of Open Admissions. It was their judgment that the best way of determining whether a potential student can benefit from college work is to admit him to college, provide him with the learning assistance he needs, and then evaluate his performance.

Beginning with the class of June 1970, every New York City resident who received a high school diploma from a public or private high school was guaranteed a place in one of the colleges of City University.

7. Of the following, the BEST title for the above passage is 7.____
   A. A Brief History of the City University
   B. High Schools and the City University
   C. The Components of the University
   D. Tuition-free Colleges

8. According to the above passage, which one of the following colleges of the City University was ORIGINALLY called the Free Academy? 8.____
   A. Brooklyn College B. City College
   C. Hunter College D. Queens College

9. According to the above passage, the system of municipal colleges became the City University of New York in 9.____
   A. 1926 B. 1955 C. 1961 D. 1969

10. According to the above passage, Staten Island Community College came under the jurisdiction of the Board of Higher Education 10.____
    A. 6 years after a Graduate Division was organized
    B. 8 years before the adoption of the Open Admissions Policy
    C. 29 years after Brooklyn and Queens Colleges
    D. 29 years after City and Hunter Colleges

11. According to the above passage, the Staten Island Community College is 11.____
    A. a graduate division center B. a senior college
    C. a two-year college D. an upper division college

12. According to the above passage, the TOTAL number of colleges, divisions, and affiliated branches of the City University is 12.____
    A. 18 B. 19 C. 20 D. 21

13. According to the above passage, the Open Admissions Policy is designed to determine whether a potential student will benefit from college by PRIMARILY 13.____
    A. discouraging competition for placement in the City University among high school students
    B. evaluating his performance after entry into college
    C. lowering admission standards
    D. providing learning assistance before entry into college

14. According to the above passage, the FIRST class to be affected by the Open Admissions Policy was the 14.____
    A. high school class which graduated in January 1970
    B. City University class which graduated in June 1970
    C. high school class when graduated in June 1970
    D. City University class when graduated in June 1970

15. According to the above passage, one of the reasons that the Board of Higher Education initiated the policy of Open Admission was to 15.____
    A. enable high school graduates with a background of limited educational opportunities to enter college
    B. expand the growth of the City University so as to increase the number and variety of degrees offered
    C. provide a social resource to the qualified youth of the City
    D. revise admission standards to meet the needs of the City

Questions 16-18.

DIRECTIONS: Questions 16 through 18 are to be answered SOLELY on the basis of the following passage.

Hereafter, all probationary students interested in transferring to community college career programs (associate degrees) from liberal arts programs in senior colleges (bachelor degrees) will be eligible for such transfers if they have completed no more than three semesters.

For students with averages 1.5 or above, transfer will be automatic. Those with 1.0 to 1.5 averages can transfer provisionally and will be required to make substantial progress during the first semester in the career program. Once transfer has taken place, only those courses in which passing grades were received will be computed in the community college grade-point average.

No request for transfer will be accepted from probationary students wishing to enter the liberal arts programs at the community college.

16. According to the above passage, the one of the following which is the BEST statement concerning the transfer of probationary students is that a probationary student 16.____
    A. may transfer to a career program at the end of one semester
    B. must complete three semester hours before he is eligible for transfer
    C. is not eligible to transfer to a career program
    D. is eligible to transfer to a liberal arts program

17. Which of the following is the BEST statement of academic evaluation for transfer purposes in the case of probationary students? 17.____
    A. No probationary student with an average under 1.5 may transfer.
    B. A probationary student with an average of 1.3 may not transfer.
    C. A probationary student with an average of 1.6 may transfer.
    D. A probationary student with an average of .8 may transfer on a provisional basis.

18. It is MOST likely that, of the following, the next degree sought by one who already holds the Associate in Science degree would be a(n) _____ degree. 18.____
    A. Assistantship in Science
    B. Associate in Applied Science
    C. Bachelor of Science
    D. Doctor of Philosophy

Questions 19-20.

DIRECTIONS: Questions 19 and 20 are to be answered SOLELY on the basis of the following passage.

Auto: Auto travel requires prior approval by the President and/or appropriate Dean and must be indicated in the *Request for Travel Authorization* form. Employees authorized to use personal autos on official College business will be reimbursed at the rate of 28¢ per mile for the first 500 miles driven and 18¢ per mile for mileage driven in excess of 500 mile. The Comptroller's Office may limit the amount of reimbursement to the expenditure that would have been made if a less expensive mode of transportation (railroad, airplane, bus, etc.) had been utilized. If this occurs, the traveler will have to pick up the excess expenditure as a personal expense.

Tolls, Parking Fees, and Parking Meter Fees are not reimbursable and many not be claimed.

19. Suppose that Professor T gives the office assistant the following memorandum: Used car for official trip to Albany, New York, and return. Distance from New York to Albany is 148 miles. Tolls were $3.50 each way. Parking garage cost $3.00. When preparing the Travel Expense Voucher for Professor T, the figure which should be claimed for transportation is 19.____
    A. $120.88 B. $113.88 C. $82.88 D. $51.44

20. Suppose that Professor V gives the office assistant the following memorandum: Used car for official trip to Pittsburgh, Pennsylvania, and return. Distance from New York to Pittsburgh is 350 miles. Tolls were $3.30, $11.40 going, and $3.30, $2.00 returning. 20.____
    When preparing the Travel Expense Voucher for Professor V, the figure which should be claimed for transportation is
    A. $225.40 B. $176.00 C. $127.40 D. $98.00

Questions 21-25.

DIRECTIONS: Questions 21 through 25 are to be answered SOLELY on the basis of the following passage.

For a period of nearly fifteen years, beginning in the mid-1950's, higher education sustained a phenomenal rate of growth. The factor principally responsible were continuing improvement in the rate of college entrance by high school graduates, a 50 percent increase in the size of the college-age (eighteen to twenty-one) group and—until about 1967—a rapid expansion of university research activity supported by the Federal government.

Today, as one looks ahead to the year 2010, it is apparent that each of these favorable stimuli will either be abated or turn into a negative factor. The rate of growth of the college-age group has already diminished; and from 2000 to 2005, the size of the college-age group has shrunk annually almost as fast as it grew from 1965 to 1970. From 2005 to 2010, this annual decrease will slow down so that by 2010 the age group will be about the same size as it was in 2009. This substantial net decrease in the size of the college-age group (from 1995 to 2010) will dramatically affect college enrollments since, currently, 83 percent of undergraduates are twenty-one and under, and another 11 percent are twenty-to to twenty-four.

21. Which one of the following factors is NOT mentioned in the above passage as contributing to the high rate of growth of higher education? 21.____
    A. A large increase in the size of the eighteen to twenty-one age group
    B. The equalization of educational opportunities among socio-economic groups
    C. The Federal budget impact on research and development spending in the higher education sector
    D. The increasing rate at which high school graduates enter college

22. Based on the information in the above passage, the size of the college-age group in 2010 will be 22.____
    A. larger than it was in 2009
    B. larger than it was in 1995
    C. smaller than it was in 2005
    D. about the same as it was in 2000

23. According to the above passage, the tremendous rate of growth of higher education started around 23.____
    A. 1950
    B. 1955
    C. 1960
    D. 1965

24. The percentage of undergraduates who are over age 24 is MOST NEARLY 24.____
    A. 6%
    B. 8%
    C. 11%
    D. 17%

25. Which one of the following conclusions can be substantiated by the information given in the above passage? 25.____
    A. The college-age group was about the same size in 2000 as it was in 1965.
    B. The annual decrease in the size of the college-age group from 2000 to 2005 is about the same as the annual increase from 1965 to 1970.
    C. The overall decrease in the size of the college-age group from 2000 to 2005 will be followed by an overall increase in its size from 2005 to 2010.
    D. The size of the college-age group is decreasing at a fairly constant rate from1995 to 2010.

---

# KEY (CORRECT ANSWERS)

| | | | |
|---|---|---|---|
| 1. | A | 11. | C |
| 2. | B | 12. | C |
| 3. | A | 13. | B |
| 4. | B | 14. | C |
| 5. | B | 15. | A |
| 6. | B | 16. | A |
| 7. | A | 17. | C |
| 8. | B | 18. | C |
| 9. | C | 19. | C |
| 10. | D | 20. | B |

| | |
|---|---|
| 21. | B |
| 22. | C |
| 23. | B |
| 24. | A |
| 25. | B |

# INTERPRETING STATISTICAL DATA GRAPHS, CHARTS, AND TABLES

## EXAMINATION SECTION

## TEST 1

DIRECTIONS: Each question or incomplete statement is followed by several suggested answers or completions. Select the one that BEST answers the question or completes the statement. *PRINT THE LETTER OF THE CORRECT ANSWER IN THE SPACE AT THE RIGHT.*

Questions 1-5.

DIRECTIONS: Questions 1 through 5 are to be answered SOLELY on the basis of the following table.

| ANNUAL SALARIES PAID TO SELECTED CLERICAL TITLES IN FIVE MAJOR CITIES IN 2017 AND 2019 | | | | | |
|---|---|---|---|---|---|
| | | | 2019 | | |
| | Clerk | Typist | Steno | Legal Steno | Computer Operator |
| Newton | $33,900 | $34,800 | $36,300 | $43,800 | $35,400 |
| Barton | $32,400 | $34,200 | $35,400 | $43,500 | $24,200 |
| Phelton | $32,400 | $32,400 | $34,200 | $42,000 | $33,000 |
| Washburn | $33,600 | $34,800 | $35,400 | $43,800 | $34,800 |
| Biltmore | $33,000 | $34,200 | $35,100 | $43,500 | $34,500 |
| | | | 2017 | | |
| Newton | $31,800 | $33,600 | $35,400 | $41,400 | $34,500 |
| Barton | $30,000 | $31,500 | $33,000 | $39,600 | $31,500 |
| Phelton | $29,400 | $30,600 | $31,800 | $37,800 | $31,200 |
| Washburn | $30,600 | $32,400 | $33,600 | $40,200 | $32,400 |
| Biltmore | $30,000 | $31,800 | $33,00 | $39,600 | $32,100 |

1. Assume that the value of the fringe benefits offered to clerical employees in 2019 amounted to 14% of their annual salaries in Newton, 17% in Barton, 18% in Phelton, 15% in Washburn, and 16% in Biltmore. 1.____
The total cost of employing a computer operator for 2019 was GREATEST in
A. Newton B. Barton C. Phelton D. Washburn

2. During negotiations for their 2020 contract, the stenographers of Biltmore are demanding that their rate of pay be fixed at 85% of the legal stenographer salary. 2.____
If this demand is granted and if the legal stenographer salary increases by 7% in 2020, the 2020 stenographer salary will be MOST NEARLY
A. $36,972 B. $37,560 C. $39,564 D. $40,020

3. Of the following, the GREATEST percentage increase in salary from 2017 to 2019 was gained by 3.____
   A. clerks in Newton
   B. stenographers in Barton
   C. legal stenographers in Washburn
   D. computer operators in Biltmore

4. The title which achieved the SMALLEST average percentage increase in salary from 2017 to 2019 was 4.____
   A. clerk
   B. typist
   C. stenographer
   D. legal stenographer

5. Assume that, in 2019, clerks accounted for 60% of the clerical work force in Barton. The clerical work force consists of 140 employees. In 2017, the clerks accounted for 65% of the clerical work force in Barton. The clerical work force then consisted of 120 employees. 5.____
   The difference between the 2017 and 2019 payroll for clerks in Barton is MOST NEARLY
   A. $120,000
   B. $240,000
   C. $360,000
   D. $480,000

## KEY (CORRECT ANSWERS)

1. A
2. C
3. C
4. C
5. C

# TEST 2

DIRECTIONS: Each question or incomplete statement is followed by several suggested answers or completions. Select the one that BEST answers the question or completes the statement. *PRINT THE LETTER OF THE CORRECT ANSWER IN THE SPACE AT THE RIGHT.*

Questions 1-9.

DIRECTIONS: Questions 1 through 9 are to be answered SOLELY on the basis of the facts given in the following table, which contains certain information about employees in a city bureau.

| RECORD OF EMPLOYEES IN A CITY BUREAU | | | | | |
|---|---|---|---|---|---|
| NAME | TITLE | AGE | ANNUAL SALARY | YEARS OF SERVICE | EXAMINATION RATING |
| Jones | Clerk | 34 | $40,800 | 10 | 82 |
| Smith | Stenographer | 25 | $38,400 | 2 | 72 |
| Black | Typist | 19 | $28,800 | 1 | 71 |
| Brown | Stenographer | 36 | $50,400 | 12 | 88 |
| Thomas | Accountant | 49 | $82,400 | 21 | 91 |
| Gordon | Clerk | 31 | $60,000 | 8 | 81 |
| Johnson | Stenographer | 26 | $52,800 | 5 | 75 |
| White | Accountant | 53 | $72,000 | 30 | 90 |
| Spencer | Clerk | 42 | $55,200 | 19 | 85 |
| Taylor | Typist | 24 | $43,200 | 5 | 74 |
| Simpson | Accountant | 37 | $100,000 | 1 | 87 |
| Reid | Typist | 20 | $24,000 | 2 | 72 |
| Fulton | Accountant | 55 | $110,000 | 31 | 100 |
| Chambers | Clerk | 22 | $31,200 | 4 | 75 |
| Calhoun | Stenographer | 48 | $57,600 | 16 | 80 |

1. The name of the employee whose salary would be the middle one if all the salaries were ranked in order of magnitude is 1.____
   A. White B. Johnson C. Brown D. Spencer

2. The combined monthly salary of all the stenographers EXCEEDS the combined monthly salary of all the clerks by 2.____
   A. $12,000 B. $1,000 C. $45,600 D. $1,200

3. The age of the employee who received the HIGHEST rating in the examination among those who have less than 10 years of service is _____ years. 3.____
   A. 22 B. 31 C. 55 D. 34

4. The average examination rating of those employees who had 15 years of service or more as compared with the average examination rating of those employees who had 5 years of service or less is MOST NEARLY _____ points _____. 4.____

   A. 16; greater  B. 7; greater  C. 10; less  D. 25; greater

5. The name of the youngest employee whose monthly salary is more than $2,000 per month and who has more than one year of service is 5.____

   A. Reid  B. Black  C. Chambers  D. Taylor

6. The name of the employee who received an examination rating of over 85%, who has more than 15 years of service, and who earns a yearly salary of more than $50,000 but less than $80,000 is 6.____

   A. Thomas  B. Spencer  C. Calhoun  D. White

7. The annual salary of the HIGHEST paid stenographer is 7.____

   A. more than twice as great as the salary of the youngest employee
   B. greater than the salary of the oldest typist but not as great as the salary of the oldest clerk
   C. greater than the salary of the highest paid typist but not as great as the salary of the lowest paid accountant
   D. less than the combined salaries of the two youngest typists

8. The number of employees whose annual salary is more than $31,200 but less than $57,600 and who have at least 5 years of service is 8.____

   A. 11  B. 8  C. 6  D. 5

9. Of the following, it would be MOST accurate to state that the 9.____

   A. youngest employee is lowest with respect to number of years of service, examination rating, and salary
   B. oldest employee is highest with respect to number of years of service, examination rating, but not with respect to salary
   C. annual salary of the youngest clerk is $2,400 more than the annual salary of the youngest typist and $4,800 less than the annual salary of the youngest stenographer
   D. difference in age between the youngest and oldest typist is less than one-fourth the difference in age between the youngest and oldest stenographer

# KEY (CORRECT ANSWERS)

| | | | |
|---|---|---|---|
| 1. | B | 6. | D |
| 2. | B | 7. | C |
| 3. | B | 8. | D |
| 4. | A | 9. | D |
| 5. | C | | |

# TEST 3

DIRECTIONS: Each question or incomplete statement is followed by several suggested answers or completions. Select the one that BEST answers the question or completes the statement. *PRINT THE LETTER OF THE CORRECT ANSWER IN THE SPACE AT THE RIGHT.*

Questions 1-10.

DIRECTIONS: Questions 1 through 10 are to be answered SOLELY on the basis of the Personnel Record of Division X shown below.

DIVISION X
PERSONNEL RECORD – CURRENT YEAR

| Employee | Bureau in Which Employed | Title | Annual Salary | No. of Days Absent: On Vacation | No. of Days Absent: On Sick Leave | No. of Times Late |
|---|---|---|---|---|---|---|
| Abbot | Mail | Clerk | $31,200 | 18 | 0 | 1 |
| Barnes | Mail | Clerk | $25,200 | 25 | 3 | 7 |
| Davis | Mail | Typist | $24,000 | 21 | 9 | 2 |
| Adams | Payroll | Accountant | $42,500 | 10 | 0 | 2 |
| Bell | Payroll | Bookkeeper | $31,200 | 23 | 2 | 5 |
| Duke | Payroll | Clerk | $27,600 | 24 | 4 | 3 |
| Gross | Payroll | Clerk | $21,600 | 12 | 5 | 7 |
| Lane | Payroll | Stenographer | $26,400 | 19 | 16 | 20 |
| Reed | Payroll | Typist | $22,800 | 15 | 11 | 11 |
| Arnold | Record | Clerk | $32,400 | 6 | 15 | 9 |
| Cane | Record | Clerk | $24,500 | 14 | 3 | 4 |
| Fay | Record | Clerk | $21,100 | 20 | 0 | 4 |
| Hale | Record | Typist | $25,200 | 18 | 2 | 7 |
| Baker | Supply | Clerk | $30,000 | 20 | 3 | 2 |
| Clark | Supply | Clerk | $27,600 | 25 | 6 | 5 |
| Ford | Supply | Typist | $22,800 | 25 | 4 | 22 |

1. The percentage of the total number of employees who are clerks is MOST NEARLY 1.____
   A. 25% B. 33% C. 38% D. 56%

2. Of the following employees, the one who receives a monthly salary of $2,100 is 2.____
   A. Barnes B. Gross C. Reed D. Clark

3. The difference between the annual salary of the highest paid clerk and that of the lowest paid clerk is 3.____
   A. $6,000 B. $8,400 C. $11,300 D. $20,900

4. The number of employees receiving more than $25,000 a year but less than $40,000 a year is 4.____
   A. 6 B. 9 C. 12 D. 15

5. The TOTAL annual salary of the employees of the Mail Bureau is _____ the total annual salary of the employees of the _____. 5.____
   A. one-half of; Payroll Bureau
   B. less than; Record Bureau by $21,600
   C. equal to; Supply Bureau
   D. less than; Payroll Bureau by $71,600

6. The average annual salary of the employees who are not clerks is MOST NEARLY 6.____
   A. $23,700 B. $25,450 C. $26,800 D. $27,850

7. If all the employees were given a 10% increase in pay, the annual salary of Lane would then be 7.____
   A. *greater* than that of Barnes by $1,320
   B. *less* than that of Bell by $4,280
   C. *equal to* that of Clark
   D. *greater* than that of Ford by $3,600

8. Of the clerks who earned less than $30,000 a year, the one who was late the FEWEST number of times was late _____ time(s). 8.____
   A. 1 B. 2 C. 3 D. 4

9. The bureau in which the employees were late the FEWEST number of times on an average is the _____ Bureau. 9.____
   A. Mail B. Payroll C. Record D. Supply

10. The MOST accurate of the following statements is that 10.____
   A. Reed was late more often than any other typist
   B. Bell took more time off for vacation than any other employee earning $30,000 or more annually
   C. of the typists, Ford was the one who was absent the fewest number of times because of sickness
   D. three clerks took no time off because of sickness

# KEY (CORRECT ANSWERS)

| | | | |
|---|---|---|---|
| 1. | D | 6. | D |
| 2. | A | 7. | A |
| 3. | C | 8. | C |
| 4. | B | 9. | A |
| 5. | C | 10. | B |

# TEST 4

DIRECTIONS: Each question or incomplete statement is followed by several suggested answers or completions. Select the one that BEST answers the question or completes the statement. *PRINT THE LETTER OF THE CORRECT ANSWER IN THE SPACE AT THE RIGHT.*

Questions 1-10.

DIRECTIONS: Questions 1 through 10 are to be answered SOLELY on the basis of the Weekly Payroll Record shown below of Bureau X in a public agency. In answering these questions, note that gross weekly salary is the salary before deductions have been made; take-home pay is the amount remaining after all indicated weekly deductions have been made from the gross weekly salary. In answering questions involving annual amounts, compute on the basis of 52 weeks per year.

BUREAU X
WEEKLY PAYROLL PERIOD

| Unit in Which Employed | Employee | Title | Gross Weekly Salary (Before Deductions) | Weekly Deductions From Gross Salary | | |
|---|---|---|---|---|---|---|
| | | | | Medical Insurance | Income Tax | Pension System |
| Accounting | Allen | Accountant | $950 | $14.50 | $125.00 | $53.20 |
| Accounting | Barth | Bookkeeper | $720 | $19.00 | $62.00 | $40.70 |
| Accounting | Keller | Clerk | $580 | $6.50 | $82.00 | $33.10 |
| Accounting | Peters | Typist | $560 | $6.50 | $79.00 | $35.30 |
| Accounting | Simons | Stenographer | $610 | $14.50 | $64.00 | $37.80 |
| Information | Brown | Clerk | $560 | $13.00 | $56.00 | $42.20 |
| Information | Smith | Clerk | $590 | $14.50 | $61.00 | $58.40 |
| Information | Turner | Typist | $580 | $13.00 | $59.00 | $62.60 |
| Information | Williams | Stenographer | $620 | $19.00 | $44.00 | $69.40 |
| Mail | Conner | Clerk | $660 | $13.00 | $74.00 | $55.40 |
| Mail | Farrell | Typist | $540 | $6.50 | $75.00 | $34.00 |
| Mail | Johnson | Stenographer | $580 | $19.00 | $36.00 | $37.10 |
| Records | Dillon | Clerk | $640 | $6.50 | $94.00 | $58.20 |
| Records | Martin | Clerk | $540 | $19.00 | $29.00 | $50.20 |
| Records | Standish | Typist | $620 | $14.50 | $67.00 | $60.10 |
| Records | Wilson | Stenographer | $690 | $6.50 | $101.00 | $75.60 |

1. Dillon's annual take-home pay is MOST NEARLY 1.____
   A. $25,000 B. $27,000 C. $31,000 D. $33,000

2. The difference between Turner's gross annual salary and his annual take-home pay is MOST NEARLY 2.____
   A. $3,000 B. $5,000 C. $7,000 D. $9,000

3. Of the following, the employee whose weekly take-home pay is CLOSEST to that of Keller's is 3.____
   A. Peters B. Brown C. Smith D. Turner

4. The average gross annual salary of the typists is 4.____
   A. less than $27,500
   B. more than $27,500 but less than $30,000
   C. more than $30,000 but less than $32,500
   D. more than $32,500

5. The average gross weekly salary of the stenographers EXCEEDS the gross weekly salary of the clerk by 5.____
   A. $20 B. $30 C. $40 D. $50

6. Of the following employees in Accounting Unit, the one who pays the HIGHEST percentage of his gross weekly salary for the Pension System is 6.____
   A. Barth B. Keller C. Peters D. Simons

7. For all of the Accounting Unit employees, the total annual deductions for Medical Insurance are less than the total annual deductions for the Pension System by MOST NEARLY 7.____
   A. $6,000 B. $7,000 C. $8,000 D. $9,000

8. Of the following, the employee whose total weekly deductions are MOST NEARLY 27% of his gross weekly salary is 8.____
   A. Barth B. Brown C. Martin D. Wilson

9. The total amount of the gross weekly salaries of all the employees in the Records Unit is MOST NEARLY 9.____
   A. 95% of the total amount of the gross weekly salaries of all the employees in the Information Unit
   B. 10% greater than the total amount of the gross weekly salaries of all the employees in the Mail Unit
   C. 75% of the total amount of the gross weekly salaries of all the employees in the Accounting Unit
   D. four times as great as the total amount deducted weekly for tax for all the employees in the Records Unit

10. For the employees in the Information Unit, the AVERAGE weekly deductions for Income Tax _____ the average weekly deduction for _____. 10.____
    A. exceeds; Income Tax for the employees in the Records Unit
    B. is less than; the Pension System for the employees in the Mail Unit
    C. exceeds; Income Tax for the employees in the Accounting Unit
    D. is less than; the Pension System for the employees in the Records Unit

# KEY (CORRECT ANSWERS)

| | | | |
|---|---|---|---|
| 1. | A | 6. | C |
| 2. | C | 7. | B |
| 3. | C | 8. | D |
| 4. | B | 9. | C |
| 5. | B | 10. | D |

# TEST 5

DIRECTIONS: Each question or incomplete statement is followed by several suggested answers or completions. Select the one that BEST answers the question or completes the statement. *PRINT THE LETTER OF THE CORRECT ANSWER IN THE SPACE AT THE RIGHT.*

Questions 1-9.

DIRECTIONS: Questions 1 through 9 are to be answered SOLELY on the basis of the following information.

Assume that the following rules for computing service ratings are to be used experimentally in determining service ratings of seven permanent city employees. (Note that these rules are hypothetical and are NOT to be confused with the existing method of computing service ratings for city employees). The personnel record of each of these seven employees is given in Table II. You are to determine the answer to each of the questions on the basis of the rules given below for computing service ratings and the data contained in the personnel records of these seven employees.

All computations should be made as of the close of the rating period ending March 31, 2017.

Service Rating

The service rating of each permanent competitive class employee shall be computed by adding the following three scores: (1) a basic score, (2) the employee's seniority score, and (3) the employee's efficiency score.

Seniority Score

An employee's seniority score shall be computed by crediting him with ½% per year for each year of service starting with the date of the employee's entrance as a permanent employee into the competitive class, up to a maximum of 15 years (7½%).

A residual fractional period of eight months or more shall be considered as a full year and credited with ½%. A residual fraction of from four to, but not including, eight months shall be considered as half-year and credited with ¼%. A residual fraction of less than four months shall receive no credit in the seniority score.

For example, a person who entered the competitive class as a permanent employee on August 1, 2014 would, as of March 31, 2017, be credited with a seniority score of 1½% for his 2 years and 8 months of service.

Efficiency Score

An employee's efficiency score shall be computed by adding the annual efficiency ratings received by him during his service in his present position. (Where there are negative efficiency ratings, such ratings shall be subtracted from the sum of the positive efficiency ratings.) An employee's annual efficiency rating shall be based on the grade he receives from his supervisor for his work performance during the annual efficiency rating period.

Basic Score

A basic score of 70% shall be given to each employee upon permanent appointment to a competitive class position.

An employee shall receive a grade of A for performing work of the highest quality and shall be credited with an efficiency rating of plus (+)3%. An employee shall receive a grade of F for performing work of the lowest quality and shall receive an efficiency rating of minus (-)2%. Table I, entitled BASS FOR DETERMINING ANNUAL EFFICIENCY RATINGS, lists the six grades of work performance with their equivalent annual efficiency ratings. Table I also lists the efficiency ratings to be assigned for service in a position for less than a year during the annual efficiency rating period.

The annual efficiency rating period shall run from April 1 to March 31, inclusive.

| TABLE I – BASIS FOR DETERMINING ANNUAL EFFICIENCY RATINGS | | | | |
|---|---|---|---|---|
| | | | | |
| | | | Annual Efficiency Rating for Service in a Position For | |
| Quality of Work Performed | Grade Assigned | 8 Months to a Full Year | At Least 4 Months But Less Than 8 Months | Less Than 4 Months |
| Highest | A | +3% | +1½% | 0% |
| Good | B | +2% | +1% | 0% |
| Standard | C | +1% | + ½% | 0% |
| Substandard | D | 0% | 0% | 0% |
| Poor | E | -1% | -4% | 0% |
| Lowest | F | -2% | -1% | 0% |

<u>Appointment or Promotion During an Efficiency Rating Period</u>

An employee who has been appointed or promoted during an efficiency rating period shall receive for that period an efficiency rating only for work performed by him during the portion of the period that he served in the position to which he was appointed or promoted. His efficiency rating for the period shall be determined in accordance with Table I.

<u>Sample Computation of Service Rating</u>

John Smith entered the competitive class as a permanent employee on December 1, 2012 and was promoted to his present position as a Clerk, Grade 3, on November 1, 2015. As a Clerk, Grade 3, he received a grade of B for work performed during the five-month period extending from November 1, 2015 to March 31, 2016 and a grade of C for work performed during the full annual period extending from April 1, 2016 to March 31, 2017.

On the basis of the RULES FOR COMPUTING SERVICE RATINGS, John Smith should be credited with:

70% Basic Score
2¼% Seniority Score – for 4 years and 4 months of service (from 12/1/12 to 3/31/17)
2% Efficiency Score – for 5 months of B service and a full _____ year of C service
74¼%

TABLE II
PERSONNEL RECORD OF SEVEN PERMANENT
COMPETITIVE CLASS EMPLOYEES

| Employee | Present Position | Date of Appointment or Promotion to Present Position | Date of Entry as Permanent Employment in Competitive Class |
|---|---|---|---|
| Allen | Clerk, Gr. 5 | 6-1-13 | 7-1-00 |
| Brown | Clerk, Gr. 4 | 1-1-15 | 7-1-17 |
| Cole | Clerk, Gr. 3 | 9-1-13 | 11-1-10 |
| Fox | Clerk, Gr. 3 | 10-1-13 | 9-1-08 |
| Green | Clerk, Gr. 2 | 12-1-11 | 12-1-11 |
| Hunt | Clerk, Gr. 2 | 7-1-12 | 7-1-12 |
| Kane | Steno, Gr. 3 | 11-16-14 | 3-1-11 |

GRADES RECEIVED ANNUALLY FOR WORK
PERFORMED IN PRESENT POSITION

| Employee | 4-1-11 to 3-31-12 | 4-1-12 to 3-31-13 | 4-1-13 to 3-31-14 | 4-1-14 to 3-31-15 | 4-1-15 to 3-31-16 | 4-1-16 to 3-31-17 |
|---|---|---|---|---|---|---|
| Allen | | | C* | C | B | C |
| Brown | | | | C* | C | B |
| Cole | | | A* | B | C | C |
| Fox | | | C* | C | D | C |
| Green | C* | D | C | D | C | C |
| Hunt | | C* | C | E | C | C |
| Kane | | | | B* | B | C |

EXPLANATORY NOTES
* Served in present position for less than a full year during this rating period. (Note date of appointment, or promotion, to present position.)
All seven employees have served continuously as permanent employees since their entry into the competitive class.

Questions 1 through 9 refer to the employees listed in Table II. You are to answer these questions SOLELY on the basis of the preceding RULES FOR COMPUTING SERVICE RATINGS and on the information concerning these seven employees given in Table II. You are reminded that all computations are to be made as of the close of the rating period ending March 31, 2017. Candidates may find it helpful to arrange their computations on their scratch paper in an orderly manner since the computations for one question may also be utilized in answering another question.

1. The seniority score of Allen is 1.____
   A. 7½% B. 8½% C. 8% D. 8¼%

2. The seniority score of Fox EXCEEDS that of Cole by 2.____
   A. 1½% B. 2% C. 1% D. ¾%

3. The seniority score of Brown is 3.____
   A. *equal* to Hunt's
   B. *twice* Hunt's
   C. *more* than Hunt's by 1½%
   D. *less* than by Hunt's by ½%

4. Green's efficiency score is 4.____
   A. *twice* that of Kane
   B. *equal* to that of Kane
   C. *less* than Kane's by ½%
   D. *less* than Kane's by 1%

5. Of the following employees, the one who has the LOWEST efficiency score is 5.____
   A. Brown
   B. Fox
   C. Hunt
   D. Kane

6. A comparison of Hunt's efficiency score with his seniority score reveals that his efficiency score is 6.____
   A. *less* than his seniority score by ½%
   B. *less* than his seniority score by ¾%
   C. *equal* to his seniority score
   D. *greater* than his seniority score by ½%

7. Fox's service rating is 7.____
   A. 72½%
   B. 74%
   C. 76½%
   D. 76¾%

8. Brown's service rating is 8.____
   A. less than 78%
   B. 78%
   C. 78¼%
   D. more than 78¼%

9. Cole's service rating EXCEEDS Kane's by 9.____
   A. less than 2%
   B. 2%
   C. 2¼%
   D. more than 2¼%

---

## KEY (CORRECT ANSWERS)

| | | | |
|---|---|---|---|
| 1. | A | 6. | D |
| 2. | C | 7. | D |
| 3. | B | 8. | B |
| 4. | C | 9. | A |
| 5. | B | | |

# DOCUMENTS AND FORMS
# PREPARING WRITTEN MATERIALS
# EXAMINATION SECTION
# TEST 1

DIRECTIONS : Each question or incomplete statement is followed by several suggested answers or completions. Select the one that BEST answers the question or completes the statement. *PRINT THE LETTER OF THE CORRECT ANSWER IN THE SPACE AT THE RIGHT.*

1. The office layout chart is a sketch of the physical arrangement of the office to which has been added the flow lines of the principal work performed there. 1.____
   Which one of the following states the BEST advantage of superimposing the work flow onto the desk layout?

   A. Lighting and acoustics can be improved.
   B. Line and staff relationships can be determined.
   C. Obvious misarrangements can be corrected.
   D. The number of delays can be determined.

2. An advantage of the multiple process chart over the flow process chart is that the multiple process chart shows the 2.____

   A. individual worker's activity
   B. number of delays
   C. sequence of operations
   D. simultaneous flow of work in several departments

3. Of the following, which is the MAJOR advantage of a microfilm record retention system? 3.____

   A. Filing can follow the terminal digit system.
   B. Retrieving documents from the files is faster.
   C. Significant space is saved in storing records.
   D. To read a microfilm record, a film reader is not necessary.

4. Assume that you are in the process of eliminating unnecessary forms. 4.____
   The answer to which one of the following questions would be LEAST relevant?

   A. Could the information be obtained elsewhere?
   B. Is the form properly designed?
   C. Is the form used as intended?
   D. Is the purpose of the form essential to the operation?

5. Use of color in forms adds to their cost. Sometimes, however, the use of color will greatly simplify procedure and more than pay for itself in time saved and errors eliminated. 5.____
   This is ESPECIALLY true when

   A. a form passes through many reviewers
   B. considerable sorting is required
   C. the form is other than a standard size
   D. the form will not be sent through the mail

6. Of the following techniques, the one *generally* employed and considered BEST in forms design is to provide writing lines into boxes with captions printed in small type 6.____

A. centered in the lower part of the box
B. centered in the upper part of the box
C. in the upper left-hand corner of the box
D. in the lower right-hand corner of the box

7. Many forms authorities advocate the construction of a functional forms file or index. 7.____
If such a file is set up, the MOST effective way of classifying forms for such an index is classification by

A. department
B. form number
C. name or type of form
D. subject to which the form applies

8. Of the following, the symbol as used in a systems flow chart denotes 8.____

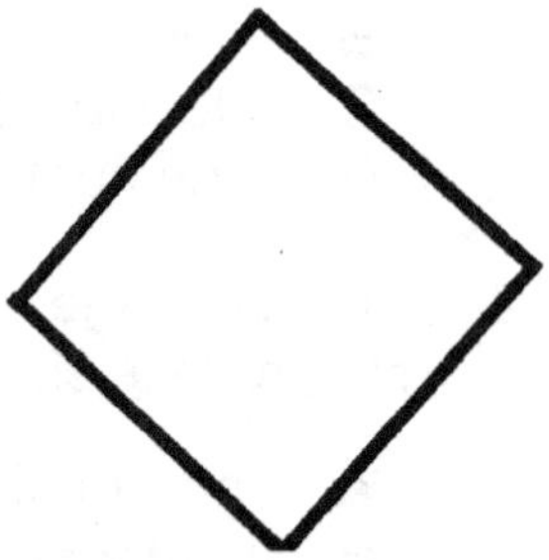

A. decision
B. document
C. manual operation
D. process

9. Assume you are assigned to analyze the details of the procedures a clerk follows in order to complete filling out an invoice or a requisition. Your purpose is to simplify and shorten the procedure he has been trained to use. 9.____
The BEST appropriate chart for this purpose would be the

A. block flow diagram
B. flow process chart
C. forms flow chart
D. work distribution chart

10. What *generally* is the PRINCIPAL objection to the use of form letters? The 10.____

A. difficulty of developing a form letter to serve the purpose
B. excessive time involved in selecting the proper form letter
C. errors in selecting form letters
D. impersonality of form letters

11. In process charting, the symbol which is used when conditions (except those which intentionally change the physical or chemical characteristics of the object) do not permit or require immediate performance, is 11.____

A. 
B. 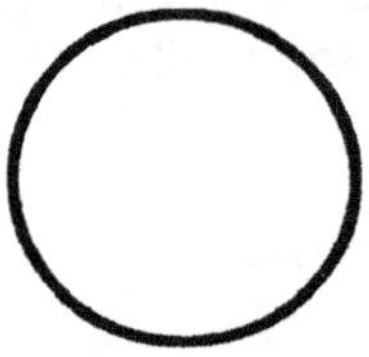
C. 
D. 

12. Assume that you are making a study of a central headquarters office which processes claims received from a number of district offices. You notice the following problems: Some employees are usually busy, while others doing the same kind of work in the same grade have little to do; high level professional people frequently spend considerable time searching for files in the file room. Which of the following charts would be MOST useful to record and analyze the data needed to help solve these problems? 12.____

A. Forms distribution chart
B. Process chart
C. Space layout chart
D. Work distribution chart

13. Which of the following questions.has the LEAST significant bearing on the analysis of the paperwork flow? 13.____

A. How is the work brought into the department and how is it taken away?
B. How many work stations are involved in processing the work within the department?
C. Is the work received and removed in the proper quantity?
D. Where is the supervisor's desk located in relationship to those he supervises?

14. Which of the following does NOT have significant bearing on the arrangement, sequence, and zoning of information into box captions? The 14.____

A. layout of the source documents from which the information is taken
B. logical flow of data
C. needs of forms to be prepared from this form
D. type of print to be employed

15. In determining the space requirements of a form and the size of the boxes to be used, PRIMARY consideration should be given to the 15.____

A. distribution of the form
B. method of entry, i.e., handwritten or machine, and type of machine
C. number of copies
D. number of items to be entered

16. Of the following, the BEST technique to follow when providing instructions for the completion and routing of a form is to 16.____

A. imprint the instructions on the face of the form
B. imprint the instructions on the back of the form
C. provide a written procedure to accompany the form
D. provide verbal instructions when issuing the form

17. A forms layout style where a separate space in the shape of a box is provided for each item of information requested and the caption or question for each item is shown in the upper left-hand corner of each box, is known as the 17.____

A. box style
B. check box style
C. check list style
D. check box and check list style

18. The BEST type of chart to use in showing the absolute movement or change of a continuous series of data over a period of time, such as changes in prices, employment or expenses, is *usually* a 18.____

A. bar chart
B. line chart
C. multiple bar chart
D. pie chart

19. In order to secure information on several specific points from all the tenants of a project, it has been suggested that a questionnaire be distributed to be completed and returned by the tenants. 19.____
The use of such a procedure is, *generally,*

A. *desirable,* because it is a valuable means of building the cooperative relationship which should exist between tenants and management
B. *desirable,* because it provides a written record of each tenant's reply
C. *undesirable,* because distribution and collection of questionnaires is time-consuming
D. *undesirable,* because it makes no provision for the expression of related information or viewpoints

20. A functional forms file is a collection of forms which are grouped by 20.____

A. purpose
B. department
C. title
D. subject

21. All of the following are reasons to consult a records retention schedule EXCEPT one. Which one is that? To determine 21.____

A. whether something should be filed
B. how long something should stay in file
C. who should be assigned to filing
D. when something on file should be destroyed

22. Listed below are four of the steps in the process of preparing correspondence for filing. If they were to be put in logical sequence, the SECOND step would be 22.____

A. preparing cross-reference sheets or cards
B. coding the correspondence using a classification system
C. sorting the correspondence in the order to be filed
D. checking for follow-up action required and preparing a follow-up slip

23. New material added to a file folder should *usually* be inserted 23.____

A. in the order of importance (the most important in front)
B. in the order of importance (the most important in back)
C. chronologically (most recent in front)
D. chronologically (most recent in back)

24. An individual is looking for a name in the white pages of a telephone directory. Which of the following BEST describes the system of filing found there? A(n) 24.____

A. alphabetic file
B. sequential file
C. locator file
D. index file

25. The MAIN purpose of a tickler file is to 25.____

A. help prevent overlooking matters that require future attention
B. check on adequacy of past performance
C. pinpoint responsibility for recurring daily tasks
D. reduce the volume of material kept in general files

# KEY (CORRECT ANSWERS)

1. C
2. D
3. C
4. B
5. B
6. C
7. D
8. A
9. B
10. D
11. C
12. D
13. D
14. D
15. B
16. A
17. A
18. B
19. B
20. A
21. C
22. A
23. C
24. A
25. A

# TEST 2

1. A *good* record-keeping system includes all of the following procedures EXCEPT the 1.____

   A. filing of useless records
   B. destruction of certain files
   C. transferring of records from one type of file to another
   D. creation of inactive files

2. A new program is being set up for which certain new forms will be needed. You have been asked to design these forms. 2.____
   Of the following, the FIRST step you should take in planning the forms is

   A. finding out the exact purpose for which each form will be used
   B. deciding what size of paper should be used for each form
   C. determining whether multiple copies will be needed for any of the forms
   D. setting up a new filing system to handle the new forms

3. Assume that your department is being moved to new and larger quarters, and that you have been asked to suggest an office layout for the central clerical office. 3.____
   Of the following, your FIRST step in planning the new layout should *ordinarily* be to

   A. find out how much money has been budgeted for furniture and equipment
   B. make out *work-flow* and *traffic-flow* charts for the clerical operations
   C. measure each piece of furniture and equipment that is presently in use
   D. determine which files should be moved to a storage area or destroyed

4. In modern office layouts, screens and dividers are often used instead of walls to set off working groups. Advantages given for this approach have included *all* of the following EXCEPT 4.____

   A. more frequent communication between different working groups
   B. reduction in general noise level
   C. fewer objections from employees who are transferred to different groups
   D. cost savings from increased sharing of office equipment

5. Of the following, the CHIEF reason for moving less active material from active to inactive files is to 5.____

   A. dispose of material that no longer has any use
   B. keep the active files down to a manageable size
   C. make sure that no material over a year old remains in active files
   D. separate temporary records from permanent records

6. On a general organization chart, staff positions NORMALLY should be pictured 6.____

   A. directly above the line positions to which they report
   B. to the sides of the main flow lines
   C. within the box of the highest level subordinate positions pictured
   D. directly below the line positions which report to them

7. When an administrator is diagramming an office layout, of the following, his PRIMARY job, *generally,* should be to indicate the 7.____

A. lighting intensities that will be required by each operation
B. noise level that will be produced by the various equipment employed in the office
C. direction of the work flow and the distance involved in each transfer
D. durability of major pieces of office equipment currently in use or to be utilized

8. One common guideline or rule-of-thumb ratio for evaluating the efficiency of files is the number of records requested divided by the number of records filed. 8.____
*Generally,* if this ratio is very low, it would point MOST directly to the need for

A. improving the indexing and coding system
B. improving the charge-out procedures
C. exploring the need for transferring records from active storage to the archives
D. exploring the need to encourage employees to keep more records in their private files

9. The GREATEST percentage of money spent on preparing and keeping the usual records in an office, *generally,* is expended for which one of the following? 9.____

A. Renting space in which to place the record-keeping equipment
B. Paying salaries of record-preparing and record-keeping personnel
C. Depreciation of purchased record-preparation and record-keeping equipment
D. Paper and forms upon which to place the records

10. The MAXIMUM number of 2 3/4" *x* 4 1/4" size forms which may be obtained from two reams of 17" *x* 22" paper is 10.____

A. 4,000 B. 8,000 C. 16,000 D. 32,000

11. Word processing computer applications (i.e. Microsoft Word) generally provide all of the following advantages as compared to electric word processors EXCEPT 11.____

A. documents save to disk automatically
B. ability to include customized graphs and charts in a document
C. wider selection of available fonts
D. easily customized page orientation

12. Generally, the actual floor space occupied by a standard letter-size office file cabinet, when closed, is, *most nearly,* 12.____

A. 1/2 square foot B. 3 square feet
C. 7 square feet D. 11 square feet

13. In general, the CHIEF economy of using multicopy forms is in 13.____

A. the paper on which the form is printed
B. printing the form
C. employee time
D. carbon paper

14. Suppose your supervisor has asked you to develop a form to record certain information needed. The FIRST thing you should do is to 14.____

    A. determine the type of data that will be recorded repeatedly, so that it can be pre-printed
    B. study the relationship of the form to the job to be accomplished, so that the form can be planned
    C. determine the information that will be recorded in the same place on each copy of the form, so that it can be used as a check
    D. find out who will be responsible for supplying the information so that space can be provided for their signatures

15. Of the following, which is usually the MOST important guideline in writing business letters? A letter should be 15.____

    A. neat
    B. written in a formalized style
    C. written in clear language intelligible to the reader
    D. written in the past tense

16. Suppose you are asked to edit a policy statement. You note that personal pronouns like *you*, *we*, and *I* are used freely. 16.____
    Which of the following statements BEST applies to this use of personal pronouns? It

    A. is proper usage because written business language should not be different from carefully spoken business language
    B. requires correction because it is ungrammatical
    C. is proper because it is clearer and has a warmer tone
    D. requires correction because policies should be expressed in an impersonal manner

17. Good business letters are coherent. To be *coherent* means to 17.____

    A. keep only one unifying idea in the message
    B. present the total message
    C. use simple, direct words for the message
    D. tie together the various ideas in the message

18. Proper division of a letter into paragraphs requires that the writer of business letters should, as much as possible, be sure that 18.____

    A. each paragraph is short
    B. each paragraph develops discussion of just one topic
    C. each paragraph repeats the theme of the total message
    D. there are at least two paragraphs for every message

19. An editor is given a letter with this initial paragraph *We have received your letter, which we read with interest, and we are happy to respond to your question. In fact, we talked with several people in our office to get ideas to send to you.* 19.____
    Which of the following is it MOST reasonable for the editor to conclude? The paragraph is

    A. concise
    B. communicating something of value
    C. unnecessary
    D. coherent

20. Suppose that one of your duties is to dictate responses to routine requests from the public for information. A letter writer asks for information which, as expressed in a one-sentence, explicit agency rule, cannot be given out to the public. 20.____
Of the following ways of answering the letter, which is the MOST efficient?

A. Quote verbatim that section of the agency rules which prohibits giving this information to the public
B. Without quoting the rule, explain why you cannot accede to the request and suggest alternative sources
C. Describe how carefully the request was considered before classifying it as subject to the rule forbidding the issuance of such information
D. Acknowledge receipt of the letter and advise that the requested information is not released to the public

21. Suppose you have been asked to write and to prepare for reproduction new departmental vacation leave regulations. After you have written the new regulations, all of which fit on one page, which one of the following would be the BEST method of reproducing 800 copies? 21.____

A. An outside private printer, because you can best maintain confidentiality using this technique
B. Using your own computer's printer/copier, because it is most convenient
C. Giving the job to a coworker in another department who does this type of work more frequently, since the coworker is more familiar with the process
D. Using a high-volume color copier, because it is fastest and of highest quality

22. The files in your office have been overcrowded and difficult to work with since you started working there. One day your supervisor is transferred and another assistant in your office decides to discard three drawers of the oldest materials. 22.____
For him to take this action is

A. *desirable;* it will facilitate handling the more active materials
B. *desirable;* no file should be removed from its point of origin
C. *desirable;* there is no need to burden a new supervisor with unnecessary information
D. *undesirable;* no file should be discarded without first noting what material has been discarded

23. You have been criticized by the general supervisor because of spelling errors in some of your typing. You have only copied the reports as written and you realize that the errors occurred in work given to you by your immediate supervisor. 23.____
Of the following, the BEST way for you to handle this situation is to

A. tell the general supervisor that the spelling errors are your immediate supervisor's, not yours, because they occur only when you type his reports
B. tell the general supervisor that you only type the reports as given to you, without indicating anyone
C. inform your immediate supervisor that you have been unjustly criticized because of his spelling errors and politely request that he be more careful in the future
D. use a dictionary whenever you have doubt regarding spelling

24. You have recently found several items misfiled. You believe that this occurred because a new assistant in your section has been making mistakes. 24.____
The BEST course of action for you to take is to

A. refile the material and say nothing about it
B. send your supervisor an anonymous note of complaint about the filing errors
C. show the errors to the new assistant and tell him why they are errors in filing
D. tell your supervisor that the new assistant makes a lot of errors in filing

---

# KEY (CORRECT ANSWERS)

| | | | |
|---|---|---|---|
| 1. | A | 11. | A |
| 2. | A | 12. | B |
| 3. | B | 13. | C |
| 4. | B | 14. | B |
| 5. | B | 15. | C |
| 6. | B | 16. | D |
| 7. | C | 17. | D |
| 8. | C | 18. | B |
| 9. | B | 19. | C |
| 10. | D | 20. | A |

21. D
22. D
23. D
24. C

---

# PREPARING WRITTEN MATERIAL

## PARAGRAPH REARRANGEMENT COMMENTARY

The sentences that follow are in scrambled order. You are to rearrange them in proper order and indicate the letter choice containing the correct answer at the space at the right.

Each group of sentences in this section is actually a paragraph presented in scrambled order. Each sentence in the group has a place in that paragraph; no sentence is to be left out. You are to read each group of sentences and decide upon the best order in which to put the sentences so as to form a well-organized paragraph.

The questions in this section measure the ability to solve a problem when all the facts relevant to its solution are not given.

More specifically, certain positions of responsibility and authority require the employee to discover connection between events sometimes, apparently, unrelated. In order to do this, the employee will find it necessary to correctly infer that unspecified events have probably occurred or are likely to occur. This ability becomes especially important when action must be taken on incomplete information.

Accordingly, these questions require competitors to choose among several suggested alternatives, each of which presents a different sequential arrangement of the events. Competitors must choose the MOST logical of the suggested sequences.

In order to do so, they may be required to draw on general knowledge to infer missing concepts or events that are essential to sequencing the given events. Competitors should be careful to infer only what is essential to the sequence. The plausibility of the wrong alternatives will always require the inclusion of unlikely events or of additional chains of events which are NOT essential to sequencing the given events.

It's very important to remember that you are looking for the best of the four possible choices, and that the best choice of all may not even be one of the answers you're given to choose from.

There is no one right way to solve these problems. Many people have found it helpful to first write out the order of the sentences, as they would have arranged them, on their scrap paper before looking at the possible answers. If their optimum answer is there, this can save them some time. If it isn't, this method can still give insight into solving the problem. Others find it most helpful to just go through each of the possible choices, contrasting each as they go along. You should use whatever method feels comfortable and works for you.

While most of these types of questions are not that difficult, we've added a higher percentage of the difficult type, just to give you more practice. Usually there are only one or two questions on this section that contain such subtle distinctions that you're unable to answer confidently. And you then may find yourself stuck deciding between two possible choices, neither of which you're sure about.

---

# PARAGRAPH REARRANGEMENT COMMENTARY

# EXAMINATION SECTION

# TEST 1

DIRECTIONS: The following groups of sentences need to be arranged in an order that makes sense. Select the letter preceding the sequence that represents the BEST sentence order. *PRINT THE LETTER OF THE CORRECT ANSWER IN THE SPACE AT THE RIGHT.*

1. I. The keyboard was purposely designed to be a little awkward to slow typists down. 1.____
   II. The arrangement of letters on the keyboard of a typewriter was not designed for the convenience of the typist.
   III. Fortunately, no one is suggesting that a new keyboard be designed right away.
   IV. If one were, we would have to learn to type all over again.
   V. The reason was that the early machines were slower than the typists and would jam easily.

   The CORRECT answer is:
   A. I, III, IV, II, V
   B. II, V, I, IV, III
   C. V, I, II, III, IV
   D. II, I, V, III, IV

2. I. The majority of the new service jobs are part-time or low-paying. 2.____
   II. According to the U.S. Bureau of Labor Statistics, jobs in the service sector constitute 72% of all jobs in this country.
   III. If more and more workers receive less and less money, who will buy the goods and services needed to keep the economy going?
   IV. The service sector is by far the fastest growing part of the United States economy.
   V. Some economists look upon this trend with great concern.

   The CORRECT answer is:
   A. II, IV, I, V, III
   B. II, III, IV, I, V
   C. V, IV, II, III, I
   D. III, I, II, IV, V

3. I. They can also affect one's endurance. 3.____
   II. This can stabilize blood sugar levels, and ensure that the brain is receiving a steady, constant, supply of glucose, so that one is *hitting on all cylinders* while taking the test.
   III. By food, we mean real food, not junk food or unhealthy snacks.
   IV. For this reason, it is important not to skip a meal, and to bring food with you to the exam.
   V. One's blood sugar levels can affect how clearly one is able to think and concentrate during an exam.

   The CORRECT answer is:
   A. V, IV, II, III, I
   B. V, II, I, IV, III
   C. V, I, IV, III, II
   D. V, IV, I, III, II

4. I. Those who are the embodiment of desire are absorbed in material quests, and those who are the embodiment of feeling are warriors who value power more than possession. 4.____
   II. These qualities are in everyone, but in different degrees.
   III. But those who value understanding yearn not for goods or victory, but for knowledge.
   IV. According to Plato, human behavior flows from three main sources: desire, emotion, and knowledge.
   V. In the perfect state, the industrial forces would produce but not rule, the military would protect but not rule, and the forces of knowledge, the philosopher kings, would reign.

   The CORRECT answer is:
   A. IV, V, I, II, III
   B. V, I, II, III, IV
   C. IV, III, II, I, V
   D. IV, II, I, III, V

5. I. Of the more than 26,000 tons of garbage produced daily in New York City, 12,000 tons arrive daily at Fresh Kills. 5.____
   II. In a month, enough garbage accumulates there to fill the Empire State Building.
   III. In 1937, the Supreme Court halted the practice of dumping the trash of New York City into the sea.
   IV. Although the garbage is compacted, in a few years the mounds of garbage at Fresh Kills will be the highest points south of Maine's Mount Desert Island on the Eastern Seaboard.
   V. Instead, tugboats now pull barges of much of the trash to Staten Island and the largest landfill in the world, Fresh Kills.

   The CORRECT answer is:
   A. III, V, IV, I, II
   B. III, V, II, IV, I
   C. III, V, I, II, IV
   D. III, II, V, IV, I

6. I. Communists rank equality very high, but freedom very low. 6.____
   II. Unlike communists, conservatives place a high value on freedom and a very low value on equality.
   III. A recent study demonstrated that one way to classify people's political beliefs is to look at the importance placed on two words: freedom and equality.
   IV. Thus, by demonstrating how members of these groups feel about the two words, the study has proved to be useful for political analysts in several European countries.
   V. According to the study, socialists and liberals rank both freedom and equality very high, while fascists rate both very low.

   The CORRECT answer is:
   A. III, V, I, II, IV
   B. V, IV, III, I, II
   C. III, V, IV, II, I
   D. III, I, II, IV, V

7. I. "Can there be anything more amazing than this?" 7.____
   II. If the riddle is successfully answered, his dead brothers will be brought back to life.
   III. "Even though man sees those around him dying every day," says Dharmaraj, "he still believes and acts as if he were immortal."
   IV. "What is the cause of ceaseless wonder?" asks the Lord of the Lake.
   V. In the ancient epic, The Mahabharata, a riddle is asked of one of the Pandava brothers.

   The CORRECT answer is:
   A. V, II, I, IV, III
   B. V, IV, III, I, II
   C. V, II, IV, III, I
   D. V, II, IV, I, III

8. I. On the contrary, the two main theories—the cooperative (neoclassical) theory and the radical (labor theory)—clearly rest on very different assumptions, which have very different ethical overtones. 8.____
   II. The distribution of income is the primary factor in determining the relative levels of material well-being that different groups or individuals attain.
   III. Of all issues in economics, the distribution of income is one of the most controversial.
   IV. The neoclassical theory tends to support the existing income distribution (or minor changes), while the labor theory ends to support substantial changes in the way income is distributed.
   V. The intensity of the controversy reflects the fact that different economic theories are not purely neutral, *detached* theories with no ethical or moral implications.

   The CORRECT answer is:
   A. II, I, V, IV, III
   B. III, II, V, I, IV
   C. III, V, II, I, IV
   D. III, V, IV, I, II

9. I. The pool acts as a broker and ensures that the cheapest power gets used first. 9.____
   II. Every six seconds, the pool's computer monitors all of the generating stations in the state and decides which to ask for more power and which to cut back.
   III. The buying and selling of electrical power is handled by the New York Power Pool in Guilderland, New York.
   IV. This is to the advantage of both the buying and selling utilities.
   V. The pool began operation in 1970, and consists of the state's eight electric utilities.

   The CORRECT answer is:
   A. V, I, II, III, IV
   B. IV, II, I, III, V
   C. III, V, I, IV, II
   D. V, III, IV, II, I

10. I. Modern English is much simpler grammatically than Old English. 10.____
    II. Finnish grammar is very complicated; there are some fifteen cases, for example.
    III. Chinese, a very old language, may seem to be the exception, but it is the great number of characters/words that must be mastered that makes it so difficult to learn, not its grammar.
    IV. The newest literary language—that is, written as well as spoken—is Finish, whose literary roots go back only to about the middle of the nineteenth century.
    V. Contrary to popular belief, the longer a language is been in use the simpler its grammar—not the reverse.

    The CORRECT answer is:
    A. IV, I, II, III, V
    B. V, I, IV, II, III
    C. I, II, IV, III, V
    D. IV, II, III, I, V

---

# KEY (CORRECT ANSWERS)

| | | | |
|---|---|---|---|
| 1. | D | 6. | A |
| 2. | A | 7. | C |
| 3. | C | 8. | B |
| 4. | D | 9. | C |
| 5. | C | 10. | B |

---

# TEST 2

DIRECTIONS: This type of question tests your ability to recognize accurate paraphrasing, well-constructed paragraphs, and appropriate style and tone. It is important that the answer you select contains only the facts or concepts given in the original sentences. It is also important that you be aware of incomplete sentences, inappropriate transitions, unsupported opinions, incorrect usage, and illogical sentence order. Paragraphs that do not include all the necessary facts and concepts, that distort them, or that add new ones are not considered correct.

The format for this section may vary. Sometimes, long paragraphs are given, and emphasis is placed on style and organization. Our first five questions are of this type. Other times, the paragraphs are shorter, and there is less emphasis on style and more emphasis on accurate representation of information. Our second group of five questions are of this nature.

For each of Questions 1 through 10, select the paragraph that BEST expresses the ideas contained in the sentences above it. *PRINT THE LETTER OF THE CORRECT ANSWER IN THE SPACE AT THE RIGHT.*

1. I. Listening skills are very important for managers. 1.____
   II. Listening skills are not usually emphasized.
   III. Whenever managers are depicted in books, manuals or the media, they are always talking, never listening.
   IV. We'd like you to read the enclosed handout on listening skills and to try to consciously apply them this week.
   V. We guarantee they will improve the quality of your interactions.

   A. Unfortunately, listening skills are not usually emphasized for managers. Managers are always depicted as talking, never listening. We'd like you to read the enclosed handout on listening skills. Please try to apply these principles this week. If you do, we guarantee they will improve the quality of your interactions.
   B. The enclosed handout on listening skills will be important improving the quality of your interactions. We guarantee it. All you have to do is take sometime this week to read and to consciously try to apply the principles. Listening skills are very important for manages, but they are not usually emphasized. Whenever managers are depicted in books, manuals or the media, they are always talking, never listening.
   C. Listening well is one of the most important skills a manager can have, yet it's not usually given much attention. Think about any representation of managers in books, manuals, or in the media that you may have seen. They're always talking, never listening. We'd like you to read the enclosed handout on listening skills and consciously try to apply them the rest of the week. We guarantee you will see a difference in the quality of your interactions.

D. Effective listening, one very important tool in the effective manager's arsenal, is usually not emphasized enough. The usual depiction of managers in books, manuals or the media is one in which they are always talking, never listening. We'd like you to read the enclosed handout and consciously try to apply the information contained therein throughout the rest of the week. We feel sure that you will see a marked difference in the quality of your interactions.

2. I. Chekhov wrote three dramatic masterpieces which share certain themes and formats: Uncle Vanya, The Cherry Orchard, and The Three Sisters. 2.____

II. They are primarily concerned with the passage of time and how this erodes human aspirations.

III. The plays are haunted by the ghosts of the wasted life.

IV. The characters are concerned with life's lesser problems; however, such as the inability to make decisions, loyalty to the wrong cause, and the inability to be clear.

V. This results in sweet, almost aching, type of a sadness referred to as Chekhovian.

A. Chekhov wrote three dramatic masterpieces: Uncle Vanya, The Cherry Orchard, and The Three Sisters. These masterpieces share certain themes and formats: the passage of time, how time erodes human aspirations, and the ghosts of wasted life. Each masterpiece is characterized by a sweet, almost aching, type of sadness that has become known as Chekhovian. The sweetness of this sadness hinges on the fact that it is not the great tragedies of life which are destroying these characters, but their minor flaws: indecisiveness, misplaced loyalty, unclarity.

B. The Cherry Orchard, Uncle Vanya, and The Three Sisters are three dramatic masterpieces written by Chekhov that use similar formats to explore a common theme. Each is primarily concerned with the way that passing time wears down human aspirations, and each is haunted by the ghosts of the wasted life. The characters are shown struggling futilely with the lesser problems of life: indecisiveness, loyalty to the wrong cause, and the inability to be clear. These struggles create a mood of sweet, almost aching, sadness that has become known as Chekhovian.

C. Chekhov's dramatic masterpieces are, along with The Cherry Orchard, Uncle Vanya, and The Three Sisters. These plays share certain thematic and formal similarities. They are concerned most of all with the passage of time and the way in which time erodes human aspirations. Each play is haunted by the specter of the wasted life. Chekhov's characters are caught, however, by life's lesser snares: indecisiveness, loyalty to the wrong cause, and unclarity. The characteristic mood is a sweet, almost aching type of sadness that has come to be known as Chekhovian.

D. A Chekhovian mood is characterized by sweet, almost aching, sadness. The term comes from three dramatic tragedies by Chekhov which revolve around the sadness of a wasted life. The three masterpieces (Uncle Vanya, The Three Sisters, and The Cherry Orchard) share the same theme and format. The plays are concerned with how the passage of time erodes human aspirations. They are peopled with characters who are struggling with life's lesser problems. These are people who are indecisive, loyal to the wrong causes, or are unable to make themselves clear.

3. I. Movie previews have often helped producers decide which parts of movies they should take out or leave in. 3.____
II. The first 1933 preview of King Kong was very helpful to the producers because many people ran screaming from the theater and would not return when four men first attacked by Kong were eaten by giant spiders.
III. The 1950 premiere of Sunset Boulevard resulted in the filming of an entirely new beginning, and a delay of six months in the film's release.
IV. In the original opening scene, William Holden was in a morgue talking with thirty-six other "corpses" about the ways some of them had died.
V. When he began to tell them of his life with Gloria Swanson, the audience found this hilarious, instead of taking the scene seriously.

A. Movie previews have often helped producers decide what parts of movies they should leave in or take out. For example, the first preview of King Kong in 1933 was very helpful. In one scene, four men were first attacked by Kong and then eaten by giant spiders. Many members of the audience ran screaming from the theater and would not return. The premiere of the 1950 film Sunset Boulevard was also very helpful. In the original opening scene, William Holden was in a morgue with thirty-six other "corpses," discussing the ways some of them had died. When he began to tell them of his life with Gloria Swanson, the audience found this hilarious. They were supposed to take the scene seriously. The result was a delay of six months in the release of the film while a new beginning was added.
B. Movie previews have often helped producers decide whether they should change various parts of a movie. After the 1933 preview of King Kong, a scene in which four men who had been attacked by Kong were eaten by giant spiders was taken out as many people ran screaming from the theater and would not return. The 1950 premiere of Sunset Boulevard also led to some changes. In the original opening scene, William Holden was in a morgue talking with thirty-six other "corpses" about the ways some of them had died. When he began to tell them of his life with Gloria Swanson, the audience found this hilarious, instead of taking the scene seriously.
C. What do Sunset Boulevard and King Kong have in common? Both show the value of using movie previews to test audience reaction. The first 1933 preview of King Kong showed that a scene showing four men being eaten by giant spiders after having been attacked by Kong was too frightening for many people. They ran screaming from the theater and couldn't be coaxed back. The 1950 premiere of Sunset Boulevard was also a scream, but not the kind the producers intended. The movie opens

with William Holden lying in a morgue discussing the ways they had died with thirty-six other "corpses." When he began to tell them of his life with Gloria Swanson, the audience couldn't take him seriously. Their laughter caused a six-month delay while the beginning was rewritten.

D. Producers very often use movie previews to decide if changes are needed. The premiere of Sunset Boulevard in 1950 led to a new beginning and a six-month delay in film release. At the beginning, William Holden and thirty-six other "corpses" discuss the ways some of them died. Rather than taking this seriously, the audience thought it was hilarious when he began to tell them of his life with Gloria Swanson. The first 1933 preview of King Kong was very helpful for its producers because one scene so terrified the audience that many of them ran screaming from the theater and would not return. In this particular scene, four men who had first been attacked by Kong were eaten by giant spiders.

4. I. It is common for supervisors to view employees as "things" to be manipulated. 4._____

II. This approach does not motivate employees, nor does the carrot-and-stick approach because employees often recognize these behaviors and resent them.

III. Supervisors can change these behaviors by using self-inquiry and persistence.

IV. The best managers genuinely respect those they work with, are supportive and helpful, and are interested in working as a team with those they supervise.

V. They disagree with the Golden Rule that says "he or she who has the gold makes the rules."

A. Some managers act as if they think the Golden Rule means "he or she who has the gold makes the rules." They show disrespect to employees by seeing them as "things" to be manipulated. Obviously, this approach does not motivate employees any more than the carrot-and-stick approach motivates them. The employees are smart enough to spot these behaviors and resent them. On the other hand, the managers genuinely respect those they work with, are supportive and helpful, and are interested in working as a team. Self-inquiry and persistence can change even the former type of supervisor into the latter.

B. Many supervisors all into the trap of viewing employees as "things" to be manipulated, or try to motivate them by using a carrot-and-stick approach. These methods do not motivate employees, who often recognize the behaviors and resent them. Supervisors can change these behaviors, however, by using self-inquiry and persistence. The best managers are supportive and helpful, and have genuine respect for those with whom they work. They are interested in working as a team with those they supervise. To them, the Golden Rule is not "he or she who has the gold makes the rules."

C. Some supervisors see employees as "things" to be used or manipulated using a carrot-and-stick technique. These methods don't work. Employees often see through them and resent them. A supervisor who wants to change may do so. The techniques of self-inquiry and persistence can be used to turn him or her into the type of supervisor who doesn't think the Golden Rule is "he or she who has the gold makes the rules." They may become like the best managers who treat those with whom they work with respect and give them help and support. These are the manager who know how to build a team.

D. Unfortunately, many supervisors act as if their employees are objects whose movements they can position at will. This mistaken belief has the same result as another popular motivational technique—the carrot-and-stick approach. Both attitudes can lead to the same result—resentment from those employees who recognize the behaviors for what they are. Supervisors who recognize these behaviors can change through the use of persistence and the use of self-inquiry. It's important to remember that the best managers respect their employees. They readily give necessary help and support and are interested in working as a team with those they supervise. To these managers, the Golden Rule is not "he or she who has the gold makes the rules."

5. I. The first half of the nineteenth century produced a group of pessimistic poets—Byron, De Musset, Heine, Pushkin, and Leopardi. 5.____

II. It also produced a group of pessimistic composers—Schubert, Chopin, Schumann, and even the later Beethoven.

III. Above all, in philosophy, there was the profoundly pessimistic philosopher, Schopenhauer.

IV. The Revolution was dead, the Bourbons were restored, the feudal barons were reclaiming their land, and progress everywhere was being suppressed, as the great age was over.

V. "I thank God," said Goethe, "that I am not young in so thoroughly finished a world."

A. "I thank God," said Goethe, "that I am not young in so thoroughly finished a world." The Revolution was dead, the Bourbons were restored, the feudal barons were reclaiming their land, and progress everywhere was being suppressed. The first half of the nineteenth century produced a group of pessimistic poets: Byron, De Musset, Heine, Pushkin, and Leopardi. It also produced pessimistic composers: Schubert, Chopin, Schumann. Although Beethoven came later, he fits into this group, too. Finally and above all, it also produced a profoundly pessimistic philosopher, Schopenhauer. The great age was over.

B. The first half of the nineteenth century produced a group of pessimistic poets: Byron, De Musset, Heine, Pushkin, and Leopardi. It produced a group of pessimistic composers: Schubert, Chopin, Schumann, and even the later Beethoven. Above all, it produced a profoundly pessimistic philosopher, Schopenhauer. For each of these men, the great age was over. The Revolution was dead, and the Bourbons were restored. The feudal barons were reclaiming their land, and progress everywhere was being suppressed.

C. The great age was over. The Revolution was dead—the Bourbons were restored, and the feudal barons were reclaiming their land. Progress everywhere was being suppressed. Out of this climate came a profound pessimism. Poets, like Byron, De Musset, Heine, Pushkin, and Leopardi; composers, like Schubert, Chopin, Schumann, and even the later Beethoven; and above all, a profoundly pessimistic philosopher, Schopenauer. This pessimism which arose in the first half of the nineteenth century is illustrated by these words of Goethe, "I thank God that I am not young in so thoroughly finished a world."

D. The first half of the nineteenth century produced a group of pessimistic poets, Byron, De Musset, Heine, Pushkin, and Leopardi—and a group of pessimistic composers, Schubert, Chopin, Schumann, and the later Beethoven. Above it all, it produced a profoundly pessimistic philosopher, Schopenhauer. The great age was over. The Revolution was dead, the Bourbons were restored, the feudal barons were reclaiming their land, and progress everywhere was being suppressed. "I thank God," said Goethe, "that I am not young in so thoroughly finished a world."

6. I. A new manager sometimes may feel insecure about his or her competence in the new position. 6.____

II. The new manager may then exhibit defensive or arrogant behavior towards those one supervises, or the new manager may direct overly flattering behavior toward one's new supervisor.

A. Sometimes, a new manager may feel insecure about his or her ability to perform well in this new position. The insecurity may lead him or her to treat others differently. He or she may display arrogant or defensive behavior towards those he or she supervises, or be overly flattering to his or her new supervisor.

B. A new manager may sometimes feel insecure about his or her ability to perform well in the new position. He or she may then become arrogant, defensive, or overly flattering towards those he or she works with.

C. There are times when a new manager may be insecure about how well he or she can perform in the new job. The new manager may also behave defensive or act in an arrogant way towards those he or she supervises, or overly flatter his or her boss.

D. Sometimes a new manager may feel insecure about his or her ability to perform well in the new position. He or she may then display arrogant or defensive behavior towards those they supervise, or become overly flattering towards their supervisors.

7. I. It is possible to eliminate unwanted behavior by bringing it under stimulus control—tying the behavior to a cue, and then never, or rarely, giving the cue. 7.____

II. One trainer successfully used this method to keep an energetic young porpoise from coming out of her tank whenever she felt like it, which was potentially dangerous.

III. Her trainer taught her to do it for a reward, in response to a hand signal, and then rarely gave the signal.

A. Unwanted behavior can be eliminated by tying the behavior to a cue, and then never, or rarely, giving the cue. This is called stimulus control. One trainer was able to use this method to keep an energetic young porpoise from coming out of her tank by teaching her to come out for a reward in response to a hand signal, and then rarely giving the signal.
B. Stimulus control can be used to eliminate unwanted behavior. In this method, behavior is tied to a cue, and then the cue is rarely, if ever, given. One trainer was able to successfully use stimulus control to keep an energetic young porpoise from coming out of her tank whenever she felt like it—a potentially dangerous practice. She taught the porpoise to come out for a reward when she gave a hand signal, and then rarely gave the signal.
C. It is possible to eliminate behavior that is undesirable by bringing it under stimulus control by tying behavior to a signal, and then rarely giving the signal. One trainer successfully used this method to keep an energetic porpoise from coming out of her tank, a potentially dangerous situation. Her trainer taught the porpoise to do it for a reward, in response to a hand signal, and then would rarely give the signal.
D. By using stimulus control, it is possible to eliminate unwanted behavior by tying the behavior to a cue, and then rarely or never give the cue. One trainer was able to use this method to successfully stop a young porpoise from coming out of her tank whenever she felt like it. To curb this potentially dangerous practice, the porpoise was taught by the trainer to come out of the tank for a reward, in response to a hand signal, and then rarely given the signal.

8. I. There is a great deal of concern over the safety of commercial trucks, caused by their greatly increased role in serious accidents since federal deregulation in 1981. 8.____
II. Recently, 60 percent of trucks in New York and Connecticut and 70 percent of trucks in Maryland randomly stopped by state troopers failed safety inspections.
III. Sixteen states in the United States require no training at all for truck drivers.

A. Since federal deregulation in 1981, there has been a great deal of concern over the safety of commercial trucks, and their greatly increased role in serious accidents. Recently, 60 percent of trucks in New York and Connecticut, and 70 percent of trucks in Maryland failed safety inspections. Sixteen states in the United States require no training at all for truck drivers.
B. There is a great deal of concern over the safety of commercial trucks since federal deregulation in 1981. Their role in serious accidents has greatly increased. Recently, 60 percent of trucks randomly stopped in Connecticut and New York and 70 percent in Maryland failed safety inspections conducted by state troopers. Sixteen states in the United States provide no training at all for truck drivers.
C. Commercial trucks have a greatly increased role in serious accidents since federal deregulation in 1981. This has led to a great deal of concern.

Recently, 70 percent of trucks in Maryland and 60 percent of trucks in New York and Connecticut failed inspection of those that were randomly stopped by state troopers. Sixteen states in the United States require no training for all truck drivers.

D. Since federal deregulation in 1981, the role that commercial trucks have played in serious accidents has greatly increased, and this has led to a great deal of concern. Recently, 60 percent of trucks in New York and Connecticut, and 70 percent of trucks in Maryland randomly stopped by state troopers failed safety inspections. Sixteen states in the U.S. don't require any training for truck drivers.

9. I. No matter how much some people have, they still feel unsatisfied and want more, or want to keep what they have forever. 9.____

II. One recent television documentary showed several people flying from New York to Paris for a one-day shopping spree to buy platinum earrings, because they were bored.

III. In Brazil, some people were ordering coffins that cost a minimum of $45,000 and are equipping them with deluxe stereos, televisions, and other graveyard necessities.

A. Some people, despite having a great deal, still feel unsatisfied and want more, or think they can keep what they have forever. One recent documentary on television showed several people enroute from Paris to New York for a one day shopping spree to buy platinum earrings, because they were bored. Some people in Brazil are even ordering coffins equipped with such graveyard necessities as deluxe stereos and televisions. The price of the coffins start at $45,000.

B. No matter how much some people have, they may feel unsatisfied. This leads them to want more, or to want to keep what they have forever. Recently, a television documentary depicting several people flying from New York to Paris for a one day shopping spree to buy platinum earrings. They were bored. Some people in Brazil are ordering coffins that cost at least $45,000 and come equipped with deluxe televisions, stereos and other necessary graveyard items.

C. Some people will be dissatisfied no matter how much they have. They may want more, or they may want to keep what they have forever. One recent television documentary showed several people, motivated by boredom, jetting from New York to Paris for a one-day shopping spree to buy platinum earrings. In Brazil, some people are ordering coffins equipped with deluxe stereos, televisions and other graveyard necessities. The minimum price for these coffins—$45,000.

D. Some people are never satisfied. No matter how much they have they still want more, or think they can keep what they have forever. One television documentary recently showed several people flying from New York to Paris for the day to buy platinum earrings because they were bored. In Brazil, some people are ordering coffins that cost $45,000 and are equipped with deluxe stereos, televisions and other graveyard necessities.

10. I. A television signal or video signal has three parts. 10.____
II. Its parts are the black-and-white portion, the color portion, and the synchronizing (sync) pulses, which keep the picture stable.
III. Each video source, whether it's a camera or a video-cassette recorder contains its own generator of these synchronizing pulses to accompany the picture that it's sending in order to keep it steady and straight.
IV. In order to produce a clean recording, a video-cassette recorder must "lock-up" to the sync pulses that are part of the video it is trying to record, and this effort may be very noticeable if the device does not have gunlock.

A. There are three parts to a television or video signal: the black-and-white part, the color part, and the synchronizing (sync) pulses, which keep the picture stable. Whether it's a video-cassette recorder or a camera, each video source contains its own pulse that synchronizes and generates the picture it's sending in order to keep it straight and steady. A video-cassette recorder must "lock up" to the sync pulses that are part of the video it's trying to record. If the device doesn't have gunlock, this effort must be very noticeable.
B. A video signal or television is comprised of three parts: the black-and-white portion, the color portion, and the sync (synchronizing) pulses, which keep the picture stable. Whether it's a camera or a video-cassette recorder, each video source contains its own generator of these synchronizing pulses. These accompany the picture that it's sending in order to keep it straight and steady. A video-cassette recorder must "lock up" to the sync pulses that are part of the video it is trying to record in order to produce a clean recording. This effort may be very noticeable if the device does not have gunlock.
C. There are three parts to a television or video signal: the color portion, the black-and-white portion, and the sync (synchronizing pulses). These keep the picture stable. Each video source, whether it's a video-cassette recorder or a camera, generates these synchronizing pulses accompanying the picture it's sending in order to keep it straight and steady. If a clean recording is to be produced, a video-cassette recorder must store the sync pulses that are part of the video it is trying to record. This effort may not be noticeable if the device does not have gunlock.
D. A television signal or video signal has three parts: the black-and-white portion, the color portion, and the synchronizing (sync) pulses. It's the sync pulses which keep the picture stable, which accompany it and keep it steady and straight. Whether it's a camera or a video-cassette recorder, each video source contains its own generator of these synchronizing pulses. To produce a clean recording, a video-cassette recorder must "lock up" to the sync pulses that are part of the video it is trying to record. If the device does not have gunlock, this effort may be very noticeable.

# KEY (CORRECT ANSWERS)

| | | | |
|---|---|---|---|
| 1. | C | 6. | A |
| 2. | B | 7. | B |
| 3. | A | 8. | D |
| 4. | B | 9. | C |
| 5. | D | 10. | D |

# PREPARING WRITTEN MATERIALS

# EXAMINATION SECTION

## TEST 1

DIRECTIONS: Each question consists of a sentence which may be classified appropriately under one of the following four categories:

A. Incorrect because of faulty grammar or sentence structure;
B. Incorrect because of faulty punctuation;
C. Incorrect because of faulty capitalization;
D. Correct

Examine each sentence carefully. Then, in the space at the right, indicate the letter preceding the category which is the BEST of the four suggested above. Each incorrect sentence contains only one type of error. Consider a sentence correct if it contains no errors, although there may be other correct ways of expressing the same thought.

1. All the employees, in this office, are over twenty-one years old. 1.____

2. Neither the clerk nor the stenographer was able to explain what had happened. 2.____

3. Mr. Johnson did not know who he would assign to type the order. 3.____

4. Mr. Marshall called her to report for work on Saturday. 4.____

5. He might of arrived on time if the train has not been delayed. 5.____

6. Some employees on the other hand, are required to fill out these forms every month. 6.____

7. The supervisor issued special instructions to his subordinates to prevent their making errors. 7.____

8. Our supervisor Mr. Williams, expects to be promoted in about two weeks. 8.____

9. We were informed that prof. Morgan would attend the conference. 9.____

10. The clerks were assigned to the old building; the stenographers, to the new building. 10.____

11. The supervisor asked Mr. Smith and I to complete the work as quickly as possible. 11.____

12. He said, that before an employee can be permitted to leave, the report must be finished. 12.____

13. A calculator, in addition to the three computers, are needed in the new office. 13.____

14. Having made many errs in her work, the supervisor asked the typist to be more careful. 14.____

15. "If you are given an assignment," he said, "you should begin work on it as quickly as possible." 15.____

16. All the clerks, including those who have been appointed recently are required to work on the new assignment. 16.____

17. The office manager asked each employee to work one Saturday a month. 17.____

18. Neither Mr. Smith nor Mr. Jones was able to finish his assignment on time. 18.___

19. The task of filing these cards is to be divided equally between you and he. 19.____

20. He is an employee whom we consider to be efficient. 20.____

21. I believe that the new employees are not as punctual as us. 21.____

22. The employees, working in this office, are to be congratulated for their work. 22.____

23. The delay in preparing the report was caused, in his opinion, by the lack of proper supervision and coordination. 23.____

24. John Jones accidentally pushed the wrong button and then all the lights went out. 24.____

25. The investigator ought to of had the witness sign the statement. 25.____

---

# KEY (CORRECT ANSWERS)

1. B
2. D
3. A
4. C
5. A

6. B
7. D
8. B
9. C
10. D

11. A
12. B
13. A
14. A
15. D

16. B
17. C
18. D
19. A
20. D

21. A
22. B
23. D
24. D
25. A

# TEST 2

Questions 1-10.

DIRECTIONS: Each of the following sentences may be classified under one of the following four options:

A. Faulty; contains an error in grammar only
B. Faulty; contains an error in spelling only
C. Faulty; contains an error in grammar and an error in spelling
D. Correct; contains no error in grammar or in spelling

Examine each sentence carefully to determine under which of the above four options it is BEST classified. Then, in the space at the right, write the letter preceding the option which is the best of the four listed above.

1. A recognized principle of good management is that an assignment should be given to whomever is best qualified to carry it out. 1.____

2. He considered it a privilege to be allowed to review and summarize the technical reports issued annually by your agency. 2.____

3. Because the warehouse was in an inaccessible location, deliveries of electric fixtures from the warehouse were made only in large lots. 3.____

4. Having requisitioned the office supplies, Miss Brown returned to her desk and resumed the computation of petty cash disbursements. 4.____

5. One of the advantages of this chemical solution is that records treated with it are not inflamable. 5.____

6. The complaint of this employee, in addition to the complaints of the other employees, were submitted to the grievance committee. 6.____

7. A study of the duties and responsibilities of each of the various categories of employees was conducted by an unprejudiced classification analyst. 7.____

8. Ties of friendship with this subordinate compels him to withold the censure that the subordinate deserves. 8.____

9. Neither of the agencies are affected by the decision to institute a program for rehabilitating physically handi-caped men and women. 9.____

10. The chairman stated that the argument between you and he was creating an intolerable situation. 10.____

Questions 11-25.

DIRECTIONS: Each of the following sentences may be classified under one of the following four options:
A. Correct
B. Sentence contains an error in spelling
C. Sentence contains an error in grammar
D. Sentence contains errors in both grammar and spelling.

11. He reported that he had had a really good time during his vacation although the farm was located in a very inaccessible portion of the country. 11.____

12. It looks to me like he has been fasinated by that beautiful painting. 12.____

13. We have permitted these kind of pencils to accumulate on our shelves, knowing we can sell them at a profit of five cents apiece any time we choose. 13.____

14. Believing that you will want an unexagerated estimate of the amount of business we can expect, I have made every effort to secure accurate figures. 14.____

15. Each and every man, woman and child in that untrammeled wilderness carry guns for protection against the wild animals. 15.____

16. Although this process is different than the one to which he is accustomed, a good chemist will have no trouble. 16.____

17. Insensible to the fuming and fretting going on about him, the engineer continued to drive the mammoth dynamo to its utmost capacity. 17.____

18. Everyone had studied his lesson carefully and was consequently well prepared when the instructor began to discuss the fourth dimention. 18.____

19. I learned Johnny six new arithmetic problems this afternoon. 19.____

20. Athletics is urged by our most prominent citizens as the pursuit which will enable the younger generation to achieve that ideal of education, a sound mind in a sound body. 20.____

21. He did not see whoever was at the door very clearly but thinks it was the city tax appraiser. 21.____

22. He could not scarsely believe that his theories had been substantiated in this convincing fashion. 22.____

23. Although you have displayed great ingenuity in carrying out your assignments, the choice for the position still lies among Brown and Smith. 23.____

24. If they had have pleaded at the time that Smith was an accessory to the crime, it would have lessened the punishment. 24.____

25. It has proven indispensible in his compilation of the facts in the matter. 25.____

---

# KEY (CORRECT ANSWERS)

1. A
2. D
3. B
4. D
5. B

6. A
7. D
8. C
9. C
10. A

11. A
12. D
13. C
14. B
15. D

16. C
17. A
18. B
19. C
20. A

21. B
22. D
23. C
24. D
25. B

# TEST 3

Questions 1-5.

DIRECTIONS: Questions 1 through 5 consist of sentences which may or may not contain errors in grammar or spelling or both. Sentences which do not contain errors in grammar or spelling or both are to be considered correct, even though there may be other correct ways of expressing the same thought. Examine each sentence carefully. Then, in the space at the right, write the letter of the answer which is the BEST of those suggested below.

A. If the sentence is correct
B. If the sentence contains an error in spelling
C. If the sentence contains an error in grammar
D. If the sentence contains errors in both grammar and spelling.

1. Brown is doing fine although the work is irrevelant to his training. 1.____

2. The conference of sales managers voted to set its adjournment at one o'clock in order to give those present an opportunity to get rid of all merchandise. 2.____

3. He decided that in view of what had taken place at the hotel that he ought to stay and thank the benificent stranger who had rescued him from an embarassing situation. 3.____

4. Since you object to me criticizing your letter, I have no alternative but to consider you a mercenary scoundrel. 4.____

5. I rushed home ahead of schedule so that you will leave me go to the picnic with Mary. 5.____

Questions 6-15.

DIRECTIONS: Some of the following sentences contain an error in spelling, word usage, or sentence structure, or punctuation. Some sentences are correct as they stand although there may be other correct ways of expressing the same thought. All incorrect sentences contain only one error. Mark your answer to each question in the space at the right as follows:

A. If the sentence has an error in spelling
B. If the sentence has an error in punctuation or capitalization
C. If the sentence has an error in word usage or sentence structure
D. If the sentence is correct

6. Because the chairman failed to keep the participants from wandering off into irrelevant discussions, it was impossible to reach a consensus before the meeting was adjourned. 6.____

7. Certain employers have an unwritten rule that any applicant, who is over 55 years of age, is automatically excluded from consideration for any position whatsoever. 7.____

8. If the proposal to build schools in some new apartment buildings were to be accepted by the builders, one of the advantages that could be expected to result would be better communication between teachers and parents of schoolchildren. 8.____

9. In this instance, the manufacturer's violation of the law against deseptive packaging was discernible only to an experienced inspector. 9.____

10. The tenants' anger stemmed from the president's going to Washington to testify without consulting them first. 10.____

11. Did the president of this eminent banking company say; "We intend to hire and train a number of these disadvantaged youths?" 11.____

12. In addition, today's confidential secretary must be knowledgable in many different areas: for example, she must know modern techniques for making travel arrangements for the executive. 12.____

13. To avoid further disruption of work in the offices, the protesters were forbidden from entering the building unless they had special passes. 13.____

14. A valuable secondary result of our training conferences is the opportunities afforded for management to observe the reactions of the participants. 14.____

15. Of the two proposals submitted by the committee, the first one is the best. 15.____

Questions 16-25.

DIRECTIONS: Each of the following sentences may be classified MOST appropriately under one of the following three categories:

A. Faulty because of incorrect grammar
B. Faulty because of incorrect punctuation
C. Correct

Examine each sentence. Then, print the capital letter preceding the BEST choice of the three suggested above. All incorrect sentences contain only one type of error. Consider a sentence correct if it contains none of the types of errors mentioned, even though there may be other ways of expressing the same thought.

16. He sent the notice to the clerk who you hired yesterday. 16.____

17. It must be admitted, however that you were not informed of this change. 17.____

18. Only the employees who have served in this grade for at least two years are eligible for promotion. 18.____

19. The work was divided equally between she and Mary. 19.____

20. He thought that you were not available at that time. 20.____

21. When the messenger returns; please give him this package. 21.____

22. The new secretary prepared, typed, addressed, and delivered, the notices. 22.____

23. Walking into the room, his desk can be seen at the rear. 23.____

24. Although John has worked here longer than she, he produces a smaller amount of work. 24.____

25. She said she could of typed this report yesterday. 25.____

---

# KEY (CORRECT ANSWERS)

1. D
2. A
3. D
4. C
5. C

6. A
7. B
8. D
9. A
10. D

11. B
12. A
13. C
14. D
15. C

16. A
17. B
18. C
19. A
20. C

21. B
22. B
23. A
24. C
25. A

---

# TEST 4

Questions 1-5.

DIRECTIONS: Each of the following sentences may be classified MOST appropriately under one of the following three categories:
A. Faulty because of incorrect grammar
B. Faulty because of incorrect punctuation
C. Correct

Examine each sentence. Then, print the capital letter preceding the BEST choice of the three suggested above. All incorrect sentences contain only one type of error. Consider a sentence correct if it contains none of the types of errors mentioned, even though there may be other ways of expressing the same thought.

1. Neither one of these procedures are adequate for the efficient performance of this task. 1.____

2. The keyboard is the tool of the typist; the cash register, the tool of the cashier. 2.____

3. "The assignment must be completed as soon as possible" said the supervisor. 3.____

4. As you know, office handbooks are issued to all new employees. 4.____

5. Writing a speech is sometimes easier than to deliver it before an audience. 5.____

Questions 6-15.

DIRECTIONS: Each statement given in Questions 6 through 15 contains one of the faults of English usage listed below. For each, choose from the options listed the MAJOR fault contained.
A. The statement is not a complete sentence.
B. The statement contains a word or phrase that is redundant.
C. The statement contains a long, less commonly used word when a shorter, more direct word would be acceptable.
D. The statement contains a colloquial expression that normally is avoided in business writing.

6. The fact that this activity will afford an opportunity to meet your group. 6.____

7. Do you think that the two groups can join together for next month's meeting? 7.____

8. This is one of the most exciting new innovations to be introduced into our college. 8.____

9. We expect to consummate the agenda before the meeting ends tomorrow at noon. 9.____

10. While this seminar room is small in size, we think we can use it. 10.____

11. Do you think you can make a modification in the date of the Budget Committee meeting? 11.____

12. We are cognizant of the problem but we think we can ameliorate the situation. 12.____

13. Shall I call you around three on the day I arrive in the City? 13.____

14. Until such time that we know precisely that the students will be present. 14.____

15. The consensus of opinion of all the members present is reported in the minutes. 15.____

Questions 16-25.

DIRECTIONS: For each of Questions 16 through 25, select from the options given below the MOST applicable choice.

A. The sentence is correct.
B. The sentence contains a spelling error only.
C. The sentence contains an English grammar error only.
D. The sentence contains both a spelling error and an English grammar error.

16. Every person in the group is going to do his share. 16.____

17. The man who we selected is new to this University. 17.____

18. She is the older of the four secretaries on the two staffs that are to be combined. 18.____

19. The decision has to be made between him and I. 19.____

20. One of the volunteers are too young for his complicated task, don't you think? 20.____

21. I think your idea is splindid and it will improve this report considerably. 21.____

22. Do you think this is an exagerated account of the behavior you and me observed this morning? 22.____

23. Our supervisor has a clear idea of excelence. 23.____

24. How many occurences were verified by the observers? 24.____

25. We must complete the typing of the draft of the questionaire by noon tomorrow. 25.____

---

## KEY (CORRECT ANSWERS)

| | | | |
|---|---|---|---|
| 1. | A | 11. | C |
| 2. | C | 12. | C |
| 3. | B | 13. | D |
| 4. | C | 14. | A |
| 5. | A | 15. | B |
| 6. | A | 16. | A |
| 7. | B | 17. | C |
| 8. | B | 18. | C |
| 9. | C | 19. | C |
| 10. | B | 20. | D |

| | |
|---|---|
| 21. | B |
| 22. | D |
| 23. | B |
| 24. | B |
| 25. | B |

## PRINCIPLES AND PRACTICES, OF ADMINISTRATION, SUPERVISION AND MANAGEMENT

### TABLE OF CONTENTS


| | Page |
|---|---|
| GENERAL ADMINISTRATION | 1 |
| | |
| SEVEN BASIC FUNCTIONS OF THE SUPERVISOR | 2 |
| I. Planning | 2 |
| II. Organizing | 3 |
| III. Staffing | 3 |
| IV. Directing | 3 |
| V. Coordinating | 3 |
| VI. Reporting | 3 |
| VII. Budgeting | 3 |
| | |
| PLANNING TO MEET MANAGEMENT GOALS | 4 |
| I. What is Planning | 4 |
| II. Who Should Make Plans | 4 |
| III. What are the Results of Poor Planning | 4 |
| IV. Principles of Planning | 4 |
| | |
| MANAGEMENT PRINCIPLES | 5 |
| I. Management | 5 |
| II. Management Principles | 5 |
| III. Organization Structure | 6 |
| | |
| ORGANIZATION | 8 |
| I. Unity of Command | 8 |
| II. Span of Control | 8 |
| III. Uniformity of Assignment | 9 |
| IV. Assignment of Responsibility and Delegation of Authority | 9 |
| | |
| PRINCIPLES OF ORGANIZATION | 9 |
| I. Definition | 9 |
| II. Purpose of Organization | 9 |
| III. Basic Considerations in Organizational Planning | 9 |
| IV. Bases for Organization | 10 |
| V. Assignment of Functions | 10 |
| VI. Delegation of Authority and Responsibility | 10 |
| VII. Employee Relationships | 11 |

DELEGATING 11
- I. WHAT IS DELEGATING: 11
- II. TO WHOM TO DELEGATE 11

REPORTS 12
- I. DEFINITION 12
- II. PURPOSE 12
- III. TYPES 12
- IV. FACTORS TO CONSIDER BEFORE WRITING REPORT 12
- V. PREPARATORY STEPS 12
- VI. OUTLINE FOR A RECOMMENDATION REPORT 12

MANAGEMENT CONTROLS 13
- I. Control 13
- II. Basis for Control 13
- III. Policy 13
- IV. Procedure 14
- V. Basis of Control 14

FRAMEWORK OF MANAGEMENT 14
- I. Elements 14
- II. Manager's Responsibility 15
- III. Control Techniques 16
- IV. Where Forecasts Fit 16

PROBLEM SOLVING 16
- I. Identify the Problem 16
- II. Gather Data 17
- III. List Possible Solutions 17
- IV. Test Possible Solutions 18
- V. Select the Best Solution 18
- VI. Put the Solution into Actual Practice 19

COMMUNICATION 19
- I. What is Communication? 19
- II. Why is Communication Needed? 19
- III. How is Communication Achieved? 20
- IV. Why Does Communication Fail? 21
- V. How to Improve Communication 21
- VI. How to Determine If You Are Getting Across 21
- VII. The Key Attitude 22

HOW ORDERS AND INSTRUCTIONS SHOULD BE GIVEN 22
- I. Characteristics of Good Orders and Instructions 22

FUNCTIONS OF A DEPARTMENT PERSONNEL OFFICE 23

SUPERVISION 23
- I. Leadership 23
  - A. The Authoritarian Approach 23
  - B. The Laissez-Faire Approach 24
  - C. The Democratic Approach 24
- II. Nine Points of Contrast Between Boss and Leader 25

EMPLOYEE MORALE 25
- I. Some Ways to Develop and Maintain Good Employee Morale 25
- II. Some Indicators of Good Morale 26

MOTIVATION 26

EMPLOYEE PARTICIPATION 27
- I. WHAT IS PARTICIPATION 27
- II. WHY IS IT IMPORTANT? 27
- III. HOW MAY SUPERVISORS OBTAIN IT? 28

STEPS IN HANDLING A GRIEVANCE 28

DISCIPLINE 29
- I. THE DISCIPLINARY INTERVIEW 29
- II. PLANNING THE INTERVIEW 29
- III. CONDUCTING THE INTERVIEW 30

## PRINCIPLES AND PRACTICES, OF ADMINISTRATION, SUPERVISION AND MANAGEMENT

Most people are inclined to think of administration as something that only a few persons are responsible for in a large organization. Perhaps this is true if you are thinking of Administration with a capital *A*, but administration with a lower case *a* is a responsibility of supervisors at all levels each working day.

All of us feel we are pretty good supervisors and that we do a good job of administering the workings of our agency. By and large, this is true, but every so often it is good to check up on ourselves. Checklists appear from time to time in various publications which psychologists say tell whether or not a person will make a good wife, husband, doctor, lawyer, or supervisor.

The following questions are an excellent checklist to test yourself as a supervisor and administrator.

Remember, Administration gives direction and points the way but administration carries the ideas to fruition. Each is dependent on the other for its success. Remember, too, that no unit is too small for these departmental functions to be carried out. These statements apply equally as well to the Chief Librarian as to the Department Head with but one or two persons to supervise.

**GENERAL ADMINISTRATION**: General Responsibilities of Supervisors

1. Have I prepared written statements of functions, activities, and duties for my organizational unit?

2. Have I prepared procedural guides for operating activities?

3. Have I established clearly in writing, lines of authority and responsibility for my organizational unit?

4. Do I make recommendations for improvements in organization, policies, administrative and operating routines and procedures, including simplification of work and elimination of non-essential operations?

5. Have I designated and trained an understudy to function in my absence?

6. Do I supervise and train personnel within the unit to effectively perform their assignments?

7. Do I assign personnel and distribute work on such a basis as to carry out the organizational unit's assignment or mission in the most effective and efficient manner?

8. Have I established administrative controls by:

    a. Fixing responsibility and accountability on all supervisors under my direction for the proper performance of their functions and duties.

b. Preparations and submitting periodic work load and progress reports covering the operations of the unit to my immediate superior.

c. Analysis and evaluation of such reports received from subordinate units.

d. Submission of significant developments and problems arising within the organizational unit to my immediate superior.

e. Conducting conferences, inspections, etc., as to the status and efficiency of unit operations.

9. Do I maintain an adequate and competent working force?

10. Have I fostered good employee-department relations, seeing that established rules, regulations, and instructions are being carried out properly?

11. Do I collaborate and consult with other organizational units performing related functions to insure harmonious and efficient working relationships?

12. Do I maintain liaison through prescribed channels with city departments and other governmental agencies concerned with the activities of the unit?

13. Do I maintain contact with and keep abreast of the latest developments and techniques of administration (professional societies, groups, periodicals, etc.) as to their applicability to the activities of the unit?

14. Do I communicate with superiors and subordinates through prescribed organizational channels?

15. Do I notify superiors and subordinates in instances where bypassing is necessary as soon thereafter as practicable?

16. Do I keep my superior informed of significant developments and problems?

**SEVEN BASIC FUNCTIONS OF THE SUPERVISOR**

I. PLANNING

This means working out goals and means to obtain goals. What needs to be done, who will do it, how, when, and where it is to be done.

SEVEN STEPS IN PLANNING

A. Define job or problem clearly.
B. Consider priority of job.
C. Consider time-limit—starting and completing.
D. Consider minimum distraction to, or interference with, other activities.
E. Consider and provide for contingencies—possible emergencies.
F. Break job down into components.

G. Consider the 5 W's and H:
WHY..........is it necessary to do the job? (Is the purpose clearly defined?)
WHAT........needs to be done to accomplish the defined purpose?
.........is needed to do the job? (Money, materials, etc.)
WHO..........is needed to do the job?
..........will have responsibilities?
WHERE......is the work to be done?
WHEN........is the job to begin and end? (Schedules, etc.)
HOW..........is the job to bed done? (Methods, controls, records, etc.)

II. ORGANIZING

This means dividing up the work, establishing clear lines of responsibility and authority and coordinating efforts to get the job done.

III. STAFFING

The whole personnel function of bringing in and training staff, getting the right man and fitting him to the right job—the job to which he is best suited.

In the normal situation, the supervisor's responsibility regarding staffing normally includes providing accurate job descriptions, that is, duties of the jobs, requirements, education and experience, skills, physical, etc.; assigning the work for maximum use of skills; and proper utilization of the probationary period to weed out unsatisfactory employees.

IV. DIRECTING

Providing the necessary leadership to the group supervised. Important work gets done to the supervisor's satisfaction.

V. COORDINATING

The all-important duty of inter-relating the various parts of the work.
The supervisor is also responsible for controlling the coordinated activities. This means measuring performance according to a time schedule and setting quotas to see that the goals previously set are being reached. Reports from workers should be analyzed, evaluated, and made part of all future plans.

VI. REPORTING

This means proper and effective communication to your superiors, subordinates, and your peers (in definition of the job of the supervisor). Reports should be read and information contained therein should be used, not be filed away and forgotten. Reports should be written in such a way that the desired action recommended by the report is forthcoming.

VII. BUDGETING
This means controlling current costs and forecasting future costs. This forecast is based on past experience, future plans and programs, as well as current costs.

You will note that these seven functions can fall under three topics:

| | | |
|---|---|---|
| Planning ) Organizing ) Make a plan | Staffing ) Directing ) Controlling ) Get things done | Reporting ) Budgeting ) Watch it work |

**PLANNING TO MEET MANAGEMENT GOALS**

I. WHAT IS PLANNING?

A. Thinking a job through before new work is done to determine the best way to do it
B. A method of doing something
C. Ways and means for achieving set goals
D. A means of enabling a supervisor to deliver with a minimum of effort, all details involved in coordinating his work

II. WHO SHOULD MAKE PLANS?

Everybody!
All levels of supervision must plan work. (Top management, heads of divisions or bureaus, first line supervisors, and individual employees.) The higher the level, the more planning required.

III. WHAT ARE THE RESULTS OF POOR PLANNING?

A. Failure to meet deadline
B. Low employee morale
C. Lack of job coordination
D. Overtime is frequently necessary
E. Excessive cost, waste of material and manhours

IV. PRINCIPLES OF PLANNING

A. Getting a clear picture of your objectives. What exactly are you trying to accomplish?
B. Plan the whole job, then the parts, in proper sequence.
C. Delegate the planning of details to those responsible for executing them.
D. Make your plan flexible.
E. Coordinate your plan with the plans of others so that the work may be processed with a minimum of delay.
F. Sell your plan before you execute it.
G. Sell your plan to your superior, subordinate, in order to gain maximum participation and coordination.
H. Your plan should take precedence. Use knowledge and skills that others have brought to a similar job.
I. Your plan should take account of future contingencies; allow for future expansion.
J. Plans should include minor details. Leave nothing to chance that can be anticipated.
K. Your plan should be simple and provide standards and controls. Establish quality and quantity standards and set a standard method of doing the job. The controls will indicate whether the job is proceeding according to plan.
L. Consider possible bottlenecks, breakdowns, or other difficulties that are likely to arise.

V. Q. WHAT ARE THE YARDSTICKS BY WHICH PLANNING SHOULD BE MEASURED?

A. Any plan should:

—Clearly state a definite course of action to be followed and goal to be achieved, with consideration for emergencies.
— Be realistic and practical.
— State what's to be done, when it's to be done, where, how, and by whom.
— Establish the most efficient sequence of operating steps so that more is accomplished in less time, with the least effort, and with the best quality results.
— Assure meeting deliveries without delays.
— Establish the standard by which performance is to be judged.

Q. WHAT KINDS OF PLANS DOES EFFECTIVE SUPERVISION REQUIRE?

A. Plans should cover such factors as:

— Manpower: right number of properly trained employees on the job
— Materials: adequate supply of the right materials and supplies
— Machines: full utilization of machines and equipment, with proper maintenance
— Methods: most efficient handling of operations
— Deliveries: making deliveries on time
— Tools: sufficient well-conditioned tools
— Layout: most effective use of space
— Reports: maintaining proper records and reports
— Supervision: planning work for employees and organizing supervisor's own time

## MANAGEMENT PRINCIPLES

I. MANAGEMENT

Q. What do we mean by management?

A. Getting work done through others.

Management could also be defined as planning, directing, and controlling the operations of a bureau or division so that all factors will function properly and all persons cooperate efficiently for a common objective.

II. MANAGEMENT PRINCIPLES

A. There should be a hierarchy—wherein authority and responsibility run upward and downward through several levels—with a broad base at the bottom and a single head at the top.

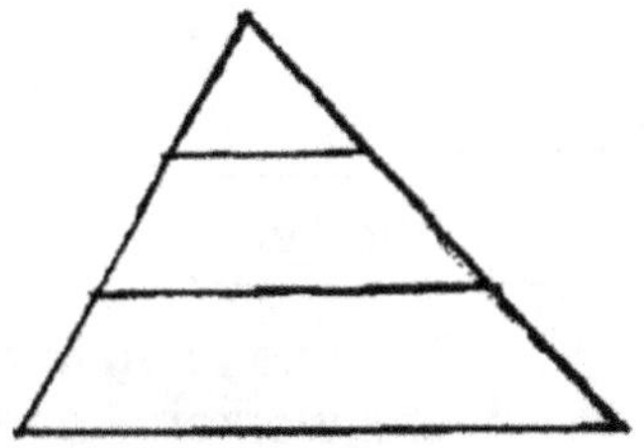

B. Each and every unit or person in the organization should be answerable ultimately to the manager at the apex. In other words, *The buck stops here!*

C. Every necessary function involved in the bureau's objectives is assigned to a unit in that bureau.

D. Responsibilities assigned to a unit are specifically clear-cut and understood.

E. Consistent methods of organizational structure should be applied at each level of the organization.

F. Each member of the bureau from top to bottom knows: to whom he reports and who reports to him.

G. No member of one bureau reports to more than one supervisor. No dual functions.

H. Responsibility for a function is matched by authority necessary to perform that function. Weight of authority.

I. Individuals or units reporting to a supervisor do not exceed the number which can be feasibly and effectively coordinated and directed. Concept of *span of control.*

J. Channels of command (management) are not violated by staff units, although there should be staff services to facilitate and coordinate management functions.

K. Authority and responsibility should be decentralized to units and individuals who are responsible for the actual performance of operations.
Welfare – down to Welfare Centers
Hospitals – down to local hospitals

L. Management should exercise control through attention to policy problems of exceptional performance, rather than through review of routine actions of subordinates.

M. Organizations should never be permitted to grow so elaborate as to hinder work accomplishments.

III. ORGANIZATION STRUCTURE

Types of Organizations
The purest form is a leader and a few followers, such as:

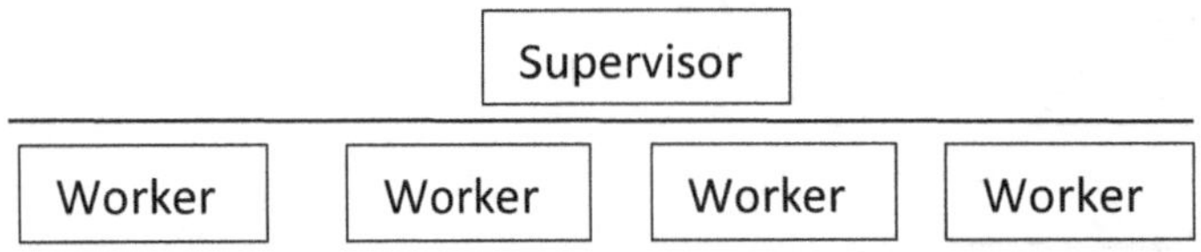


(Refer to organization chart) from supervisor to workers.

The line of authority is direct, The workers know exactly where they stand in relation to their boss, to whom they report for instructions and direction.

Unfortunately, in our present complex society, few organizations are similar to this example of a pure line organization. In this era of specialization, other people are often needed in the simplest of organizations. These specialists are known as staff. The sole purpose for their existence (staff) is to assist, advise, suggest, help or counsel line organizations. Staff has no authority to direct line people—nor do they give them direct instructions.

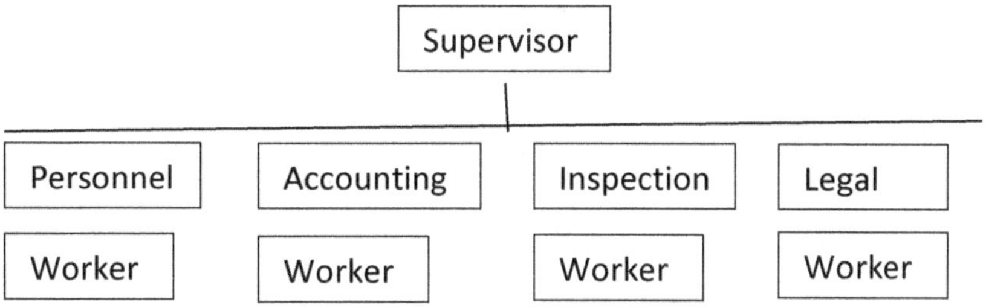


Line Functions
1. Directs
2. Orders
3. Responsibility for carrying out activities from beginning to end
4. Follows chain of command
5. Is identified with what it does
6. Decides when and how to use staff advice
7. Line executes

Staff Functions
1. Advises
2. Persuades and sells
3. Staff studies, reports, recommends but does not carry out
4. May advise across department lines
5. May find its ideas identified with others
6. Has to persuade line to want its advice
7. Staff: Conducts studies and research. Provides advice and instructions in technical matters. Serves as technical specialist to render specific services.

Types and Functions of Organization Charts
An organization chart is a picture of the arrangement and inter-relationship of the subdivisions of an organization.

A. Types of Charts:
   1. Structural: basic relationships only
   2. Functional: includes functions or duties
   3. Personnel: positions, salaries, status, etc.
   4. Process Chart: work performed
   5. Gantt Chart: actual performance against planned
   5. Flow Chart: flow and distribution of work

B. Functions of Charts:
   1. Assist in management planning and control
   2. Indicate duplication of functions
   3. Indicate incorrect stressing of functions
   4. Indicate neglect of important functions
   5. Correct unclear authority
   6. Establish proper span of control

C. Limitations of Charts:
   1. Seldom maintained on current basis
   2. Chart is oversimplified
   3. Human factors cannot adequately be charted

D. Organization Charts should be:
   1. Simple
   2. Symmetrical
   3. Indicate authority
   4. Line and staff relationship differentiated
   5. Chart should be dated and bear signature of approving officer
   6. Chart should be displayed, not hidden

**ORGANIZATION**

There are four basic principles of organization:
1. Unity of command
2. Span of control
3. Uniformity of assignment
4. Assignment of responsibility and delegation of authority

I. UNITY OF COMMAND

Unity of command means that each person in the organization should receive orders from one, and only one, supervisor. When a person has to take orders from two or more people, (a) the orders may be in conflict and the employee is upset because he does not know which he should obey, or (b) different orders may reach him at the same time and he does not know which he should carry out first.

Equally as bad as having two bosses is the situation where the supervisor is bypassed. Let us suppose you are a supervisor whose boss bypasses you (deals directly with people reporting to you). To the worker, it is the same as having two bosses; but to you, the supervisor, it is equally serious. Bypassing on the part of your boss will undermine your authority, and the people under you will begin looking to your boss for decisions and even for routine orders.

You can prevent bypassing by telling the people you supervise that if anyone tries to give them orders, they should direct that person to you.

II. SPAN OF CONTROL

Span of control on a given level involves:
A. The number of people being supervised
B. The distance
C The time involved in supervising the people. (One supervisor cannot supervise too many workers effectively.)

Span of control means that a supervisor has the right number (not too many and not too few) of subordinates that he can supervise well.

III. UNIFORMITY OF ASSIGNMENT

In assigning work, you as the supervisor should assign to each person jobs that are similar in nature. An employee who is assigned too many different types of jobs will waste time in going from one kind of work to another. It takes time for him to get to top production in one kind of task and, before he does so, he has to start on another.
When you assign work to people, remember that:

A. Job duties should be definite. Make it clear from the beginning what they are to do, how they are to do it, and why they are to do it. Let them know how much they are expected to do and how well they are expected to do it.
B. Check your assignments to be certain that there are no workers with too many unrelated duties, and that no two people have been given overlapping responsibilities. Your aim should be to have every task assigned to a specific person with the work fairly distributed and with each person doing his part.

IV. ASSIGNMENT OF RESPONSIBILITY AND DELEGATION OF AUTHORITY

A supervisor cannot delegate his final responsibility for the work of his department. The experienced supervisor knows that he gets his work done through people. He can't do it all himself. So he must assign the work and the responsibility for the work to his employees. Then they must be given the authority to carry out their responsibilities.

By assigning responsibility and delegating authority to carry out the responsibility, the supervisor builds in his workers initiative, resourcefulness, enthusiasm, and interest in their work. He is treating them as responsible adults. They can find satisfaction in their work, and they will respect the supervisor and be loyal to the supervisor.

**PRINCIPLES OF ORGANIZATION**

I. DEFINITION

Organization is the method of dividing up the work to provide the best channels for coordinated effort to get the agency's mission accomplished.

II. PURPOSE OF ORGANIZATION

A. To enable each employee within the organization to clearly know his responsibilities and relationships to his fellow employees and to organizational units
B. To avoid conflicts of authority and overlapping of jurisdiction.
C. To ensure teamwork.

III. BASIC CONSIDERATIONS IIN ORGANIZATIONAL PLANNING

A. The basic plans and objectives of the agency should be determined, and the organizational structure should be adapted to carry out effectively such plans and objectives.
B. The organization should be built around the major functions of the agency and not individuals or groups of individuals.

C. The organization should be sufficiently flexible to meet new and changing conditions which may be brought about from within or outside the department.
D. The organizational structure should be as simple as possible and the number of organizational units kept at a minimum.
E. The number of levels of authority should be kept at a minimum. Each additional management level lengthens the chain of authority and responsibility and increases the time for instructions to be distributed to operating levels and for decisions to be obtained from higher authority.
F. The form of organization should permit each executive to exercise maximum initiative within the limits of delegated authority.

IV. BASES FOR ORGANIZATION

A. Purpose (Examples: education, police, sanitation)
B. Process (Examples: accounting, legal, purchasing)
C. Clientele (Examples: welfare, parks, veteran)
D. Geographic (Examples: borough offices, precincts, libraries)

V. ASSIGNMENTS OF FUNCTIONS

A. Every function of the agency should be assigned to a specific organizational unit. Under normal circumstances, no single function should be assigned to more than one organizational unit.
B. There should be no overlapping, duplication, or conflict between organizational elements.
C. Line functions should be separated from staff functions, and proper emphasis should be placed on staff activities.
D. Functions which are closely related or similar should normally be assigned to a single organizational unit.
E. Functions should be properly distributed to promote balance, and to avoid overemphasis of less important functions and underemphasis of more essential functions.

VI. DELEGATION OF AUTHORITY AND RESPONSIBILITY

A. Responsibilities assigned to a specific individual or organizational unit should carry corresponding authority, and all statements of authority or limitations thereof should be as specific as possible.
B. Authority and responsibility for action should be decentralized to organizational units and individuals responsible for actual performance to the greatest extent possible, without relaxing necessary control over policy or the standardization of procedures. Delegation of authority will be consistent with decentralization of responsibility but such delegation will not divest an executive in higher authority of his overall responsibility.
C. The heads of organizational units should concern themselves with important matters and should delegate to the maximum extent details and routines performed in the ordinary course of business.
D. All responsibilities, authorities, and relationships should be stated in simple language to avoid misinterpretation.
E. Each individual or organizational unit charged with a specific responsibility will be held responsible for results.

VII. EMPLOYEE RELATIONSHIPS

A. The employees reporting to one executive should not exceed the number which can be effectively directed and coordinated. The number will depend largely upon the scope and extent of the responsibilities of the subordinates.
B. No person should report to more than one supervisor. Every supervisor should know who reports to him, and every employee should know to whom he reports. Channels of authority and responsibility should not be violated by staff units.
C. Relationships between organizational units within the agency and with outside organizations and associations should be clearly stated and thoroughly understood to avoid misunderstanding.

**DELEGATING**

I. WHAT IS DELEGATING?
Delegating is assigning a job to an employee, giving him the authority to get that job done, and giving him the responsibility for seeing to it that the job is done.

A. What To Delegate
1. Routine details
2. Jobs which may be necessary and take a lot of time, but do not have to be done by the supervisor personally (preparing reports, attending meetings, etc.)
3. Routine decision-making (making decisions which do not require the supervisor's personal attention)

B. What Not To Delegate
1. Job details which are *executive functions* (setting goals, organizing employees into a good team, analyzing results so as to plan for the future)
2. Disciplinary power (handling grievances, preparing service ratings, reprimands, etc.)
3. Decision-making which involves large numbers of employees or other bureaus and departments
4. Final and complete responsibility for the job done by the unit being supervised

C. Why Delegate?
1. To strengthen the organization by developing a greater number of skilled employees
2. To improve the employee's performance by giving him the chance to learn more about the job, handle some responsibility, and become more interested in getting the job done
3. To improve a supervisor's performance by relieving him of routine jobs and giving him more time for *executive functions* (planning, organizing, controlling, etc.) which cannot be delegated

II. TO WHOM TO DELEGATE
People with abilities not being used. Selection should be based on ability, not on favoritism.

## REPORTS

I. DEFINITION
A report is an orderly presentation of factual information directed to a specific reader for a specific purpose

II. PURPOSE
The general purpose of a report is to bring to the reader useful and factual information about a condition or a problem. Some specific purposes of a report may be:

A. To enable the reader to appraise the efficiency or effectiveness of a person or an operation
B. To provide a basis for establishing standards
C. To reflect the results of expenditures of time, effort, and money
D. To provide a basis for developing or altering programs

III. TYPES

A. Information Report: Contains facts arranged in sequence
B. Summary (Examination) Report: Contains facts plus an analysis or discussion of the significance of the facts. Analysis may give advantages and disadvantages or give qualitative and quantitative comparisons
C. Recommendation Report: Contains facts, analysis, and conclusion logically drawn from the facts and analysis, plus a recommendation based upon the facts, analysis, and conclusions

IV. FACTORS TO CONSIDER BEFORE WRITING REPORT

A. Why write the report?: The purpose of the report should be clearly defined.
B. Who will read the report?: What level of language should be used? Will the reader understand professional or technical language?
C. What should be said?: What does the reader need or want to know about the subject?
D. How should it be said?: Should the subject be presented tactfully? Convincingly? In a stimulating manner?

V. PREPARATORY STEPS

A. Assemble the facts: Find out who, why, what, where, when, and how.
B. Organize the facts: Eliminate unnecessary information
C. Prepare an outline: Check for orderliness, logical sequence
D. Prepare a draft: Check for correctness, clearness, completeness, conciseness, and tone
E. Prepare it in final form: Check for grammar, punctuation, appearance

VI. OUTLINE FOR A RECOMMENDATION REPORT

Is the report:
A. Correct in information, grammar, and tone?
B. Clear?
C. Complete?

D. Concise?
E. Timely?
F. Worth its cost?

Will the report accomplish its purpose?

## MANAGEMENT CONTROLS

I. CONTROL
What is control? What is controlled? Who controls?

The essence of control is action which adjusts operations to predetermined standards, and its basis is information in the hands of managers. Control is checking to determine whether plans are being observed and suitable progress toward stated objectives is being made, and action is taken, if necessary, to correct deviations.

We have a ready-made model for this concept of control in the automatic systems which are widely used for process control in the chemical land petroleum industries. A process control system works this way. Suppose, for example, it is desired to maintain a constant rate of flow of oil through a pipe at a predetermined or set-point value. A signal, whose strength represents the rate of flow, can be produced in a measuring device and transmitted to a control mechanism. The control mechanism, when it detects any deviation of the actual from the set-point signal, will reposition the value regulating flow rate.

II. BASIS FOR CONTROL

A process control mechanism thus acts to adjust operations to predetermined standards and does so on the basis of information it receives. In a parallel way, information reaching a manager gives him the opportunity for corrective action and is his basis for control. He cannot exercise control without such information, and he cannot do a complete job of managing without controlling.

III. POLICY

What is policy?

Policy is simply a statement of an organization's intention to act in certain ways when specified types of circumstances arise. It represents a general decision, predetermined and expressed as a principle or rule, establishing a normal pattern of conduct for dealing with given types of business events—usually recurrent. A statement is therefore useful in economizing the time of managers and in assisting them to discharge their responsibilities equitably and consistently.

Policy is not a means of control, but policy does generate the need for control.

Adherence to policies is not guaranteed nor can it be taken on faith. It has to be verified. Without verification, there is no basis for control. Policy and procedures, although closely related and interdependent to a certain extent, are not synonymous. A policy may be adopted, for example, to maintain a materials inventory not to exceed one million dollars.

A procedure for inventory control could interpret that policy and convert it into methods for keeping within that limit, with consideration, too, of possible but foreseeable expedient deviation.

IV. PROCEDURE

What is procedure?

A procedure specifically prescribes:

A. What work is to be performed by the various participants
B. Who are the respective participants
C. When and where the various steps in the different processes are to be performed
D. The sequence of operations that will insure uniform handling of recurring transactions
E. The paper that is involved, its origin, transition, and disposition

Necessary appurtenances to a procedure are:

A. Detailed organizational chart
B. Flow charts
C. Exhibits of forms, all presented in close proximity to the text of the procedure

V. BASIS OF CONTROL – INFORMATION IN THE HANDS OF MANAGERS

If the basis of control is information in the hands of managers, then reporting is elevated to a level of very considerable importance.

Types of reporting may include:

A. Special reports and routine reports
B. Written, oral, and graphic reports
C. Staff meetings
D. Conferences
E. Television screens
F. Non-receipt of information, as where management is by exception
G. Any other means whereby information is transmitted to a manager as a basis for control action

**FRAMEWORK OF MANAGEMENT**

I. ELEMENTS

A. Policy: It has to be verified, controlled.

B. Organization is part of the giving of an assignment. The organizational chart gives to each individual in his title, a first approximation of the nature of his assignment and orients him as being accountable to a certain individual. Organization is not in a true sense a means of control. Control is checking to ascertain whether the assignment is executed as intended and acting on the basis of that information.

C. Budgets perform three functions:
   1. They present the objectives, plans, and programs of the organization in financial terms.

2. They report the progress of actual performance against these predetermined objectives, plans, and programs.
3. Like organizational charts, delegations of authority, procedures, and job descriptions, they define the assignments which have flowed from the Chief Executive. Budgets are a means of control in the respect that they report progress of actual performance against the program. They provide information which enables managers to take action directed toward bringing actual results into conformity with the program.

D. Internal Check provides in practice for the principle that the same person should not have responsibility for all phases of a transaction. This makes it clearly an aspect of organization rather than of control. Internal Check is static, or built-in.

E. Plans, Programs, Objectives
People must know what they are trying to do. Objectives fulfill this need. Without them, people may work industriously and yet, working aimlessly, accomplish little. Plans and Programs complement Objectives, since they propose how and according to what time schedule the objectives are to be reached.

F. Delegations of Authority
Among the ways we have for supplementing the titles and lines of authority of an organizational chart are delegations of authority. Delegations of authority clarify the extent of authority of individuals and in that way serve to define assignments. That they are not means of control is apparent from the very fact that wherever there has been a delegation of authority, the need for control increases. This could hardly be expected to happen if delegations of authority were themselves means of control.

II. MANAGER'S RESPONSIBILITY

Control becomes necessary whenever a manager delegates authority to a subordinate because he cannot delegate and then simply sit back and forget4 about it. A manager's accountability to his own superior has not diminished one whit as a result of delegating part of his authority to a subordinate. The manager must exercise control over actions taken under the authority so delegated. That means checking serves as a basis for possible corrective action.

Objectives, plans, programs, organizational charts, and other elements of the managerial system are not fruitfully regarded as either controls or means of control. They are pre-established standards or models of performance to which operations are adjusted by the exercise of management control. These standards or models of performance are dynamic in character for they are constantly altered, modified, or revised. Policies, organizational set-up, procedures, delegations, etc. are constantly altered but, like objectives and plans, they remain in force until they are either abandoned or revised. All of the elements (or standards or models of performance), objectives, plans, and programs, policies, organization, etc. can be regarded as a *framework of management*.

III. CONTROL TECHNIQUES

Examples of control techniques:

A. Compare against established standards
B. Compare with a similar operation
C. Compare with past operations
D. Compare with predictions of accomplishment

IV. WHERE FORECASTS FIT

Control is after-the-fact while forecasts are before. Forecasts and projections are important for setting objectives and formulating plans.

Information for aiming and planning does not have to be before-the-fact. It may be an after-the-fact analysis proving that a certain policy has been impolitic in its effect on the relation of the company or department with customer, employee, taxpayer, or stockholder; or that a certain plan is no longer practical, or that a certain procedure is unworkable.

The prescription here certainly would not be in control (in these cases, control would simply bring operations into conformity with obsolete standards) but the establishment of new standards, a new policy, a new plan, and a new procedure to be controlled too.

Information is, of course, the basis for all communication in addition to furnishing evidence to management of the need for reconstructing the framework of management.

**PROBLEM SOLVING**

The accepted concept in modern management for problem solving is the utilization of the following steps:

A. Identify the problem
B. Gather data
C. List possible solutions
D. Test possible solutions
E. Select the best solution
F. Put the solution into actual practice

Occasions might arise where you would have to apply the second step of gathering data before completing the first step.

You might also find that it will be necessary to work on several steps at the same time.

I. IDENTIFY THE PROBLEM

Your first step is to define as precisely as possible the problem to be solved. While this may sound easy, it is often the most difficult part of the process.

It has been said of problem solving that you are halfway to the solution when you can write out a clear statement of the problem itself.

Our job now is to get below the surface manifestations of the trouble and pinpoint the problem. This is usually accomplished by a logical analysis, by going from the general to the particular; from the obvious to the not-so-obvious cause.

Let us say that production is behind schedule. WHY? Absenteeism is high. Now, is absenteeism the basic problem to be tackled, or is it merely a symptom of low morale among the workforce? Under these circumstances, you may decide that production is not the problem; the problem is *employee morale.*

In trying to define the problem, remember there is seldom one simple reason why production is lagging, or reports are late, etc.

Analysis usually leads to the discovery that an apparent problem is really made up of several subproblems which must be attacked separately.

Another way is to limit the problem, and thereby ease the task of finding a solution, and concentrate on the elements which are within the scope of your control.

When you have gone this far, write out a tentative statement of the problem to be solved.

II. GATHER DATA

In the second step, you must set out to collect all the information that might have a bearing on the problem. Do not settle for an assumption when reasonable fact and figures are available.

If you merely go through the motions of problem-solving, you will probably shortcut the information-gathering step. Therefore, do not stack the evidence by confining your research to your own preconceived ideas.

As you collect facts, organize them in some form that helps you make sense of them and spot possible relationships between them. For example, plotting cost per unit figures on a graph can be more meaningful than a long column of figures.

Evaluate each item as you go along. Is the source material absolutely, reliable, probably reliable, or not to be trusted.

One of the best methods for gathering data is to go out and look the situation over carefully. Talk to the people on the job who are most affected by this problem.

Always keep in mind that a primary source is usually better than a secondary source of information.

III. LIST POSSIBLE SOLUTIONS

This is the creative thinking step of problem solving. This is a good time to bring into play whatever techniques of group dynamics the agency or bureau might have developed for a joint attack on problems.

Now the important thing for you to do is: Keep an open mind. Let your imagination roam freely over the facts you have collected. Jot down every possible solution that occurs to you. Resist the temptation to evaluate various proposals as you go along. List seemingly absurd ideas along with more plausible ones. The more possibilities you list during this step, the less risk you will run of settling for merely a workable, rather than the best, solution.

Keep studying the data as long as there seems to be any chance of deriving additional ideas, solutions, explanations, or patterns from it.

IV. TEST POSSIBLE SOLUTIONS

Now you begin to evaluate the possible solutions. Take pains to be objective. Up to this point, you have suspended judgment but you might be tempted to select a solution you secretly favored all along and proclaim it as the best of the lot.

The secret of objectivity in this phase is to test the possible solutions separately, measuring each against a common yardstick. To make this yardstick try to enumerate as many specific criteria as you can think of. Criteria are best phrased as questions which you ask of each possible solution. They can be drawn from these general categories:

| | |
|---|---|
| Suitability – | Will this solution do the job?<br>Will it solve the problem completely or partially?<br>Is it a permanent or a stopgap solution? |
| Feasibility - | Will this plan work in actual practice?<br>Can we afford this approach?<br>How much will it cost? |
| Acceptability - | Will the boss go along with the changes required in the plan?<br>Are we trying to drive a tack with a sledge hammer? |

V. SELECT THE BEST SOLUTION

This is the area of executive decision.

Occasionally, one clearly superior solution will stand out at the conclusion of the testing process. But often it is not that simple. You may find that no one solution has come through all the tests with flying colors.

You may also find that a proposal, which flunked miserably on one of the essential tests, racked up a very high score on others.

The best solution frequently will turn out to be a combination.

Try to arrange a marriage that will bring together the strong points of one possible solution with the particular virtues of another. The more skill and imagination that you apply, the greater is the likelihood that you will come out with a solution that is not merely adequate and workable, but is the best possible under the circumstances.

VI. PUT THE SOLUTION INTO ACTUAL PRACTICE

As every executive knows, a plan which works perfectly on paper may develop all sorts of bugs when put into actual practice.

Problem-solving does not stop with selecting the solution which looks best in theory. The next step is to put the chosen solution into action and watch the results. The results may point towards modifications.

If the problem disappears when you put your solution into effect, you know you have the right solution.

If it does not disappear, even after you have adjusted your plan to cover unforeseen difficulties that turned up in practice, work your way back through the problem-solving solutions.

> Would one of them have worked better?
> Did you overlook some vital piece of data which would have given you a different slant on the whole situation? Did you apply all necessary criteria in testing solutions? If no light dawns after this much rechecking, it is a pretty good bet that you defined the problem incorrectly in the first place.

You came up with the wrong solution because you tackled the wrong problem.

Thus, step six may become step one of a new problem-solving cycle.

## COMMUNICATION

I. WHAT IS COMMUNICATION?
We communicate through writing, speaking, action, or inaction. In speaking to people face-to-face, there is opportunity to judge reactions and to adjust the message. This makes the supervisory chain one of the most, and in many instances the most, important channels of communication.

In an organization, communication means keeping employees informed about the organization's objectives, policies, problems, and progress. Communication is the free interchange of information, ideas, and desirable attitudes between and among employees and between employees and management.

II. WHY IS COMMUNICATION NEEDED?

A. People have certain social needs
B. Good communication is essential in meeting those social needs
C. While people have similar basic needs, at the same time they differ from each other
D. Communication must be adapted to these individual differences

An employee cannot do his best work unless he knows why he is doing it. If he has the feeling that he is being kept in the dark about what is going on, his enthusiasm and productivity suffer.

Effective communication is needed in an organization so that employees will understand what the organization is trying to accomplish; and how the work of one unit contributes to or affects the work of other units in the organization and other organizations.

III. HOW IS COMMUNICATION ACHIEVED?

Communication flows downward, upward, sideways.

A. Communication may come from top management down to employees. This is downward communication.

Some means of downward communication are:
1. Training (orientation, job instruction, supervision, public relations, etc.)
2. Conferences
3. Staff meetings
4. Policy statements
5. Bulletins
6. Newsletters
7. Memoranda
8. Circulation of important letters

In downward communication, it is important that employees be informed in advance of changes that will affect them.

B. Communications should also be developed so that the ideas, suggestions, and knowledge of employees will flow upward to top management.

Some means of upward communication are:
1. Personal discussion conferences
2. Committees
3. Memoranda
4. Employees suggestion program
5. Questionnaires to be filled in giving comments and suggestions about proposed actions that will affect field operations.

Upward communication requires that management be willing to listen, to accept, and to make changes when good ideas are present. Upward communication succeeds when there is no fear of punishment for speaking out or lack of interest at the top. Employees will share their knowledge and ideas with management when interest is shown and recognition is given.

C. The advantages of downward communication:
1. It enables the passing down of orders, policies, and plans necessary to the continued operation of the station.
2. By making information available, it diminishes the fears and suspicions which result from misinformation and misunderstanding.
3. It fosters the pride people want to have in their work when they are told of good work.
4. It improves the morale and stature of the individual to be *in the know.*

5. It helps employees to understand, accept, and cooperate with changes when they know about them in advance.

D. The advantages of upward communication:
1. It enables the passing upward of information, attitudes, and feelings.
2. It makes it easier to find out how ready people are to receive downward communication.
3. It reveals the degree to which the downward communication is understood and accepted.
4. It helps to satisfy the basic social needs.
5. It stimulates employees to participate in the operation of their organization.
6. It encourage employees to contribute ideas for improving the efficiency and economy of operations.
7. It helps to solve problem situations before they reach the explosion point.

IV. WHY DOES COMMUNICATION FAIL?

A. The technical difficulties of conveying information clearly
B. The emotional content of communication which prevents complete transmission
C. The fact that there is a difference between what management needs to say, what it wants to day, and what it does say
D. The fact that there is a difference between what employees would like to say, what they think is profitable or safe to say, and what they do say

V. HOW TO IMPROVE COMMUNICATION

As a supervisor, you are a key figure in communication. To improve as a communicator, you should:

A. Know: Knowing your subordinates will help you to recognize and work with individual differences.
B. Like: If you like those who work for you and those for whom you work, this will foster the kind of friendly, warm, work atmosphere that will facilitate communication.
C. Trust: Showing a sincere desire to communicate will help to develop the mutual trust and confidence which are essential to the free flow of communication.
D. Tell: Tell your subordinates and superiors *what's doing*. Tell your subordinates *why* as well as *how*.
E. Listen: By listening, you help others to talk and you create good listeners. Don't forget that listening implies action.
F. Stimulate: Communication has to be stimulated and encouraged. Be receptive to ideas and suggestions and motivate your people so that each member of the team identifies himself with the job at hand.
G. Consult: The most effective way of consulting is to let your people participate, insofar as possible, in developing determinations which affect them or their work.

VI. HOW TO DETERMINE WHETHER YOU ARE GETTING ACROSS

A. Check to see that communication is received and understood
B. Judge this understanding by actions rather than words
C. Adapt or vary communication, when necessary
D. Remember that good communication cannot cure all problems

VII. THE KEY ATTITUDE

Try to see things from the other person's point of view. By doing this, you help to develop the permissive atmosphere and the shared confidence and understanding which are essential to effective two-way communication.

Communication is a two-way process:

A. The basic purpose of any communication is to get action.
B. The only way to get action is through acceptance.
C. In order to get acceptance, communication must be humanly satisfying as well as technically efficient.

**HOW ORDERS AND INSTRUCTIONS SHOULD BE GIVEN**

I. CHARACTERISTICS OF GOOD ORDERS AND INSTRUCTIONS

A. Clear
Orders should be definite as to
—What is to be done
—Who is to do it
—When it is to be done
—Where it is to be done
—How it is to be done

B. Concise
Avoid wordiness. Orders should be brief and to the point.

C. Timely
Instructions and orders should be sent out at the proper time and not too long in advance of expected performance.

D. Possibility of Performance
Orders should be feasible:
1. Investigate before giving orders
2. Consult those who are to carry out instructions before formulating and issuing them

E. Properly Directed
Give the orders to the people concerned. Do not send orders to people who are not concerned. People who continually receive instructions that are not applicable to them get in the habit of neglecting instructions generally.

F. Reviewed Before Issuance
Orders should be reviewed before issuance:
1. Test them by putting yourself in the position of the recipient
2. If they involve new procedures, have the persons who are to do the work review them for suggestions.

G. Reviewed After Issuance
Persons who receive orders should be allowed to raise questions and to point out unforeseen consequences of orders.

H. Coordinated
Orders should be coordinated so that work runs smoothly.

I. Courteous
Make a request rather than a demand. There is no need to continually call attention to the fact that you are the boss.

J. Recognizable as an Order
Be sure that the order is recognizable as such.

K. Complete
Be sure recipient has knowledge and experience sufficient to carry out order. Give illustrations and examples.

**A DEPARTMENTAL PERSONNEL OFFICE IS RESPONSIBLE FOR THE FOLLOWING FUNCTIONS**

1. Policy
2. Personnel Programs
3. Recruitment and Placement
4. Position Classification
5. Salary and Wage Administration
6. Employee performance Standards and Evaluation
7. Employee Relations
8. Disciplinary Actions and Separations
9. Health and Safety
10. Staff Training and Development
11. Personnel Records, Procedures, and Reports
12. Employee Services
13. Personnel Research

**SUPERVISION**

I. LEADERSHIP

All leadership is based essentially on authority. This comes from two sources: It is received from higher management or it is earned by the supervisor through his methods of supervision. Although effective leadership has always depended upon the leader's using his authority in such a way as to appeal successfully to the motives of the people supervised, the conditions for making this appeal are continually changing. The key to today's problem of leadership is flexibility and resourcefulness on the part of the leader in meeting changes in conditions as they occur.

Three basic approaches to leadership are generally recognized:

A. The Authoritarian Approach
1. The methods and techniques used in this approach emphasize the *I* in leadership and depend primarily on the formal authority of the leader. This authority is sometimes exercised in a hardboiled manner and sometimes in a benevolent

manner, but in either case the dominating role of the leader is reflected in the thinking, planning, and decisions of the group.

2. Group results are to a large degree dependent on close supervision by the leader. Usually, the individuals in the group will not show a high degree of initiative or acceptance of responsibility and their capacity to grow and develop probably will not be fully utilized. The group may react with resentment or submission, depending upon the manner and skill of the leader in using his authority.
3. This approach develops as a natural outgrowth of the authority that goes with the leader's job and his feeling of sole responsibility for getting the job done. It is relatively easy to use and does not require must resourcefulness.
4. The use of this approach is effective in times of emergencies, in meeting close deadline as a final resort, in settling some issues, in disciplinary matters, and with dependent individuals and groups.

B. The Laissez-Faire or Let 'em Alone Approach

1. This approach generally is characterized by an avoidance of leadership responsibility by the leader. The activities of the group depend largely on the choice of its members rather than the leader.
2. Group results probably will be poor. Generally, there will be disagreements over petty things, bickering, and confusion. Except for a few aggressive people, individuals will not show much initiative and growth and development will be retarded. There may be a tendency for informal leaders to take over leadership of the group.
3. This approach frequently results from the leader's dislike of responsibility, from his lack of confidence, from failure of other methods to work, from disappointment or criticism. It is usually the easiest of the three to use and requires both understanding and resourcefulness on the part of the leader.
4. This approach is occasionally useful and effective, particularly in forcing dependent individuals or groups to rely on themselves, to give someone a chance to save face by clearing his own difficulties, or when action should be delayed temporarily for good cause.

C. The Democratic Approach

1. The methods and techniques used in this approach emphasize the *we* in leadership and build up the responsibility of the group to attain its objectives. Reliance is placed largely on the earned authority of the leader.
2. Group results are likely to be good because most of the job motives of the people will be satisfied. Cooperation and teamwork, initiative, acceptance of responsibility, and the individual's capacity for growth probably will show a high degree of development.
3. This approach grows out of a desire or necessity of the leader to find ways to appeal effectively to the motivation of his group. It is the best approach to build up inside the person a strong desire to cooperate and apply himself to the job. It is the most difficult to develop, and requires both understanding and resourcefulness on the part of the leader.
4. The value of this approach increases over a long period where sustained efficiency and development of people are important. It may not be fully effective in all situations, however, particularly when there is not sufficient time to use it properly or where quick decisions must be made.

All three approaches are used by most leaders and have a place in supervising people. The extent of their use varies with individual leaders, with some using one approach predominantly. The leader who uses these three approaches, and varies their use with time and circumstance, is probably the most effective. Leadership which is used predominantly with a democratic approach requires more resourcefulness on the part of the leader but offers the greatest possibilities in terms of teamwork and cooperation.

The one best way of developing democratic leadership is to provide a real sense of participation on the part of the group, since this satisfies most of the chief job motives. Although there are many ways of providing participation, consulting as frequently as possible with individuals and groups on things that affect them seems to offer the most in building cooperation and responsibility. Consultation takes different forms, but it is most constructive when people feel they are actually helping in finding the answers to the problems on the job.

There are some requirements of leaders in respect to human relations which should be considered in their selection and development. Generally, the leader should be interested in working with other people, emotionally stable, self-confident, and sensitive to the reactions of others. In addition, his viewpoint should be one of getting the job done through people who work cooperatively in response to his leadership. He should have a knowledge of individual and group behavior, but, most important of all, he should work to combine all of these requirements into a definite, practical skill in leadership.

II. NINE POINTS OF CONTRAST BETWEEN *BOSS* AND *LEADER*

A. The boss drives his men; the leader coaches them.
B. The boss depends on authority; the leader on good will.
C. The boss inspires fear; the leader inspires enthusiasm.
D. The boss says I; the leader says *We*.
E. The boss says *Get here on time*; the leader gets there ahead of time.
F. The boss fixes the blame for the breakdown; the leader fixes the breakdown.
G. The boss knows how it is done; the leader shows how.
H. The boss makes work a drudgery; the leader makes work a game.
I. The boss says *Go*; the leader says *Let's go.*

**EMPLOYEE MORALE**

Employee morale is the way employees feel about each other, the organization or unit in which they work, and the work they perform.

I. SOME WAYS TO DEVELOP AND MAINTAIN GOOD EMPLYEE MORALE

A. Give adequate credit and praise when due.
B. Recognize importance of all jobs and equalize load with proper assignments, always giving consideration to personality differences and abilities.
C. Welcome suggestions and do not have an *all-wise* attitude. Request employees' assistance in solving problems and use assistants when conducting group meetings on certain subjects.
D. Properly assign responsibilities and give adequate authority for fulfillment of such assignments.

E. Keep employees informed about matters that affect them.
F. Criticize and reprimand employees privately.
G. Be accessible and willing to listen.
H. Be fair.
I. Be alert to detect training possibilities so that you will not miss an opportunity to help each employee do a better job, and if possible with less effort on his part.
J. Set a good example.
K. Apply the golden rule.

II. SOME INDICATIONS OF GOOD MORALE

A. Good quality of work
B. Good quantity
C. Good attitude of employees
D. Good discipline
E. Teamwork
F. Good attendance
G. Employee participation

**MOTIVATION**

DRIVES

A drive, stated simply, is a desire or force which causes a person to do or say certain things. These are some of the most usual drives and some of their identifying characteristics recognizable in people motivated by such drives:

A. Security (desire to provide for the future)
Always on time for work
Works for the same employer for many years
Never takes unnecessary chances
Seldom resists doing what he is told

B. Recognition (desire to be rewarded for accomplishment)
Likes to be asked for his opinion
Becomes very disturbed when he makes a mistake
Does things to attract attention
Likes to see his name in print

C. Position (desire to hold certain status in relation to others)
Boasts about important people he knows
Wants to be known as a key man
Likes titles
Demands respect
Belongs to clubs, for prestige

D. Accomplishment (desire to get things done)
   Complains when things are held up
   Likes to do things that have tangible results
   Never lies down on the job
   Is proud of turning out good work

E. Companionship (desire to associate with other people)
   Likes to work with others
   Tells stories and jokes
   Indulges in horseplay
   Finds excuses to talk to others on the job

F. Possession (desire to collect and hoard objects)
   Likes to collect things
   Puts his name on things belonging to him
   Insists on the same location

Supervisors may find that identifying the drives of employees is a helpful step toward motivating them to self-improvement and better job performance. For example: An employee's job performance is below average. His supervisor, having previously determined that the employee is motivated by a drive for security, suggests that taking training courses will help the employee to improve, advance, and earn more money. Since earning more money can be a step toward greater security, the employee's drive for security would motivate him to take the training suggested by the supervisor. In essence, this is the process of charting an employee's future course by using his motivating drives to positive advantage.

**EMPLOYEE PARTICIPATION**

I. WHAT IS PARTICIPATION

Employee participation is the employee's giving freely of his time, skill, and knowledge to an extent which cannot be obtained by demand.

II. WHY IS IT IMPORTANT?

The supervisor's responsibility is to get the job done through people. A good supervisor gets the job done through people who work willingly and well. The participation of employees is important because:

A. Employees develop a greater sense of responsibility when they share in working out operating plans and goals.
B. Participation provides greater opportunity and stimulation for employees to learn, and to develop their ability.
C. Participation sometimes provides better solutions to problems because such solutions may combine the experience and knowledge of interested employees who want the solutions to work.
D. An employee or group may offer a solution which the supervisor might hesitate to make for fear of demanding too much.

E. Since the group wants to make the solution work, they exert pressure in a constructive way on each other.
F. Participation usually results in reducing the need for close supervision.

II. HOW MAY SUPERVISORS OBTAIN IT?

Participation is encouraged when employees feel that they share some responsibility for the work and that their ideas are sincerely wanted and valued. Some ways of obtaining employee participation are:

A. Conduct orientation programs for new employees to inform them about the organization and their rights and responsibilities as employees.
B. Explain the aims and objectives of the agency. On a continuing basis, be sure that the employees know what these aims and objectives are.
C. Share job successes and responsibilities and give credit for success.
D. Consult with employees, both as individuals and in groups, about things that affect them.
E. Encourage suggestions for job improvements. Help employees to develop good suggestions. The suggestions can bring them recognition. The city's suggestion program offers additional encouragement through cash awards.

The supervisor who encourages employee participation is not surrendering his authority. He must still make decisions and initiate action, and he must continue to be ultimately responsible for the work of those he supervises. But, through employee participation, he is helping his group to develop greater ability and a sense of responsibility while getting the job done faster and better.

**STEPS IN HANDLING A GRIEVANCE**

1. Get the Facts
   a. Listen sympathetically
   b. Let him talk himself out
   c. Get his story straight
   d. Get his point of view
   e. Don't argue with him
   f. Give him plenty of time
   g. Conduct the interview privately
   h. Don't try to shift the blame or pass the buck

2. Consider the Facts
   a. Consider the employee's viewpoint
   b. How will the decision affect similar cases
   c. Consider each decision as a possible precedent
   d. Avoid snap judgments—don't jump to conclusions

3. Make or Get a Decision
   a. Frame an effective counter-proposal
   b. Make sure it is fair to all
   c. Have confidence in your judgment
   d. Be sure you can substantiate your decision

4. Notify the Employee of Your Decision
   Be sure he is told; try to convince him that the decision is fair and just.

5. Take Action When Needed and If Within Your Authority
   Otherwise, tell employee that the matter will be called to the attention of the proper person or that nothing can be done, and why it cannot.

6. Follow through to see that the desired result is achieved.

7. Record key facts concerning the complaint and the action taken.

8. Leave the way open to him to appeal your decision to a higher authority.

9. Report all grievances to your superior, whether they are appealed or not.

**DISCIPLINE**

Discipline is training that develops self-control, orderly conduct, and efficiency.

To discipline does not necessarily mean to punish.

To discipline does mean to train, to regulate, and to govern conduct.

I. THE DISCIPLINARY INTERVIEW

Most employees sincerely want to do what is expected of them. In other words, they are self-disciplined. Some employees, however, fail to observe established rules and standards, and disciplinary action by the supervisor is required.

The primary purpose of disciplinary action is to improve conduct without creating dissatisfaction, bitterness, or resentment in the process.

Constructive disciplinary action is more concerned with causes and explanations of breaches of conduct than with punishment. The disciplinary interview is held to get at the causes of apparent misbehavior and to motivate better performance in the future.

It is important that the interview be kept on an impersonal a basis as possible. If the supervisor lets the interview descend to the plane of an argument, it loses its effectiveness.

II. PLANNING THE INTERVIEW

Get all pertinent facts concerning the situation so that you can talk in specific terms to the employee.

Review the employee's record, appraisal ratings, etc.

Consider what you know about the temperament of the employee. Consider your attitude toward the employee. Remember that the primary requisite of disciplinary action is fairness.

Don't enter upon the interview when angry.

Schedule the interview for a place which is private and out of hearing of others.

III. CONDUCTING THE INTERVIEW

A. Make an effort to establish accord.
B. Question the employee about the apparent breach of discipline. Be sure that the question is not so worded as to be itself an accusation.
C. Give the employee a chance to tell his side of the story. Give him ample opportunity to talk.
D. Use understanding—listening except where it is necessary to ask a question or to point out some details of which the employee may not be aware. If the employee misrepresents facts, make a plain, accurate statement of the facts, but don't argue and don't engage in personal controversy.
E. Listen and try to understand the reasons for the employee's (mis)conduct. First of all, don't assume that there has been a breach of discipline. Evaluate the employee's reasons for his conduct in the light of his opinions and feelings concerning the consistency and reasonableness of the standards which he was expected to follow. Has the supervisor done his part in explaining the reasons for the rule? Was the employee's behavior unintentional or deliberate? Does he think he had real reasons for his actions? What new facts is he telling? Do the facts justify his actions? What causes, other than those mentioned, could have stimulated the behavior?
F. After listening to the employee's version of the situation, and if censure of his actions is warranted, the supervisor should proceed with whatever criticism is justified. Emphasis should be placed on future improvement rather than exclusively on the employee's failure to measure up to expected standards of job conduct.
G. Fit the criticism to the individual. With one employee, a word of correction may be all that is required.
H. Attempt to distinguish between unintentional error and deliberate misbehavior. An error due to ignorance requires training and not censure.
I. Administer criticism in a controlled, even tone of voice, never in anger. Make it clear that you are acting as an agent of the department. In general, criticism should refer to the job or the employee's actions and not to the person. Criticism of the employee's work is not an attack on the individual.
J. Be sure the interview does not destroy the employee's self-confidence. Mention his good qualities and assure him that you feel confident that he can improve his performance.
K. Wherever possible, before the employee leaves the interview, satisfy him that the incident is closed, that nothing more will be said on the subject unless the offense is repeated.

www.ingramcontent.com/pod-product-compliance
Lightning Source LLC
Chambersburg PA
CBHW081803300426
44116CB00014B/2227
* 9 7 8 1 7 9 9 3 1 7 8 2 1 *